Matchbox® *and Lledo*™ *Toys*

Dr. Edward Force

With
Price Guide
and
Variations List

1469 Morstein Road, West Chester, Pennsylvania 19380

Certain information on Lledo Models of Days Gone has been gathered from the following copyrighted publications with permission:

Lledo Calling, Vol. I, No. 1 (1984) through Vol. II, No. 2 (1988), Ray Bush, editor, 1 Tor Road, Plymouth England.

Certain information on Lledo and Matchbox products has been confirmed by consulting the following copyrighted publications.

Lledo USA, Vol. I, No. 1 (1983) through Vol. IV, No. 11 (1988), and

Matchbox USA, Vol. V, No. 6 (1982) through Vol. XI, No. 6 (1988), Charles Mack, editor, RR 3, Box 216, Durham, Connecticut.

as well as by consultation with Neil Waldmann of Old Bethpage, New York, Mark Henderson of Vincentown, New Jersey, and other collectors and dealers.

The bulk of the information in this book came from the models in the author's own collection of miniature vehicles and his records of his collection.

Contents

Acknowledgments

There are numerous people whom I would like to thank for their help in my strivings to add models to my collection and information to my archives, including:

Michael Boss of Runabout,
Bob Brennen of Miniature Toys,
Ray Bush of "Lledo Calling",
Fred Clausen,
Bruce Cohen,
Martin Cowlyn of Rarities,
Patricia Ann Cox,
Vic Davey,
Preston Fries,
David Hacku,
Mark Henderson of Specialty Diecast,
Pasquale and Gary Lamagna,
Bill Layer,
Ed Lemieux,
Charles Mack of "Lledo USA" and "Matchbox USA",
James Nagle,
Peter Retelstorf,

Jo and Chris Roper,
Robert Vander Schans,
Neil Waldmann of Neil's Wheels,
James Wieland of Miniature Auto Sales,
and everybody who ought to be on this list but isn't, plus The Reverend Charles Gelbach for helping me at many toyshows while I went in quest of models, Pat, Lisa and Ellen for their forbearance while I wrote this book, and Peter and Nancy Schiffer, Doug the photographer, and all their staff for all their help in making this book become real. And thank you, not only for buying this book but for reading this far!

If you have any comments or questions, feel free to write.

Dr. Edward Force
42 Warham Street
Windsor, CT 06095

Introduction

Matchbox® Series

The story of Matchbox cars since 1982 has been a complex and challenging one—challenging for the collector, dealer and historian alike because of its complexity. Of course, it was in 1982 that Lesney Products ceased to exist, and the purchase of Matchbox by Universal International of Hong Kong was bound to bring changes. But it was one policy change that came into view at the very start of 1982 that has done the most to make the Matchbox story mind-boggling. For in that year the 1-75 Matchbox series sold in the United States was, for the first time in history, not identical to that offered in the United Kingdom and the rest of the world. Since 1982 there have been two Matchbox series of 75 models, with some models being common to both series and using the same catalog number in both, others appearing in both series but under two different numbers, and still others being part of one series but not the other, or in some cases being introduced into one series only after having been in the other for one or more years. Not long ago I hoped this practice was on the way out, but my research for this book has disabused me of such wishful thinking.

It must be noted that in recent years Japan has had its own Matchbox Series, differing completely in catalog numbers, as in many other details, from the British and American series. Details can be found in the pages of MATCHBOX USA, but not in this book. To include it here, I would have had to copy the material in the journal, which copyright laws forbid.

Another factor in the complexity of Matchbox has been the fact that the new parent company has spread production among several countries in various parts of the world. Time was when we took it for granted that "Made in England" would be seen on any Matchbox base. During the Eighties, though, production has gone on in Hong Kong, China, Macau, Bulgaria—and probably other countries that have failed to register in this writer's spinning head. This fact, cast into Matchbox baseplates of varying colors, caused a wave of culture shock when it first hit the collecting world. I have a vivid memory of those days: a collector came to the table next to mine at a toy show and was delighted to see the newest Matchbox cars on sale—until he read "Made in Macau" on their bases and rejected them—for to him, Matchbox was "Made in England" and that was that. Fortunately for the hobby (to say nothing of the manufacturers), most collectors have not rejected Matchbox cars from the ends of the earth, though many have bemoaned the proliferation of variations that has resulted.

Then too, the manufacturers have produced numerous versions for national markets, many promotional and other non-standard issues, and several new series of models, not to mention other types of toys and related articles that are beyond our province here. This all adds up to a veritable deluge of new Matchbox data since the publication of Nancy Schiffer's MATCHBOX TOYS, which brought the story up to about the middle of 1982.

And before we say anything else on the subject, let me extend to all of you my apologies for not offering you complete data on everything. I had hoped to acquire thorough data, but it was not to be, and perhaps it is just as well. An entire book could well be written in the next few years just to update the already published information. I hope such a book will be written—but please, Lord, not by me! The unexpected job of making up a list of major variations has been quite enough of a challenge for me, and I fervently hope that this book will, if not satisfying you completely, at least give you food for thought and collecting "until the real thing comes along".

My major sources of information in compiling this listing have been my own collection and the records I have kept in the process of collecting, plus the yearly collectors' catalogs published by the manufacturers of Matchbox. When I have needed additional data on such facts as colors and years of issue, I have consulted Matchbox expert Neil Waldmann, proprietor of Neil's Wheels, and other fellow collectors, plus the pages of MATCHBOX USA, a journal published monthly by a club that needs no introduction to many of you. (If you are not familiar with the club, write to Matchbox USA, c/o Charles Mack, Rural Route 3, Box 216, Saw Mill Road, Durham CT 06422 USA.) Since the text of this journal is copyrighted, I have not taken from it anything more specific than what can be regarded as public knowledge, and I have not consulted any other collectors' club journals (such as A.I.M., U.K. MATCHBOX, etc.) at all. The reader is encouraged to consult such publications for more thorough data than can be offered here, and to make the acquaintance of veteran collectors in his or her home area. There are Matchbox collectors almost everywhere, and a visit to a nearby toy meet or two will lead to one's becoming a member of a big family in which information and models are often swapped, to the benefit of everybody involved.

This is not to say that all is sweet and pure in the Matchbox world. Sooner or later one will hear of cases in which a zealous newcomer has been sold a model that is not what it claims to be. The best defense against being cheated is to be informed: find out what is genuine and what is not, find out who can or cannot be trusted to deal fairly, and learn what "Code Three" means!

That last term is part of a system developed by Ray Bush in the early days of U.K. Matchbox, and every collector ought to know the code. Code One models are fully made and sanctioned by the manufacturers and are fully legitimate. Code Two models are not fully made by the manufacturers, but the other parties who finished the job did so (usually by adding decals or labels) with the manufacturers' knowledge and consent; thus these models, though not regular Matchbox issues, still bear the seal of approval. Code Three models are those finished without the manufacturers' knowledge and consent, thus lacking the legitimate status of Code One and Two items.

This should not be taken to mean that models in one code are collectable and others are not! You as an individual collector can collect whatever you choose. You are free to set your own criteria. Even within the scope of Code One, there are many possibilities, from collecting only the most major variations to collecting every minor one you can find. The richness of Matchbox models gives you a tremendous lot to choose from. Perhaps some people can find the time, space and money to collect everything that ever bore the name of Matchbox. But most of us cannot, and I would urge you to decide at the start what you want to collect, set realistic limits for yourself and stick to them, expanding them only in the highly unlikely case of their proving to have been too narrow. Within those limits you can accomplish a great deal—and spend a great deal too.

But before you spend too much, inform yourself! Learn as much as you can, and never stop learning. Soon you will find you have gone far beyond the material in this book—and have had a lot more excitement, adventure and jolly good fun than you ever expected.

Just a few words about the Matchbox listings: they are meant to provide basic information, but not to give every detail of a model; what is given should suffice to distinguish one variation from another. The numbers and letters continue the system published in MATCHBOX TOYS but do not necessarily correspond to those used in MATCHBOX USA or any other journal, where many more variations have been listed. The letters US and GB refer to the American and British Matchbox Series existing since 1982, and every effort has been made to cross-index all models that have appeared in the two series under different numbers. (It must be noted that some variations have been offered in one series but not in the other.) Various lines of models will be introduced with a few comments as to their nature and history.

I am the first to admit that a few models listed here may not exist precisely as I have described them, simply because I have not seen them and have had to rely on pictures in Matchbox catalogs for information. Most of the descriptions, though, are of models in my own collection or in those of friends, and can be trusted as far as they go.

The rest is up to you. And whatever path you choose to follow in our hobby, may you find plenty of happiness and fulfillment in it. Happy hobbying to you all!

The Photographs

The 96 color photographs will show most of the models listed in the book. I would like to express my gratitude to Neil Waldmann of Neil's Wheels for kindly lending me more than thirty models from his collection for photographing. All the other models shown here are from my own collection.

The Lledo models, with the exception of a few last-minute arrivals, are arranged basically in order of their listing. The purist may object to finding Days Gone, Lledo Promotional and even the few Code Three models I own shown together, but I have written this part of the book for ALL Lledo collectors, not for just a certain few. I have stated elsewhere in this book that each of you is free to decide what to collect, so what irritates you may be vitally important to another hobbyist.

The Matchbox models are likewise presented in order—that of their catalog numbers, with a few exceptions to avoid breaking up families—and for the purpose of offering as much information as possible. Here, though, as in the Matchbox listing, only major variations are included. The specialist collector who wants more minute details is urged to join a collectors' club and acquire a greater depth of information from its journals.

I have added a few Matchbox and Yesteryear variations that were produced shortly before 1982, and shown in Nancy Schiffer's MATCHBOX TOYS, for the sake of continuity. In cases where the first version of a model came just before the scope of this book, it seemed practical to include it in the photo along with its younger siblings, for your convenience. In a few cases, a casting change is thereby illustrated.

Like the Lledo section, the Matchbox portion of the book is intended to serve all of you, and I hope that you will all find something interesting and informative in it.

Row 1. 01-DOW-DG **Downtown**, 01-MAI-DG **Main Street** (green and brown), 01-MAN-LP **Manly Jazz Festival**.

Row 2. 01-NAT-DG **National Tramway Museum**, 01-WES-DG **Westminster**, 03-CAR-C3 **Theophilus Cartlidge**, 03-CRU-C3 **Ebenezer Cruickshank.**

Row 3. 02-CEL-DG **Celtic Dairies**, 02-CHA-DG **Chambourcy**, 02-CLI-DG **Clifford & Sons**, 02-EXP-DG **Express Dairy**, 02-GRY-SP **Gray.**

Row 4. 03-GRY-SP **Gray**, 03-COC-DG **Coca-Cola**, 03-FIN-DG **Fine Lady Bakeries**, 03-HAM-DG **Hamleys**, 03-LCM-DG **Lledo Club Member.**

Row 1. 03-LEA-C3 **Elias Lear**, 03-LSW-DG **L.S.W.R.**, 03-NOR-DG **Matthew Norman**, 03-PEP-DG **Pepperidge Farm.**
Row 2. 03-PHO-LP **Phoenix**, 03-ROB-DG **Robertsons**, 03-ROY-DG **Royal Mail**, 03-TIR-C3 **J. Tirrell.**
Row 3. 03-STA-DG **Staffordshire** (two body colors), 03-TRI-DG **Tri-Sum**, 03-WIN-DG **Windmill Bakery.**
Row 4. 04-BRI-LP **Bridlington**, 04-EXC-LP **Exchange & Mart**, 04-GRY-SP **Gray**, 04-HAM-DG **Hamleys.**

Row 1. 04-HIG-DG **High Chapparal**, 04-LBR-DG & 04-LBG-DG **Lipton's/Bowery-Broadway** red and green, 04-LVK-DG **Lipton's/Victoria** with green logo on white.

Row 2. 04-MAD-DG **Madame Tussaud's** (original & new castings), 04-MAS-DG **Mason's Pantry** (correct & reversed logo).

Row 3. 04-OAK-DG **Oakey's** (regular & additional logo), 04-PVK-DG **Pears/Victoria** (original & new castings)

Row 4. 05-BIF-DG **BIFBAC II**, 05-CHI-DG **Chicago**, 05-COV-LP **Coventry**, 05-GRY-SP **Gray.**

11

Row 1. 05-GUI-DG **Guildford** (gold and black boilers), 05-GUI/LP **Guilfdord**, 05-GWR-DG **G. W. R.**

Row 2. 05-HKF-DG **Hong Kong** (gold boiler), 05-HUL-LP **Hull Police**, 05-LAK-DG **Lake City**, 05-MET-LP **Metropolitan.**

Row 3. 05-LON-DG **London** (original casting with gold & unpainted boilers; new casting), 05-PHI-DG **Philadelphia.**

Row 4. **Ruby Wedding Set:** 04-BAL-DG, 12-WIN-DG, 13-ROY-DG, 15-RAE-DG, 19-QEP-DG.

Row 1. 06-AER-DG **Acroplane Jelly**, 06-ALT-DG **Alton Towers**, 06-ANM-LP **Anderson & McAuley**, 06-AUE-DG **Automodel Exchange**, 06-BAR-DG **Barclay's Bank.**

Row 2. 06-AUS-DG **Australian** (two roof colors), 06-BAS-LP **Bassetts**, 06-BAY-DG **Bay to Birdwood**, 06-BBB-LP **Better Bit o' Butter.**

Row 3. 06-BEA-LP **Beamish**, 06-BEU-LP **Beaulieu**, 06-BKP-VV **Blackpool**, 06-BRB-LP **British Bacon**, 06-BRD-LP **Bridlington.**

Row 4. 06-BRH-LP **British Hovercraft**, 06-BRM-DG **British Meat** (two chassis & roof colors), 06-BRT-LP **Brit Tyres**, 06-CAA-LP **Cada Toys.**

13

Row 1. 06-CAB-DG **Cadbury's-Bournville** (original & darker body), 06-CAC-DG **Cadbury's**, 06-CAN-DG **Canadian Travel Show 1986**, 06-CAP-LP **Canadian Travel Show 1987**.

Row 2. 06-CAM-VV **Cambridge**, 06-CAS-LP **Castrol**, 06-CHA-LP **Champion Spark Plugs**, 06-CHE-VV **Chester**, 06-CAR-VV **Carlisle**.

Row 3. 06-CLA-DG **City of London Ambulance**, 06-CLF-LP **W. Clifford**, 06-CLP-LP **Clarkson Puckle**, 06-COA-DG **Coca-Cola** (darker Code 2 & lighter Code 1 versions).

Row 4. 06-COB-DG **Coca-Cola**, 06-COC-DG red **Coca-Cola**, 06-COD-DG green **Coca-Cola**, 06-COH-LP **Cook & Hickman**, 06-CON-LP **Conestoga**.

Row 1. 06-COO-DG **Cookie Coach** (two logo colors), 06-CRA-DG **Craft & Hobby Showcase**, 06-CWM-DG Cwm **Dale Spring** (red & blue chassis).

Row 2. 06-CUM-LP **Cumberland News**, 06-DAI-DG **Daily/Sunday Express**, 06-DAS-DG **Days Gone Club**, 06-DAY-DG **Days Gone Toy Fairs** (1986 & 1987 versions).

Row 3. 06-DEL-LP **Deltic Preservation**, 06-DHT-LP **DH-Trans BV**, 06-ECH-DG **Echo Centenary**, 06-EDP-LP **Eastern Daily Press**, 06-EPS-LP **Epsom Stamp Co.**

Row 4. 06-EVC-DG **Evening Chronicle**, 06-EVE-LP **Everton**, 06-EXC-LP **Exchange & Mart**, 06-EXM-LP **Exchange & Mart**, 06-FAI-DG **Fairy Soap.**

Row 1. 06-FAM-LP **Famous Menswear**, 06-FAR-LP **Farnham Maltings 1985**, 06-FIS-LP **Fishermen's Friend**, 06-FOT-LP **Fotorama** (white & silver body).

Row 2. 06-FPA-LP **Franklin Pro-Am 1986 & 1987**, 06-FUR-LP **Furniss of Truro**, 06-GAR-LP **Gardner Merchant Catering**, 06-GRY-SP **Gray.**

Row 3. 06-HAJ-DG **Hardware Journal**, 06-HAM-DG **Hamleys**, 06-HAT-LP **Hatfields**, 06-HAY-LP **W. Haydon**, 06-HED-DG **Hedges & Butler.**

Row 4. 06-HER-LP **Heritage Homes**, 06-HLC-LP **Herts Lledo Collectors**, 06-HME-LP **Hendy Motor Engineers**, 06-HRA-DG **Harry Ramsden**, 06-HOM-DG **Home Ales.**

Row 1. 06-HOR-LP **Hornby Railways**, 06-HUD-LP **Huddersfield Daily Examiner**, 06-HUM-LP **Humi-Serv**, 06-IGF-DG **International Garden Festival**, 06-ILL-DG **Illinois Toy Show**.

Row 2. 06-IPM-DG **I.P.M.S.**, 06-JON-LP **T. Jones**, 06-JST-DG **John Smith's**, 06-JWM-LP **Juwelier Wagner Madler**, 06-KIT-LP **Kit Kat**.

Row 3. 06-KOD-DG **Kodak**, 06-KOY-LP **Koyanagi**, 06-KRO-LP **Krondorf Wine**, 06-LAN-LP **Lancashire Evening Post** (brown & magenta body).

Row 4. 06-LEG-LP **Legal & General**, 06-LIN-DG **Chocolat Lindt** (light & dark roof), 06-LON-VV **London (Tower & Big Ben versions)**.

17

Row 1. 06-LON-VV **London (Guardsman)**, 06-MAG-DG **Magasin du Nord**, 06-MAL-FS **Malibu or Bust**, 06-MAR-DG **Marcol Products** (tan & yellow body).

Row 2. 06-MAS-DG **Marks & Spencer**, 06-MFF-LP **Mastiff Association**, 06-MIL-LP **Miller of Nottingham**, 06-MIT-LP **Mitre 10**, 06-MOO-LP **Moorside School.**

Row 3. 06-MUR-DG **Murphy's Crisps**, 06-MUS-LP **Mustard Shop**, 06-NCH-LP **Naional Children's Home**, 06-NCJ-LP **N. C. Jewellery**, 06-NGF-LP **National Garden Festival.**

Row 4. 06-NRF-LP **Norfolk 5th Swapmeet**, 06-NRM-DG **Northern Daily Mail**, 06-NRS-C3 **Norfolk 7th Swapmeet**, 06-OTT-LP **Ottawa Citizen**, 06-PEJ-DG **Perrier-Jouet.**

Row 1. 06-OVA-DG **Ovaltine** (two logo colors), 06-OVE-DG **Ovaltine 75 Years**, 06-PER-LP **Persil**, 06-RAF-DG **Royal Air Force**.
Row 2. 06-PHA-DG **Philadelphia Ambulance**, 06-PHB-DG **Philadelphia Rescue**, 06-REA-DG **Railway Express**, 06-RED-LP **Reddicap Heath**, 06-REE-DG **Reese's Pieces**.
Row 3. 06-ROS-DG **Rose & Crown**, 06-ROU-LP **Round Table**, 06-ROY-DG **Royal Mail**, 06-SAL-LP **Salvation Army**, 06-SCA-VV **Scarborough**.
Row 4. 06-SCH-LP **Schweppes**, 06-SCO-LP **Scotch Corner**, 06-SHP-LP **Shipstones**, 06-SHR-LP **Shredded Wheat**, 06-SJP-LP **St. John Party**.

19

Row 1. 06-SPG-LP **Spring Garden Show**, 06-STD-LP **Strand**, 06-STF-LP **Staffordshire County Show**, 06-STP-LP **Staffordshire Police**, 06-SWT-C3 **Southwestern Bell System**.

Row 2. 06-STR-DG **Stretton Spring Water** (blue & green), 06-TAL-LP **Talyllyn Railway**, 06-TAY-LP **Taylors of Gloucester**, 06-TEL-LP **Telemedia Golf**.

Row 3. 06-TEN-LP **Tennent''s Lager**, 06-THR-C3 **Three Cocks**, 06-THR-LP **Thruway**, 06-TIZ-DG **Tizer**, 06-TRU-LP **True Value**.

Row 4. 06-UNW-LP **Unwin's Wine**, 06-WEH-LP **Western Evening Herald**, 06-WEL-DG **Wells Drinks**, 06-WER-LP **Werrington Patisserie**, 06-WES-LP **Western Auto Supply**.

Row 1. 06-WEV-DG **Wells Black Velvit,** 06-WHB-LP **Whitbread,** 06-WIN-VV **Windsor,** 06-WON-DG **Wonder Bread,** 06-WOO-DG **Woodwards.**

Row 2. 06-WOR-LP **Worfield Garage** (black & red body), 06-YOB-DG **Yorkshire Biscuits,** 06-YOE-DG **Yorkshire Evening Post,** 06-YOP-DG **Yorkshire Post,** 06-YCM-LP **York Castle Museum.**

Row 3. Figures for models 001, 002, 003 & 004.

Row 4. Figures for models 007, 009, 010 & 011.

Row 1. 07-CHD-DG **Chocolates by Della**, 07-FOR-DG **Ford Sales & Service**, 07-FTS-FS **Ford Tri-State**, 07-GDF-DG **Godfrey Davis Ford**, 07-COM-DG **Commonwealth Games.**

Row 2. 07-COC-DG **Coca-Cola** (recessed & filled panel), 07-GRY-SP **Gray**, 07-HAM-DG **Hamleys**, 07-KLM-LP **KLM.**

Row 3. 07-PAT-DG **Pat's Poodle Parlour**, 07-WPT-DG **West Point Toy Show** (recessed & filled panel), Code 3 **Hofmeister & Philadelphia.**

Row 4. 09-FMF-DG **15 Millionth Ford**, 09-NYR-DG **New York-Rio**, 09-PHI-DG **Philadelphia**, 09-POL-DG **Police** (light & dark blue body).

Row 1. 08-BMF-DG **Blue Mountain**, 08-BON-LP **Bondy Oil**, 08-BPE-LP **British Petroleum**, 08-BPC-LP **B.P. Chemicals**, 08-CAS-DG **Castrol.**

Row 2. 08-COC-DG **Coca-Cola**, 08-COL-LP **Cole's**, 08-CRO-DG **Crow Carrying**, 08-ESS-DG **Esso** (wrong & right spelling).

Row 3. 08-GRY-SP **Gray**, 08-HER-DG **Hershey's**, 08-HOF-DG **Hofmeister**, 08-LIQ-FS **Liquid Bubble**, 08-MAR-LP **Marshall Trucking.**

Row 4. 08-MIL-LP **Milk**, 08-MMB-LP **Midwest Miniature Bottle**, 08-NAM-C3 **National Milk**, 08-PEN-DG **Pennzoil**, 08-RED-EC **Red Edocar.**

Row 1. 08-PHI-DG (black & white roof), 08-SHE-LP **Shell-Mex,** 08-SMW-LP **Small Wheels,** 08-WAT-DG **Water Works.**

Row 2. 10-AMS-LP **Amsterdam** (two logo types), 10-BAR-DG **Barton,** 10-BRI-DG **Brighton Belle** (cream & tan roof).

Row 3. 10-CEN-LP **Centraal Nederland,** 10-COM-DG **Commonwealth Games,** 10-DUN-LP **Dundee,** 10-GLA-LP **Glasgow,** 10-GRA-SP **Gray.**

Row 4. 10-GWM-LP **G.W.R. Museum,** 10-GWR-DG **G.W.R.,** 10-HAM-DG **Hamleys,** 10-HER-DG **Hershey's** (cream & brown chassis).

Row 1. 10-HAP-LP **Happy Days**, 10-IMP-DG **Imperial Airways**, 10-IRO-LP **Ironbridge Museums**, 10-KLM-LP **KLM**, 10-LAK-LP **Lakeside Tours**.

Row 2. 10-LNE-LP **L.N.E.R.**, 10-LOC-DG **London Country**, 10-LOT-LP **Lothian**, 10-MAI-LP **Maidstone & District**, 10-OXF-LP **Oxford**.

Row 3. 10-POT-DG **Potteries** (cream & red roof), 10-RED-DG **Redburns**, 10-SBO-FS **Oakridge School**, 10-SBU-DG **Union School**.

Row 4. 10-SIL-DG **Silver Service**, 10-SOV-DG **Southern Vectis**, 10-TAN-LP **Tandhaus**, 10-TAR-DG **Tartan Tours**, 10-THS-LP **Thorpe Hall School**.

Row 1. 10-TIL-DG **Tillingbourne Valley,** 10-TRA=DG **Trailways,** 11-GRY-SP **Gray,** 11-ABE-DG **Abels.**

Row 2. 11-BIG-DG **Big Top,** 11-BRC-LP **Branth-Chemie,** 11-DLP-LP City of London Police, 11-CLQ-LP City of London Prison **Wagon.**

Row 3. 11-COC-DG **Coca-Cola,** 11-EXC-LP **Exchange & Mart,** 11-MAC-DG **MacCosham,** 11-ROY-DG **Royal Mail.**

Row 4. 11-STA-DG **Staffordshire County Show,** 11-TEX-LP **Texas Sesquicentennial,** 11-TUR-DG **Turnbull,** 11-WIL-DG **Williams Griffin.**

Row 1. 12-AUX-DG **Auxiliary**, 12-BER-DG **Bermuda**, 12-BGD-LP **Borough Green**, 12-BOS-FS **Boston**, 12-CAR-DG **Cardiff**.
Row 2. 12-CHE-DG & 12-CHE-LP **Chelmsford**, 12-ESS-DG **Essex County**, 12-LON-DG **London** (brown & gold ladder wheels).
Row 3. 12-GRY-SP **Gray**, 12-GUI-LP **Guildford**, 12-GWR-LP **G.W.R.**, 12-LUC-DG **Luckhurst County**, 12-WAR-LP **Warrington**.
Row 4. 12-MIL-LP **Milton**, 12-NAT-LP **National**, 12-RED-EC **Red Edocar**, 12-SUR-LP **Surrey**, 12-WAL-LP **Walker**.

Row 1. 13-AIM-LP **A.I.M.**, 13-ANL-LP **Advertiser-North London**, 13-BAG-LP **Bagel World**, 13-BAS-DG **Basildon Bond**, 13-BBC-LP **B.B.C.**

Row 2. 13-BEA-LP **Beaver Lumber**, 13-BEP-LP **Bristol Evening Post**, 13-BIL-LP **Bill Switchgear**, 13-BUC-LP **Bucktrout**, 13-CAB-LP **Cadburys/Bournville**.

Row 3. 13-CAM-DG **Camp Coffee**, 13-CAR-LP **Carr's Pet**, 13-CHA-LP **Charcoal Steak House**, 13-CHE-LP **Cherry**, 13-CHI-LP **Chichester Observer**.

Row 4. 13-CHM-LP **Marocain**, 13-CHS-VV **Chester**, 13-CHU-LP **Chubb Life**, 13-CLO-LP **Clowns Convention**, 13-CPG-LP **CPGA Championship**.

Row 1. 13-COA-DG, 13-COB-DG, 13-COC-DG (two chassis colors) & 13-COD-LP **Coca-Cola.**
Row 2. 13-DUN-VV **Dunster,** 13-EDI-VV **Edinburgh,** 13-ELP-LP **El Paso,** 13-EVA-LP **Evening Argus,** 13-EVG=LP **Evening Gazette.**
Row 3. 13-EVN-DG **Evening News,** 13-EVS-DG & 13-EVS-LP **Evening Sentinel,** 13-EWC-LP **Ernie Whitt,** 13-EXC-LP **Exchange & Mart.**

29

Row 1. 13-FOT-LP **Fotorama** (white & silver body), 13-GER-LP **Gerson** (green & black), 13-GRY-SP **Gray.**
Row 2. 13-GUE-VV **Guernsey**, 13-HAM-DG **Hamleys**, 13-HAP-LP **Harold's Place**, 13-HAR-LP **Harrow 18 Plus**, 13-HGR-LP **H. & G. Restaurants.**
Row 3. 13-HER-DG & 13-HES-DG **Hershey's**, 13-HOL-LP **Holme Valley Express**, 13-HOR-LP **Hornby's Dairies**, 13-HPS-DG **H. P. Sauce.**
Row 4. 13-ILL-LP **Illinois Toy Show**, 13-IOM-LP **Isle of Man TT**, 13-IOW-VV **Isle of Wight** (two types), 13-JEL-LP **Jelly Beans.**

Row 1. 13-JEP-DG **Jersey Evening Post**, 13-JER-VV **Jersey** (two types), 13-JOL-FS **Jolly Time**, 13-KAL-LP **Kalamazoo Loose Leaf.**
Row 2. 13-KIT-LP **Kitchener Coin Machine**, 13-KLM-LP **KLM Service**, 13-KUN-LP **Kuntz**, 13-LEI-LP **Leicester Mercury**, 13-LIN-VV **Lincoln.**
Row 3. 13-LIO-LP **Lionel**, 13-LLA-VV **Llangollen**, 13-LON-VV **London** (two types), 13-MAB-DG **Mary Ann Brewery.**
Row 4. 13-MAN-LP **Manchester Evening News**, 13-MAR-VV **Margate**, 13-MIC-DG **Michelin**, 13-MIT-DG & 13-MIT-LP **Mitre 10.**

Row 1. 13-NEA-LP **James Neale**, 13-NED-LP **Nederlandse Lledo**, 13-NEP-LP **News Plus**, 13-NEY-LP **Newey & Eyre**, 13-NOF-LP **Norfran Products**.

Row 2. 13-NIA-LP **Niagara Falls** (red & blue body), 13-NTC-C3 **Northland Toy Club**, 13-OHA-LP **O'Hara Bar**, 13-OLT-LP **Old Toyland Shows**.

Row 3. 13-ONB-LP **Ontario Beaver**, 13-PEA-VV **The Peaks**, 13-PEP-LP **Peterborough Parachute**, 13-PLY-VV **Plymouth**, 13-POL-LP **Polk's Hobbies**.

Row 4. 13-POT-LP **Potter's Warehouse**, 13-ROB-DG **Robinson's**, 13-ROM-DG **Royal Mail**, 13-ROY-DG **Royal Mail 750 Years**, 13-RYD-DG **Ryder Rental**.

Row 1. 13-STI-VV **Stirling**, 13-STR-DG **Stroh's Beer**, 13-SUA-VV **Stratford-upon-Avon** (two types), 13-SWA-LP **Swan Pens**.
Row 2. 13-SWI-LP **Swiss Centre**, 13-TAY-LP **Taylors of Woodford**, 13-TEL-LP **Telegraph Centenary**, 13-TIM-LP **The Times**, 13-TUC-DG **Tucher Brau**.
Row 3. 13-TUR-LP **Turano** (brown & black), 13-VEC-LP **Vectis Models**, 13-VIM-LP **Vimto** (white & black roof).
Row 4. 13-VIW-LP **Victoria Wine**, 13-WEP-LP **Weekly Post**, 13-WIM-VV **Windermere**, 13-WIN-VV **Windsor**, 13-YOH-LP **Youngs of Hayes.**

33

Row 1. 13-WPT-LP **West Point Toy Show** (+/-blade logo), 13-YOR-VV **York**, 13-ZEA-LP **Zealley**, 14-ACM-DG **Acme.**

Row 2. 14-BEN-LP **Bennett-State Farm** (cream & black top), 14-GRA-DG **Grand Hotel**, 14-GRY-SP **Gray**, 14-HAM-DG **Hamleys.**

Row 3. 14-KLM-LP **KLM Travel**, 14-MEP-LP **Metropolitan Police**, 14-POL-FS **Police**, 14-SDF-DG & 14-SFD-FS **San Diego Fire Chief.**

Row 4. 14-STP-DG **State Penitentiary**, 14-TAX-DG, 14-TXE-EC & 14-TXI-LP **Taxis**, 14-WES-LP **Western Studios.**

Row 1. 15-ADM-LP **Admirals' Cup 1987**, 15-ALT-LP **Alton Towers**, 15-AUB-LP **Australian Bicentenary**, 15-AVD-LP **Avon Diecast Club**, 15-BAE-LP **Barclays Ealing**.

Row 2. 15-BAL-LP **Barclays** (London), 15-BAM-LP **Barclays in Milton Keynes**, 15-BAS-LP **Barclays Super Savers**, 15-BEA-LP **Beamish**, 15-BIR-LP **Bird's**.

Row 3. 15-BIS-LP **B.I.S.-Split**, 15-BRG-LP **Brigade Aid**, 15-BRK-LP **Brooklands**, 15-BTM-LP **Bournemouth** (two roof/logo colors).

Row 4. 15-BTR-LP **Bournemouth**, 15-CAS-DG **Castlemaine**, 15-CCC-LP **Catherine Cookson**, 15-CHA-LP **Chasewater**, 15-CHO-LP **Chorley Guardian**.

Row 1. 15-CIC-LP **City of Coventry**, 15-CIN-DG **Cinzano**, 15-CLB-LP **Country Life Butter**, 15-COG-DG **Coca-Cola**, 15-COM-DG **Commonwealth Games.**

Row 2. 15-COW-LP & 15-COY-LP **Cowes Museum**, 15-DNA-LP **Donington Autojumble**, 15-DUN-LP **Dundee**, 15-ETF=LP **Essex Toy Fair.**

Row 3. 15-EDM-LP **Edmonton** (blue & red body), 15-EVA-DG **Evening Argus**, 15-EXG-LP **Exchange & Mart**, 15-EXE-LP **Express & Echo.**

Row 4. 15-EXS-LP **Express & Star**, 15-FOA-LP **Fotorama Colour**, 15-FOF-LP **Fotorama Film**, 15-GEM-LP **Gemini Diecast**, 15=GLA-LP **Glasgow.**

Row 1. 15-GUA-LP **Guardian & Post**, 15-GUE-LP **Guelph** (red & yellow body), 15-GWS-LP **Great Western Society**, 15-HAM-DG **Hamleys.**

Row 2. 15-HAG-DG **Hall's Wine** (original, specimen, reissue), 15-HAH-LP **Hall's-Hastings**, 15-HAN-LP **Hanningtons.**

Row 3. 15-HAP-LP **Happy Eater**, 15-HEI-DG **Heinz-Tilling**, 15-HMQ-LP **Her Majesty the Queen**, 15-IWR-LP **Isle of Wight Steam Rally**, 15-IWS-LP **Isle of Wight Steam Railway.**

Row 4. 15-IWW-LP **Isle of Wight Weekly Post**, 15-KIT-LP **Kitchener** (red & yellow body), 15-KLM-LP **KLM**, 15-LBS-LP **Lambeth Building Society.**

Row 1. 15-LIN-LP **Lincolnshire Echo**, 15-LIV-DG **Liverpool Festival Gardens**, 15-LMC-LP **London Model Club**, 15-LOT-LP **Lothian**, 15-MAI-LP **Maidstone & District**.

Row 2. 15-MAT-DG **Madame Tussaud**, 15-MON-LP **Montreal** (blue & red body), 15-MSM-LP **MSMC**, 15-NAG-LP **National Garden Festival**.

Row 3. 15-NDM-LP **Northern Daily Mail**, 15-NEW-LP **News of the World**, 15-NIA-LP **Niagara Falls**, 15-NOR-LP **Norfolk Swapmeet**, 15-NOT-LP **Nottingham Evening Post**.

Row 4. 15-OXF-LP **Oxford Mail**, 15-PER-LP **Persil**, 15-PLA-LP **Plymouth Argyle**, 15-QUE-LP **Quebec** (blue & red body).

Row 1. 15-RAD-LP **Radio Times**, 15-RDB-LP **Redbridge**, 15-RFG-LP **Red Funnel Group**, 15-ROY-DG **Royal Wedding**, 15-RYH-LP **Ryde Harriers.**

Row 2. 15-RYR-LP **Ryde Rail**, 15-SHW-LP **Showgard**, 15-SPG-LP **Spring Garden Show**, 15-STE-LP **Stevenson's**, 15-STF-LP **Staffordshire county Show.**

Row 3. 15-STO-LP **Stockton**, 15-STR-LP **Stretton Models**, 15-SWV-DG **Swan Vestas**, 15-TOH-LP **Toronto Harbor Front** (red & yellow body).

Row 4. 15-TOR-LP **Toronto** (blue & red body), 15-TYF-LP **Toyfair at the Centre Halls**, 15-UAS-LP **United Auto Services** (+/-MBF logo).

Row 1. **15-UNP-SP Unpainted, 15-VAN-LP Vancouver** (blue & red body), **15-VIE-LP Vienna Beef** (blue & yellow roof).

Row 2. **15-VIG-LP Vigil Rescue, 15-WAT-LP Waterloo** (red & yellow body), **15 Yorkville** (red & yellow body).

Row 3. **15-VIM-LP Vimto, 15-BMO Banvil, 15-DEL-LP Delaine, 15-KOY-LP Koyanagi** (red & white body).

Row 4. **16-AIR-EC Airfix-Humbrol, 16-ALT-LP Alton Towers, 16-ALV-LP Allied Van Lines, 16-APU-LP Apura** (two logo types).

Row 1. 16-AMR-LP **A.M.R.C.**, 16-AVO-LP **Avon Diecast**, 16-BPQ-LP **British Police Quest**, 16-BUS-DG **Bushells Tea** (two front logo types).

Row 2. 16-BRD-LP **J. J. Brodsky**, 16-CAD-DG **Cadbury's**, 16-CAV-LP **Cavalier**, 16-COC-DG **Coca-Cola** (black & white wheels).

Row 3. 16-COL-LP **Cold Choice**, 16-CRO-DG **Croft Original**, 16-DUN-LP **Dunlop**, 16-EXC-LP **Exchange & Mart**, 16-FER-LP **Ferguson's**.

Row 4. 16-FYF-DG **Fyffes**, 16-GER-LP **Michael Gerson**, 16-GRE-LP **Alan Greenwood**, 16-GRY-LP **Gray**, 16-HAM-DG **Hamleys**.

Row 1. 16-HAR-LP **Harold's Place**, 16-HEG-DG **Hershey's Mr. Goodbar**, 16-HEK-DG **Hershey's Krackel**, 16-HIV-LP **Historic Comercial Vehicle Rally/Wheels of Yesterday** (left & right logo).

Row 2. 16-IDE-LP **Ideal Home**, 16-JON-LP **Jones & Son**, 16-KLM-LP **KLM**, 16-KIW-DG **Kiwi** (cream & green logo frame).

Row 3. 16-KLE-LP **Kleen-ez-e** (light & dark blue body), 16-LMS-LP **L.M.S. Parcels**, 16-LNE-DG **L.N.E.R. Parcels**, 16-MAH-LP **Manners & Harrison.**

Row 4. 16-MAY-DG **Mayflower**, 16-MIN-LP **Minster Fair**, 16-NAS-LP **National Systems**, 16-NFS-LP **National Fire Service** (red & gray body).

Row 1. 16-NOR-LP **Northland Lumber**, 16-OLT-LP **Old Toyland**, 16-OVE-LP **Over's 0f Camberley**, 16-PEA-LP **J. & B. Pearce**, 16-RRM-LP **Reading Royal Mail**.

Row 2. 16-SCA-LP **Scale Auto Enthusiast**, 16-SCF-LP **Stoney Creek**, 16-SHL-LP **Sheltons**, 16-SLU-LP **Slumberland**.

Row 3. 16-SOE-LP **South Essex**, 16-SUR-LP **Surrey Diecast**, 16-THR-LP **Threshold**, 16-TRE-DG **Trebor**, 16-VAK-LP **Vakuum Vulk**.

Row 4. 16-VAN-LP **Van Magazine**, 16-VEN-LP **VEN**, 16-VER-LP **Vers Markt**, 16-VEP-LP **Vernons Plaice**, 16-WES-LP **Westward Tools**.

Row 1. 17-ALD-LP **Aldershot**, 17-ALT-LP **Alton Towers**, 17-BIG-DG **Big Top**, 17-BLA-LP **Blackburn**.

Row 2. 17-BOA-DG **BOAC**, 17-BOU-LP **Bournemouth**, 17-BRI-LP **Bristol** (+/- Avon Diecast Club logo), 17-BUR-DG **Burnley**.

Row 3. 17-COM-DG **Commonwealth Games**, 17-DEL-LP **Delaine**, 17-DEV-LP **Devon General**, 17-DUN-LP **Dundee**.

Row 4. 17-EAB-LP **Eastbourne** (+/-gold trim), 17-EAK-LP **East Kent** (maroon & dark red body).

Row 1. 17-EUR-DG **Eurotour**, 17-EXC-LP **Exchange & Mart**, 17-GBM-LP **G. & B. Motor Service**, 17-GLA-LP **Glasgow**.
Row 2. 17-GRY-SP **Gray**, 17-HAM-DG **Hamleys**, 17-HAP-LP **Happy Days**, 17-HED-LP **Hedingham**.
Row 3. 17-IOM-LP **Isle of Man TT**, 17-LON-DG & 17-LON-LP **London Transport** (red/cream DG, green LP, red LP).
Row 4. 17-LOT-LP **Lothian**, 17-MAD-LP & 17-MAI-LP **Maidstone**, 17-MID-LP **Middlesborough**.

Row 1. 17-MOX-DG **Morrell's-Oxford**, 17-OXF-LP **Oxford**, 17-PEN-DG **Pennine**, 17-POT-LP **Potteries**.

Row 2. 17-RAF-DG **Royal Air Force**, 17-RDP-LP **RDP Collectors Guide**, 17-RIB-LP **Ribble**, 17-SOD-LP **Southdown**.

Row 3. 17-SOE-DG **Southend** (blue, red, orange body), 17-STE-LP **Stevenson's**.

Row 4. 17-SOU-LP & 17-SOV-LP **Southern Vectis** (body & roof colors), 17-SUT-LP **Sutton School**.

46

Row 1. 17-STR-DG **Stratford blue** (dark & light tires), 17-WBC-LP **West Bromwich**, 17-WHI-EC **White Edocar.**
Row 2. 17-ULS-LP **Ulster Transport**, 17-YCM-LP **York Castle Museum**, 18-AMB-DG **Ambulance** (plain & circled crosses).
Row 3. 18-AMB-EC **Edocar Ambulance**, 18-CHI-DG **Children's Hospital**, 18-COL-DG **Colman's Mustard**, 18-COM-DG **Common-wealth Games.**
Row 4. 18-EXC-LP **Exchange & Mart**, 18-FIR-DG **Firestone**, 18-JON-LP **Jon Acc**, 18-RAF-DG **Royal Air Force.**

Row 1. 18-RAP-DG **Rapid Cash Transit,** 18-STJ-LP **St. John Ambulance,** 18-WEW-LP **Western Woollens,** 18-WHS-DG **White Star.**

Row 2. 18-GRY-SP **Gray,** 19-BLK-LP **Black Rolls-Royce,** 19-BLU-LP **Blue,** 19-BUR-DG **Burgundy,** 19-GRY-SP **Gray.**

Row 3. 19-CON-LP **Congratulations,** 19-CRM-DG **Cream,** 19-GOL-DG **Gold,** 19-MAR-LP **Marilyn,** 19-OLI-DG **Olive & Wicker.**

Row 4. 19-ROY-LP **Royal Wedding,** 19-SIL-EC **Silver Edocar,** 19-WHI-LP **White,** 19-YEL-DG **Yellow.**

Row 1. 20-BBC-LP **BBC** (no logo), 20-BUR-LP **Burt's Ales**, 20-COC-DG **Coca-Cola**, 20-EAG-DG **Eagle Ale**.
Row 2. 20-GOO-DG **Goodrich**, 20-LAI-LP **Laird's Applejack**, 20-LIO-DG **Lionel**, 20-STR-DG **Stroh's Beer**.
Row 3. 20-LOW-LP **Lowcocks Lemonade** (barrels & bottle), 20-UNI-DG **Uniroyal**, 20-WHI-DG **Whitbread**.
Row 4. 20-WAT-LP **Watneys** (two logo types), 21-AAC-LP **A.A.C.A.**, 21-RDP-LP **RDP Collectors Guides**, 21-OKT-LP **Oktoberfest**.

Row 1. 21-ALL-LP **Allenburys**, 21-ANC-LP **A.N.C.**, 21-AUS-LP **Australian Model Swapmeets**, 21-CFV-LP **Canada Fruit & Vine**, 21-CIM-LP **City Museum**.

Row 2. 21-COC-DG **Coca-Cola**, 21-COM-LP **Co-Operative Milk**, 21-DEA-LP **Deane's**, 21-DRB-LP **Dr. Barnardo's**, 21-DRP-DG **Dr. Pepper**.

Row 3. 21-EDO-EC **Edocar**, 21-EXC-LP **Exchange & Mart**, 21-FOX-LP **Fox Talbot**, 21-HOS-DG **Hostess Cake**, 21-JEP-LP **Jersey Evening Post**.

Row 4. 21-LCM-DG **Lledo Club Member**, 21-LLP-LP **Lledo Promotional**, 21-LEI-DG **Leicester Mercury**, 21-SHA-DG **Sharp's Toffee**, 21-WPT-LP **West Point Toy Show**.

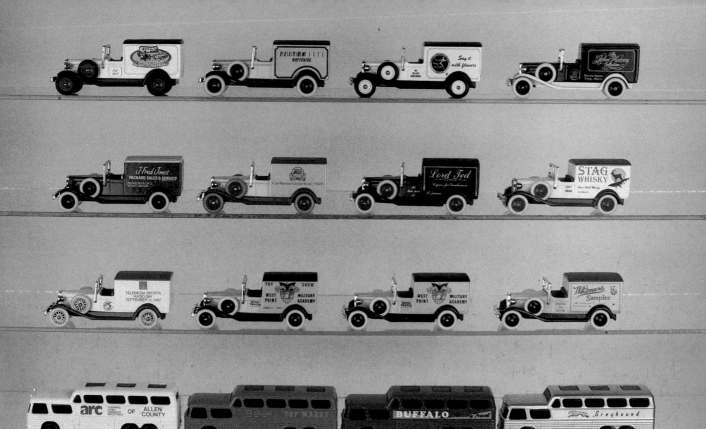

Row 1. 22-EXC-LP **Exchange & Mart**, 22-FEL-LP **Felton Worldwide**, 22-FTD-DG **F.T.D.**, 22-JHC-LP **John Harvey Collection.**
Row 2. 22-JON-LP **J. Fred Jones**, 22-LCM-DG **Lledo Club Member**, 22-LTC-DG **Lord Ted Cigars**, 22-STA-DG **Stag Whisky.**
Row 3. 22-TEL-LP **Telemedia Sports**, 22-WES-LP **West Point** (+/-Toy Show), 22-WHI-DG **Whitman's Sampler.**
Row 4. 23-ARC-LP **A.R.C.**, 23-BAT-LP **B. & A. Top Marks**, 23-BUF-DG **Buffalo**, 23-GRE-DG **Greyhound.**

Row 1. 23-BMO-LP **Banvil**, 23-FRA-LP **Frandello**, 23-STA-LP **Stagecoach**, 23-THO-LP **Thomas Tours**.
Row 2. 23-GWT-DG **Golden West Tours**, 23-TOF-LP **Töff Töff**, 26-SCH-DG **Schweppes** (light & dark body & load).
Row 3. 24-BLK-LP **Black Rolls-Royce**, 24-PUR-LP **Purple**, 24-RED-LP **Red**, 24-YEL-DG **Yellow**, 25-BLK-LP **Black**.
Row 4. 25-BLU-DG **Blue**, 25-CON-LP **Congratulations**, 25-SIL-DG **Silver**, 25-WHI-DG **White**.

Row 1. 26-LCM-DG **Lledo Club Member**, 27-A1R-DG **A1 Recovery**, Figures for models 013 & 014.
Row 2. Marathon M1: **Ensignbus, London Zoo, Pan Am,** 13-HRA-LP **Harry Ramsden's Fish & Chips.**
Row 3. **Marathon M2: Air Canada, Ghana Airways, Pan Am,** 15-AUT-LP **Autocar,** 15-EVT-LP **Evening Telegraph.**
Row 4. **Marathon M3: Island Tours, Speedlink, Gatwick,** 15-TVT-DG **TV Times.**

Row 1. 1-I1, 2 & 3 **Revin' Rebel**, 1-J1 **Jaguar XJ6**, 2-I1 & 2 **Pontiac Fiero**.

Row 2. 3-F16, 17, 18, 19 & 20 **Porsche Turbo**, 4-H6 **'57 Chevy**.

Row 3. 4-I1 **Taxi**, 5-H1 & 2 **Jeep Eagle**, 5-I1, 2 & 5 **Peterbilt Tanker**.

Row 4. 6-G1 **IMSA Mazda**, 6-H1 **Formula One**, 6-I1 & 2 **Ford Supervan II**, 7-G1 & 2 **Rompin' Rabbit**.

Row 1. 7-I2 **Porsche 959**, 8-I1 & 2 **Rover 3500**, 8-J1 **Greased Lightning**, 8-K1 & 2 **Scania T-142**.

Row 2. 8-L1 & 2 **Vauxhall Astra**, 9-G½ & 3 **Fiat Abarth**, 9-H1 **Toyota MR2**, 10-H1 **Buick LeSabre**.

Row 3. 10-G9, 10 & 11 **Plymouth police Car**, 11-J1, 2 & 3 **Lamborghini Countach**.

Row 4. 11-I1 & 2 **IMSA Cobra Mustang**, 12-G10 **Citroen CX Ambulance**, 12-H 1 & 3 **Pontiac Firebird**, 14-J1 **Jeep Laredo**.

Row 1. 13-H1, 2 & 3 **Dunes Racer**, 14-I1, 2 & 3 **'83 Corvette**.
Row 2. 15-H1, 2, 3 & 4 **Ford Sierra**, 15-I1 **Peugeot 205**, 16-I1 **Ford LTD Police Car**.
Row 3. 16-G, 16-H1, 2 & 3 **Pontiac Trans Am**, 17-H1 & 2 **AMX Pro Stocker**.
Row 4. 17-I1 & 2 **Ford Escort**, 17-J1 **Dodge Dakota**, 18-H1 & 2 **Fire Engine**, 21-G30 **Renault 5**.

Row 1. 17-G2, 3, 4, 5, 6 & 7 **London Bus.**
Row 2. 17-G9, 11, 12, 14, 15 & 16 **London Bus.**
Row 3. 17-G17, 18, 20, 22, 23 & 24 **London Bus.**
Row 4. 17-G25, 26, 28 & 29 **London Bus,** 19-H1 & 2 **Peterbilt Cement Truck.**

Row 1. 20-H1, 2, 3, 4, 5 & 6 **Volvo Container Truck.**
Row 2. 20-H7 **Volvo Container Truck,** 21-H1 **Corvette Pace Car,** 21-I1 **Breakdown Van,** 21-J1 **GMC Wrecker,** 22-G1 & 2 **Big Foot.**
Row 3. 22-H1 & 2 **Jaguar XK120,** 23-G1, 2, 3 & 4 **Audi Quattro.**
Row 4. 23-I1 **Honda ATC,** 24-H1 & 2 **Datsun 280ZX,** 24-I1, 2 & 3 **Nissan 300ZX.**

Row 1. 23-H1 & 2 **Peterbilt Tipper**, 25-L1 & 2 **Pacific Ambulance**, 26-H1 & 2 **Cable Truck.**

Row 2. 26-I1 & 2 **Volvo Covered Truck**, 27-H1 **Jeep Cherokee**, 28-I1 & 2 **Dodge Daytona**, 29-F22 **Shovel Nose Tractor.**

Row 3. 30-G2, 3, 4, 5 & 7 **Articulated Truck**, 31-I1 **Rolls-Royce Silver Cloud.**

Row 4. 30-I1 & 2 **Mercedes-Benz 280GE**, 31-H1&2 **Mazda RX7**, 33-G1 & 2 **VW Golf GTI.**

Row 1. 32-G4 **Excavator**, 33-H2 & 1 **Renault 11**, 34-G1/3, 4 & 5 **Chevy Pro Stocker**.

Row 2. 34-H1 **Ford RS200**, 35-E1 & 2 **Zoo Truck**, 36-G5 & 6 **Refuse Truck**, 39-H1 **Ford Bronco**.

Row 3. 35-H1 **Land Rover**, 37-I1 & 2 **Matra Rancho**, 37-J1 & 2 **Jeep 4x4**, 40-G1 **Rocket Transporter**.

Row 4. 39-E5 & 6 **Rolls-Royce Silver Shadow**, 39-G1, 2 & 3 **BMW Cabriolet**.

Row 1. 38-H1, 3, 4, 5, 7 & 8 **Ford Model A Truck.**
Row 2. 38-H9, 10, 11, 12, 13 & 14 **Ford Model A Truck.**
Row 3. 38-H15, 16, 20, 21, 22 & 23 **Ford Model A Truck.**
Row 4. 38-H25, 26 & 27 **Ford Model A Truck,** 40-F1, 2 & 3 **Corvette T-Top.**

Row 1. 39-F1 & 2 **Toyota Supra**, 41-G1, 2 & 3 **Kenworth Conventional Aerodyne**, 42-H1 **Mobile Crane.**

Row 2. 41-H1, 2 & 3 **Racing Porsche 935**, 42-G1, 2 & 3 **Ford Thunderbird.**

Row 3. 43-H1, 2, 3, 4, 5 & 6 **Mercedes-Benz AMG.**

Row 4. 43-G1 **Peterbilt Continental**, 44-G2, 4, 5 & 6 **Chevy Van**, 45-G1 **Ford Skip Truck.**

Row 1. 44-H2 & 3 **Citroen 15cv**, 45-F1, 2, 3 & 4 **Kenworth C.O.E. Aerodyne.**
Row 2. 44-I1 **Skoda LR130**, 46-H1 **Big Blue**, 46-I1 & 3 **Sauber Group C**, 46-J1 & 2 **Mission Helicopter.**
Row 3. 47-G1 & 2 **Jaguar SS100**, 47-H2 **School bus**, 48-I1, 2 & 3 **Vauxhall Astra.**
Row 4. 48-H1 **Unimog**, 49-F1 & 2 **Sand Digger**, 49-G1 **Peugeot Quasar**, 50-G1 **Harley-Davidson**, 50-H2 **Chevy Blazer.**

Row 1. 52-F1, 2 & 3 **BMW M1**, 53-G1, 2 & 3 **Flareside Pickup.**
Row 2. 54-G1 **NASA Command Center**, 54-H1, 2 & 3 **Foam Pumper**, 57-G1 & 2 **Carmichael Commando.**
Row 3. 56-F4 **Mercedes-Benz 450SEL**, 56-G2, 1, 6 & 7 **Peterbilt Tanker**, 58-H1 **Mercedes-Benz 300E.**
Row 4. 57-H1, 2 & 3 **Mini Pickup**, 58-G1 & 2 **Ruff Trek Pickup**, 59-G29 **Porsche 928.**

Row 1. 60-F1 & 3 **Piston Popper**, 60-H1, 2 & 3 **Pontiac Firebird**, 62-G12 **Corvette**.
Row 2. 60-I3, 4, 5, 2 & 6 **Ford Transit**, 62-I1 **Volvo 760**.
Row 3. 61-E1, 5 & 7 **Peterbilt Wrecker**, 63-H1, 2 & 3 **Snorkel Fire Engine**.
Row 4. 64-F10, 11, 12 & 13 **Caterpillar**, 65-F1 & 66-G2 **Tyrone Malone**.

Row 1. 72-G10 **Dodge Truck** (right side), 64-G4, 8 & 9 **Dodge Carvan**, 65-G1 & 2 **STP Racer**.
Row 2. 65-E20, 21, 22, 24 & 25 **Airport Coach**, 65-H2 **Airplane Transporter**.
Row 3. 65-I1 **Cadillac Allante**, 66-I1 **Rolls-Royce Silver Spirit**, 67-G1 **Flame Out**, 67-I1, 2 & 3 **Ikarus Coach**.
Row 4. 68-G1 & 2 **Camaro IROC-Z**, 69-F1 & 2 **Willys Street Rod**, 70-F1 & 2 **Ferrari 308GTB**.

Row 1. 71-G2, 3, 4 & 5 **1962 Corvette**, 72-G1 & 2 **Dodge Delivery Truck**.

Row 2. 72-G3, 4, 6, 7, 11 & 12 **Dodge Delivery Truck**.

Row 3. 72-H1 **Sand Racer**, 73-G10 & 11 **Model A Ford Coupe**, 74-G1 & 2 **Mustang GT**, 75-H1 **Ferrari Testa Rossa**.

Row 4. 72-G10 **Dodge Truck** (left side), 75-G½, 3 & 4 **Helicopter**, SF1-1 & SF2-1 **Halley's Comet cars**.

Row 1. SF1 **Mercury police,** SF2 **Pontiac Firebird,** SF3 **Porsche 928,** SF4 *Daytona Turbo,* SF5 **Mercedes-Benz AMG,** SF6 **Porsche 935.**

Row 2. SF7 **Ford Sierra,** SF8 **'62 Corvette,** SF9 **Datsun 280ZX,** SF10 **Turbo Vette,** SF11 **Ferrari 308GTV,** SF12 **Chevy Stock Car.**

Row 3. SF13 **'84 Corvette,** SF14 **BMW Cabriolet,** SF15 **Escort Cabriolet,** SF16 **Sauber Group C,** SF17 **Lamborghini Countach,** SF18 **Firebird Racer.**

Row 4. SF19 **Fiero Racer,** SF21 **Nissan 300ZX,** SF22 **Camaro IROC-Z,** SF24 **Ferrari Testa Rossa,** SF25 **Peugeot Quasar.**

Row 1. TP103-2 **Cattle Truck & Trailer**, TP106-2 **Renault & Motorcycle Trailer**, TP108-2 **Farm Tractor & Trailer**.
Row 2. TO110-2 **Matra Rancho & Lifeboat**, TP112-1 **Alpine Rescue**, TP112-2 **Unfall-Rettung Unimog & Trailer**.
Row 3. TP115-1 **Ford Escort & Boat Trailer**, TP116-1 **Cherokee & Caravan**, TP117-1 **Mercedes-Benz G-Wagon & Horse box**.
Row 4. TP118-1 **BMW & Glider Trailer**, TP119-1 **Flareside & Seafire Boat**.

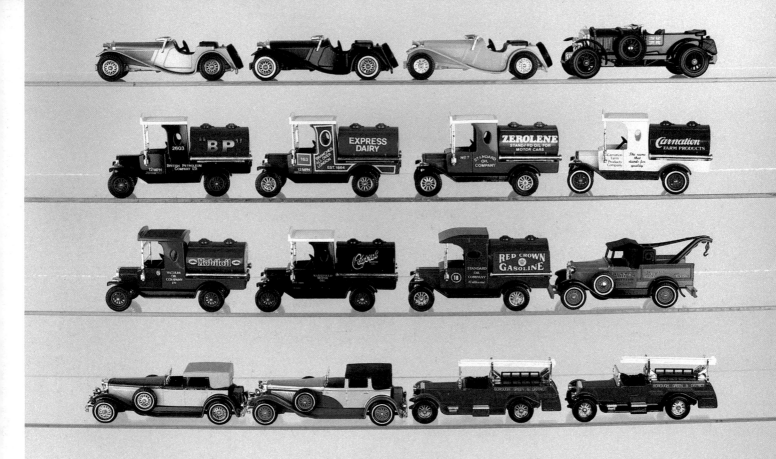

Row 1. Y1-C **Jaguar SS100:** 8 metallic blue, 9 green, 10 yellow; Y2-D1 **Bentley.**

Row 2. Y3-D **Ford Tanker:** 1 **BP**, 2 **Express Dairy**, 3 **Zerolene**, 4 **Carnation.**

Row 3. Y3-D **Ford Tanker:** 5 **Mobiloil**, 6 **Castrol**, 7 **Red Crown**; Y7-D1 **Ford Breakdown Truck.**

Row 4. Y4-D **Duesenberg:** 4 brown/tan, 5 silver/blue; Y6-D **Rolls-Royce Fire Truck:** 8 red chassis, 9 black chassis.

Row 1. Y5-D **Talbot Van:** 18 **Nestle's**, 19 **Wrights**, 20 **EverReady**, 21 **Dunlop**.
Row 2. Y5-D **Talbot Van:** 22 **Rose's**, 23 **Speelgoed Otten**, Y8-D **MG TC:** 7 blue, 8 cream.
Row 3. Y9B-9 **Simplex**, Y8-E1 Yorkshire Steam Wagon, Y9-C1 Leyland Truck, Y10-C7 **Rolls-Royce**.
Row 4. Y10-D1 **Maserati**, Y11-C7 **Lagonda**, Y11-D1 **Bugatti**, Y12-E1 Stephenson's Rocket.

Row 1. **Y12-C Ford T Van:** 12 **Bird's Custard**, 13 **Smith's Crisps**, 14 **25 Years**, 15 **Arnott's Biscuits**.
Row 2. **Y12-C Ford T Van:** 16 **Sunlight**, 17 **Harrods**, 18 **Cerebos**, 19 **Captain Morgan**.
Row 3. **Y12-C Ford T Van:** 20 **Royal Mail**, 21 **Pepsi-Cola**, 22 **Hoover**, 23 **Motor 100**.
Row 4. **Y12-C Ford T Van:** 24 **H. J. Heinz**, 25 **Rosella**; **Y12-D1 Ford T Imbach Pickup**, **Y14-C8 Stutz Bearcat**.

72

Row 1. Y13-C **Crossley Truck:** 9 **Carlsberg,** 10 white top, 11 cream top **Waring's.**
Row 2. Y15-B14 **Packard,** Y16-B8 **Mercedes SS,** Y17-A **Hispano-Suiza:** 7 blue, 8 green.
Row 3. Y15-C1 **Tramcar,** Y19-A **Auburn** ¼ tan & brown, 5 cream & black, 6 white & blue.
Row 4. Y18-B **Atkinson Steam Wagon:** 1 **Sand & Gravel,** 2 **Portland Cement,** 3 **Bass & Co.;** Y19-B1 **Fowler Showman's Engine.**

Row 1. Y20-A **Mercedes-Benz 540K:** 1 silver, 2 white, 3 red.
Row 2. Y21-A **Woody Wagon:** 1 no logo, 2 **A. & J.** box, 3 **Carter's;** Y21-B1 **Steam Roller.**
Row 3. Y22-A **Ford A Van:** 1 **Oxo,** 2 **Palm Toffee,** 3 **Toblerone,** 4 **Maggi.**
Row 4. Y22-A **Ford A Van:** 5 **Canada Post,** 6 **Spratt's,** 7 **Lyons Tea;** Y19-C1 **Morris Brasso Van.**

Row 1. Y23-A AEC **Omnibus:** 1 **Schweppes**, 3 **R.A.C.**, 4 **Maples**, 5 **Haig**.
Row 2. Y24-A **Bugatti:** 1 black/yellow, 2 gray/red; Y28-A **Unic Taxi:** 1 red, 2 blue.
Row 3. Y25-A **Renault Van:** 1 **Perrier**, 2 **James Neale**, 3 Duckhams, 4 **Eagle Pencil**.
Row 4. Y25-A **Renault Van:** 5 **Ambulance**, 6 **T. Tunnock**, 7 **Delhaize**; Y16-C1 **Ferrari**.

Row 1. Y26-A **Crossley Lorry:** 1 Löwenbräu, 2 **Romford,** 3 **Gonzalez Byass.**
Row 2. Y27-A **Foden Steam lorry:** 1 **Pickfords,** 2 **Hovis,** 3 **Tate & Lyle,** 4 **Spillers.**
Row 3. Y27-B1 **Foden & Trailer,** Y29-A **Walker Electric Van:** 1 **Harrods,** 2 **Joseph Lucas.**
Row 4. Y30-A **Mack Truck:** 1 **Acorn Storage,** 2 **Consolidated,** 3 **Arctic Ice Cream.**

Row 1. CY1A **Car Transporter**, CY2A **Rocket Transporter.**
Row 2. CY3A **Double Container: Uniroyal, Federal Express.**
Row 3. CY3B **Linfox**, CY4A **Boat Transporter.**
Row 4. CY4B **Ansett Freight**, CY5A **Interstate Trucking** (two minor variations).

Row 1. CY5A **Michelin**, CY6A **Blue Grass Farms.**
Row 2. CY7A **Supergas, Getty.**
Row 3. CY8A **Redcap, Matchbox.**
Row 4. CY9A **Midnight Xpress, IPEC, Crookes Healthcare.**

Row 1. CY10A **Tyrone Malone**, CY11A **Air Car**, CY12A **Darts**.
Row 2. CY13A **Fire Truck**, CY14A **Powerboat Transporter**.
Row 3. CY15A **NASA**, **British Telecom**.
Row 4. CY16A **Duckhams**, **7UP**, **Edwin Shirley-Sealink**.

79

Row 1. CY16A **Heinz Ketchup, Kentucky Fried Chicken.**
Row 2. CY16A **Signal Toothpaste, Wimpy.**
Row 3. **Weetabix,** CY17A **Amoco.**
Row 4. CY17A **Tizer, 7-Up.**

Row 1. CY18A **Varta, Wall's Ice Cream, Kit Kat.**
Row 2. CY18A **Rowntrees Breakaway,** CY19A **Ansett Wridgways.**
Row 3. CY20A **Taylor Woodrow, Readymix.**
Row 4. CY21A **Aircraft Transporter,** CY22A **Power Launch Transposter.**

Row 1. TM1 **Pepsi-Cola,** TM2 **Super Star.**
Row 2. TM3 **Dr. Pepper,** TM4 **Brut.**
Row 3. TM5 **7-Up,** TM6 **Duckhams.**
Row 4. CY16 **Matey Bubble Bath.**

Row 1. CY201 **Fire Rescue Set**, CY203 **Construction Set**.
Row 2. CY205 **Farm Set**, CY206 **British Telecom Set**.

83

Row 1. K15-C **London Bus:** 2 **Chesterfield Church**, 1 **Berlin**, 5 **Macleans.**
Row 2. K15-C **London bus:** 4 **Nestle Milkybar**, 11 **Berlin 750 Jahre**, 9 **Petticoat Lane.**
Row 3. K15-C **London Bus:** 7 **London Wide Tour Bus**, 6 **Telegraph & Argus**, 10 **Planetarium.**

Row 1. K11-D3 **Dodge Suchard Van,** K27-B13 **Powerboat & Transporter.**
Row 2. K31-B13 **Dr. Koch's Trink-10.**
Row 3. K31-B12 **Euro-Express.**

Row 1. K21-D7 **Bärenmarke.**
Row 2. K21-D6 **Weetabix.**
Row 3. K21-D8 **Polara.**

Row 1. K40-B4 **Bizzl-Fröhliches Durstlöschen,** K38-B2 **Notarzt Ambulance.**
Row 2. K88-A1 **Volksbank,** K88-A2 **Caisse d'Epargne,** K88-A3 **Matchbox.**
Row 3. K29-B8 **Elefanten Junge Mode,** K29-B10 **75 Express,** K29-B9 **TAA.**

Row 1. K44-Cl **Bridge Transporter.**

Row 1. K86-A **VW Golf:** 3 white, 2 ADAC, 1 black.
Row 2. K70-A3 **Porsche Turbo,** K98-B **Porsche 944:** 3 red, 2 gold.
Row 3. K95-A **Audi Quattro:** 2 white #10, 1 silver #1, 3 white #17.
Row 4. K100-A4 **Ford Sierra,** K115-A **Mercedes-Benz 190E:** 1 white, 2 silver.

Row 1. K81-A2 **Suzuki**, K110-A1 **Fire Engine**, K81-A1 **Suzuki**.
Row 2. K92-A1 **Helicopter Transporter**, K109-A1 **Petrol Tanker**.
Row 3. K104-A1 **Rancho Rescue Set**, K97-A1 **Police Range Rover**.

Row 1. K101-A2 **Racing Porsche,** K102-A1 **Race Support Set.**
Row 2. K84-A5 **Peugeot 305,** K74-A3 **Volvo Estate Car,** K84-A4 **Peugeot 305.**
Row 3. K96-A1 **Volvo Ambulance,** K90-A2 **Matra Rancho.**

Row 1. K107-A1 **Power Launch Transporter.**
Row 2. K103-A2 **Peterbilt Tanker.**
Row 3. K114-A1 **Mobile Crane,** K139-A1 **Iveco Tipper.**

Row 1. K113-A2 **Garage Transporter.**
Row 2. K135-A1 **Garage Transporter.**

Row 1. K116-A1 **Racing Car Transporter.**
Row 2. K136-A1 **Racing Car Transporter.**

Row 1. K129-A1 **Power Launch Transporter.**
Row 2. K127-A1 **Peterbilt Tanker.**
Row 3. K117-A1 **Bulldozer Transporter.**

Row 1. K130-A1 **Peterbilt Digger Transporter.**
Row 2. K124-A1 **Mercedes-Benz Refrigerator Truck.**
Row 3. K122-A1 **DAF Road Train.**

Row 1. K118-A1 **Road Construction Set.**
Row 2. K137-A1 **Road Construction set.**

Row 1. K128-A1 **DAF Aircraft Transporter.**
Row 2. K126-A1 **DAF Helicopter Transporter.**
Row 3. K134-A1 **Peterbilt Fire Spotter Transporter.**

Row 1. K121-A1 **Peterbilt Wrecker,** K141-A1 **Leyland Tipper.**
Row 2. K123-A1 **Leyland Cement Truck,** K133-A1 **Refuse Truck.**
Row 3. K120-A1 **Leyland Car Transporter,** K140-A1 **Leyland Car Recovery Vehicle.**

Row 1. K142-A2 **BMW Polizei**, K142-A1 **BMW Police**.
Row 2. K144-A1 **Frankfurt Land Rover**, K143-A1 **Bedford Ambulance**, K144-A2 **Heathrow Land Rover**.
Row 3. K131-A2 **Texaco Tanker**, K131-A1 **Shell Tanker**.

Row 1. K132-A2 **Fire Tender, NASA Countdown Set.**
Row 2. K138-A1 **Fire Rescue Set.**

Row 1. SP1-2, TS3-1 & SP2-2 **Kremer Porsche.**
Row 2. SP3-2, SP4-1 & SP4-2 **Ferrari 512BB.**
Row 3. SP5-1, SP5-2 & SP6-1 **Lancia Rally.**
Row 4. SP7-2, TS2-1 & SP8-2 **Zakspeed Mustang.**

Row 1. Dinky Toys 7 **VW Rabbit**, 9 **Fiat Abarth**, 44 **Citroen 15cv**, 51 **Pontiac Firebird**, 60 **Toyota Supra**, 69 **1984 Corvette**.
Row 2. SP9-1, SP10-1 & SP10-2 **Chevy Pro Stocker**.
Row 3. SP11-2, SP12-2 & TS1-1 **Chevrolet Camaro**.
Row 4. TS4-1 **Chevy Pro Stocker**, SP13-1 & SP14-1 **Porsche 959**.

Row 1. G5 **Federal Express Set**, G6 **Virgin Atlantic Set.**
Row 2. G10 **Pan Am Set**, G11 **Lufthansa Set.**

Row 1. **Matchbox Free Wheelin' Bonus Set.**
Row 2. **Matchbox Classy Classics Set.**

Row 1. MB12-F, **G & H Pontiac Firebird castings.**
Row 2. MB5-H2 **4x4 Jeep,** MB20-F1 **Desert Dawg,** & MB20-F2 **Laredo Jeep.**

Row 1. MB24-G, 24-H & 24-I **Nissan-Datsun castings.**
Row 2. Opposite side of MB17-G4 **Greek Bus,** the MB20-E50 **Police Patrol,** and opposite side of MB17-G16 **Staffordshire Bus.**

Row 1. DG12 **Fire Engine** with and without ladder rack tab.

Row 2. 06-HAY-LP **W. Haydon Van** on plinth, right side of 13-CHM-LP with Arabic logo, 10-SOV-DG **Southern Vectis Bus** on plinth.

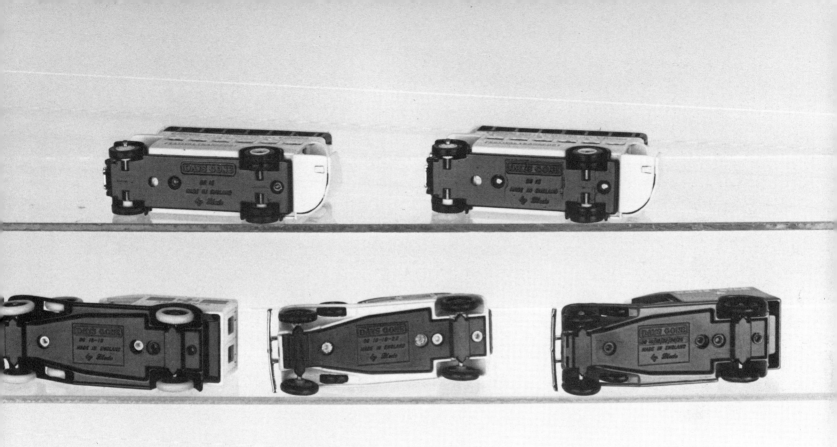

Row 1. DG15 **Double Decker Bus** with original smooth and current recessed base.
Row 2. DG18-19 base/large rear flange, DG18-19-22 base/small flange, DG18-19-22-24-25 base/medium flange. Note that the numbers on the last base are actually separated by / lines, which may or may not cross the horizontal line below them.

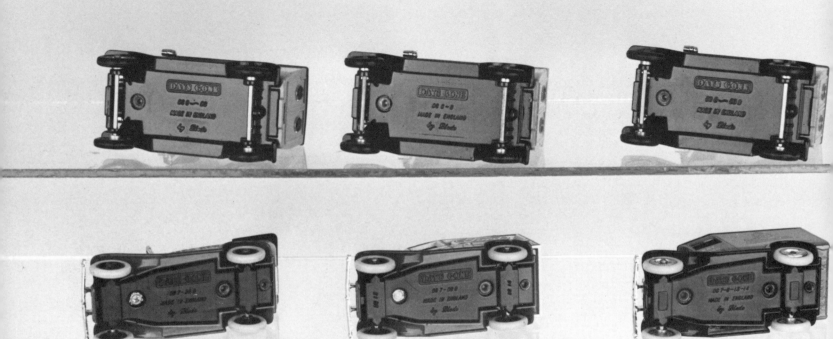

Row 1. **Model T Ford** bases: DG6-DG, DG6-DG8, & DG6-8.
Row 2. Original DG7-DG9 base, second type with DG13 & DG14 on axle covers, last type with DG7-9-13-14 on main base area and former numbers on axle covers blocked out.

Row 1. DG10-DG12 base without ridge/thin front fenders, DG10-DG12 base with ridge/thin front fenders, **Fantastic Set o' Wheels** base/thick front fenders.
Row 2. **Edocar** base/thin front fenders, DG16 base/thick front fenders, DG20 base/thin front fenders; all bases with ridge.

Row 1. Two special boxes and the usual **Lledo Promotional box.**
Row 2. Figures for **Lledo 5 & 12, 6 & 8.**

Lledo 06 **Model T Ford** promotional model: Schiffer Publishing
Ltd./Millbank Books; 1988.

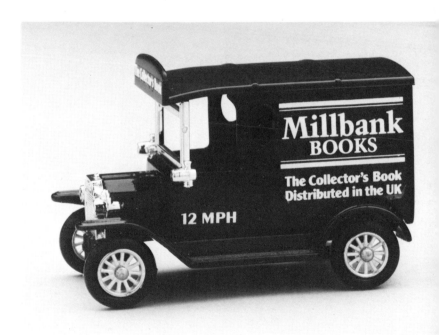

113

Matchbox® Series

1-I REVIN' REBEL 1982 GB/US
1. Orange body, white roof, blue & white trim.
2. Orange body, blue roof, blue & white trim: 1982.
3. Yellow body, black roof, Toyman logo: 1983.

1-J JAGUAR XJ6 1987 GB = 41 US
1. Metallic red body, tan interior.

2-I PONTIAC FIERO 1985 GB/US
1. White upper/blue lower body, orange trim, #85.
2. White upper/red lower body, orange trim: 1987.

3-F PORSCHE TURBO 1978 GB/US
16. Black body, gold trim, tan interior: 1984.
17. Dark blue body, Wrangler logo, #47: 1985.
18. White body, green Porsche logo, #3: 1986.
19. White body, red & black trim, "Boss", #14: 1987.
20. Black body, green and yellow BP logo, #90: 1987.

4-H '57 CHEVY 1980 GB/US
6. Black body, red hood, red & yellow trim: 1983.

4-I TAXI FX4R 1987 GB
1. Black body, gray interior.

5-H JEEP EAGLE 4x4 1982 GB/US
1. Golden brown body, black seats & roll bar.
2. Red body, yellow Golden Eagle logo: 1984 US.

5-I PETERBILT PETROL TANKER 1984 GB = 56 US
1. White body, gray tank, Shell logo.
2. White body, gray tank, red & blue Ampol logo: 1985.
3. Black body & tank, red & blue Amoco logo: 1985.
4. Black body, chrome tank, red & blue Amoco logo: 1985.
5. Black body & tank, red & blue Amoco logo: 1986.

6-G IMSA MAZDA 1983 US = 7 GB
1. Blue body, white & orange trim, red interior.

6-H FORMULA I RACING CAR 1984 GB
1. Red body, black wings & driver, #3.

6-I FORD SUPERVAN II 1986 US = 72 GB
1. White body, dark blue Ford logo.
2. White body, bright blue Ford logo: 1987.

7-G ROMPIN' RABBIT 1982 GB/US
1. White body, tan & black trim, tan interior.
2. Yellow body, blue & black trim, "Ruff Rabbit": 1983 US.

7-H IMSA MAZDA 1983 GB = 6 US
1. Blue body, white and orange trim, red interior.

7-I PORSCHE 959 1986 GB/US
1. Silver body, red & blue trim, red interior.
2. White body, red & blue trim, red interior: 1987.

8-I ROVER 3500 1983 GB
1. White body, yellow & black Police logo.
2. White body, red & blue Police logo: 1986.

8-J GREASED LIGHTNING 1983 US
1. Red body, Greased Lightning logo, #31.

8-K SCANIA T-142 TRACTOR 1985 US = 71 GB
1. White body, red chassis, orange & yellow trim.
2. White body, white chassis, red-orange-yellow trim: 1987.

8-L VAUXHALL ASTRA POLICE CAR 1987 GB
1. White body, red & blue trim, "Police".
2. White body, green hood & doors, "Polizei": 1987.

9-E AMX JAVELIN 1972 GB = 17 US
37. Maroon body, red & white trim, Dr. Pepper logo, #4: 1985.

9-G FIAT ABARTH 1982 US = 74 GB
3. White body, red & green trim, Alitalia logo: 1984.

9-H TOYOTA MR2 1986 US = 74 GB
1. White body, red & yellow trim, Pace Car logo.

9-I CATERPILLAR BULLDOZER 1986 GB = 64 US
1. Yellow body, black cab, unpainted engine and chassis.
2. Yellow body, black cab, light gray engine and chassis.

10-G PLYMOUTH POLICE CAR 1979 GB/US
9. White body, blue hoods, shield emblems: 1984.
10. White body, blue hoods, SFPD star emblem: 1985.
11. White body, red hoods & trim, "Sheriff" star: 1987.

10-H BUICK LE SABRE 1987 US
1. Black body, red interior, red-white-yellow trim, "355CID", #4.

11-I IMSA COBRA MUSTANG 1982 US = 67 GB
1. Black body, red trim, white "Mustang": 1983.
2. Black body, green-yellow-white trim: 1986.

11-J LAMBORGHINI COUNTACH 1986 GB = 67 US
1. Red body and base, tan interior.
2. Black body, red-orange-white trim, #5: 1986.
3. Red body, green & yellow BP emblems, #15: 1987.

12-G CITROEN CX 1980 GB
10. White and red body, Ambulance logo: 1983.
11. White body, blue "Marine Division" logo, as in TP109: 1984.

12-H 1982 PONTIAC FIREBIRD SE 1982 GB/US = 51 GB/60 US
1. Red body, tan interior, no logo.
2. Red body, white & red Firebird design and trim: 1983?
3. Black body, white & red Firebird emblem & trim, tan interior: 1984.
4. Orange-red interior, otherwise as type 3: 1986.
5. Red body & interior, Maaco hood & door labels: 1986.
6. Yellow body, red & blue trim, Pirelli logo, #56: 1985.

13-G SNORKEL FIRE ENGINE 1978 GB = 63 US
6. Red body, white snorkel, Metro logo: 1983.
7. Red body, white snorkel, shield emblem: 1987.

13-H 4x4 DUNES RACER 1982 US = 63 GB
1. Orange body, black rack, black & orange trim, #24. (Sponsor names on types 1 and 2 vary).
2. Dark yellow body, 4x4 lettering, otherwise as type 1: 1982.
3. White body, red rack, blue & red trim, #63: 1986.

14-I '83 CORVETTE 1983 US = 69 GB
1. Silver gray body, red & black trim, red interior.

2. Red upper/silver gray lower body, black interior: 1984.
3. White & red body, Chef Boyardee logo, Superfast wheels: 1986.

14-J   JEEP LAREDO   **1984   GB = 20 US**
1. Black body, white top, red interior, white "Laredo".
2. Red body, white top, silver gray interior: 1985.

15-H   FORD SIERRA   **1983   US = 55 GB**
1. White upper/gray lower body, red interior.
2. Silver upper/gray lower body, "Ford Sport": 1986. (British-made version is metallic silver, Macau-made is pearly silver.)
3. Yellow upper/charcoal lower body, black "XR4X4": 1986.
4. Cream yellow upper/gray lower body, black "XR4X4": 1986.

15-I   PEUGEOT 205 TURBO 16   **1984   GB**
1. White body, red-yellow-blue trim, red or black Shell trim, #205.

16-H   PONTIAC TRANS AM T-ROOF   **1982   GB = 35 US**
1. Black body, yellow emblem & lettering: 1982.
2. Black body, orange stripe Kellog logo: 1985.
3. Light gray body, red-orange-yellow trim: 1985.

16-I   FORD LTD POLICE CAR   **1987   US?**
1. White body & interior, black & silver trim, orange "PD 21".

17-G   LONDON BUS   **1982   GB = 51 US**
1. Red body, Berger Paints logo.
2. Red body, Laker Skytrain logo: 1982.
3. Dark green body, Chesterfield Transport logo: 1982.
4. White upper/blue lower body, Greek logo: 1982.
5. Red body, Matchbox London Bus logo: 1983.
6. Red body, York Festival & Mystery Plays logo: 1984.
7. Blue body, Nestle's Milky Bar logo: 1984.
8. Red body, Nestle's Milky Bar logo: 1984.
9. Dark green body, Rowntrees Fruit Gum logo: 1984.
10. Red body, Rowntrees Fruit Gum logo: 1984.
11. Dark blue body, Keddies No. 1 in Essex logo: 1984.
12. Maroon body, Rapport logo: 1984.
13. Red body, "Nice to meet you/Japan 1984" logo: 1984.
14. White upper/black lower body, Torvale Fisher logo: 1984.
15. White upper/cream lower body, W. H. Smith Travel logo: 1985.
16. Blue upper/white lower body, Staffordshire Police logo: 1985.
17. Red body, You'll Love New York logo: 1985.
18. Blue body, Sightseeing/Cityrama logo with flags: 1985.
19. Red body, Matchbox/Nürnberg logo: 1986.
20. Red body, Around London Tour Bus logo: 1986.
21. Red body, First M.I.C.A. Convention logo: 1986.
22. Blue body, National Tramway Museum/Crich logo: 1986.
23. White upper/red lower body, Midland Bus & Transport logo: 1986.
24. Dull red body, Band-Aid Plasters logo: 1986.
25. Red body, National Girobank logo: 1987.
26. Red body, Matchbox/Niagara Falls logo: 1987.
27. Red body, 26 Feria del Juguete/Valencia logo: 1987.
28. Tan upper/white lower body, tan interior, West Midlands logo: 1987.
29. White body, Second M.I.C.A. Convention logo: 1987.

17-H   AMX PRO STOCKER   **1983   US = 9 GB**
1. Silver gray body, red & black trim, #9.
2. Maroon body, red & white trim, Dr. Pepper logo, #4: 1985.

17-I   FORD ESCORT CABRIOLET   **1985   US = 37 GB**
1. White body, blue trim, gray interior.
2. Red body, Ford emblem, XR3i, gray interior: 1986.

17-J   DODGE DAKOTA PICKUP   **1987   US**
1. White body, black interior, black & white trim, "Dakota ST".

18-H   FIRE ENGINE   **1984   GB/US**
1. Red body, white ladder, no logo.
2. Red body, white ladder, shield emblem: 1987.

19-H   PETERBILT CEMENT TRUCK   **1982   GB/US**
1. Green body, orange barrel, black cradle, Big Pete logo.
2. Blue body, yellow barrel, black cradle, Kwik-Set logo: 1985.

20-E   POLICE PATROL   **1975   GB/US**
50. Tan body, black "Securite/-Rallye Paris-Dakar 83" on yellow stripe, checkered pattern: 1983.

20-F   JEEP 4x4   **1982   GB = 14 US**
1. White body, red top, black interior, red-yellow-green Desert Dawg logo.
2. Black body, white top, red interior, white "Laredo": 1983.

20-G   VOLVO CONTAINER TRUCK   **1985   GB = 23 US**
1. Blue cab, white box, Cold Fresh logo.
2. White cab & box, Scotch Corner logo: 1986.
3. Blue cab, white box, Matchbox MB75 logo: 1986.
4. Gray cab & box, Supersave Drugstores logo: 1986.
5. White cab & box, Federal Express logo: 1987.
6. Blue cab & box, red & white Crookes Healthcare logo: 1987.
7. Blue cab & box, rose-orange-yellow-blue Unic logo: 1987.
8. White cab & box, red Kellogg's/blue Milch/Lait/Latte logo: 1987.

21-H   RENAULT 5 "LE CAR"   **1978   GB**
30. White body, yellow & red trim, Radio Monte Carlo logo, #21: 1986?

21-H   CORVETTE PACE CAR   **1983   US**
1. Silver body, blue trim, red interior.

21-I   BREAKDOWN VAN   **1985   GB/US**
1. Red body, white boom, airscreen & logo.

21-J   GMC WRECKER   **1987   US**
1. White body & boom, red & orange logo, Frank's Getty logo.
2. White body & boom, Accessory Wholesalers logo: 1987.

22-G   BIG FOOT   **1982   US = 35 GB**
1. Silver body, white camper, yellow & black trim.
2. Red body, white camper, Aspen logo: 1985.

22-H   JAGUAR XK120   **1984   GB**
1. Green body, red interior.
2. Cream body, red interior, #414: 1986.

23-G   AUDI QUATTRO   **1982   US = 25 GB**
1. White body, orange & brown trim, "Audi Sport", #20.
2. White body, red & brown trim, Pirelli logo, #1: 1984.
3. Plum body, white trim: 1986.
4. Dark blue body, black interior, white & red "Audi": 1987.

23-H   PETERBILT TIPPER TRUCK   **1983   GB = 30 US**
1. Yellow cab & chassis, gray tipper, Dirty Dumper logo.
2. Pace logo, otherwise as type 1: 1985.

23-I   HONDA ATC350R   **1985   US**
1. Red body & handlebars, blue seat, yellow wheels.

23-J   VOLVO CONTAINER TRUCK   **1987   US = 20 GB**
1. White cab & box, Federal Express logo.

24-H   DATSUN 280ZX   **1982   GB/US**
1. Black body, tan interior, gold stripes, no lettering.
2. Black body, tan interior, gold trim & Turbo ZX logo: 1983.

24-I   NISSAN 300ZX   **1986   US**
1. Light gray body, gold & black trim, "Turbo" & emblem.
2. White body, red & green trim, "Fujicolor", #3: 1987.
3. White body, green & yellow BP logo, green #96: 1987.

25-K   AUDI QUATTRO   **1982   GB = 23 US**
1. White body, orange & brown trim, "Audi Sport", #20.
2. White body, red & brown trim, Pirelli logo, #1: 1984.
3. Plum body, white trim: 1986.
4. Dark blue body, black interior, white & red "Audi": 1987.

25-L   PACIFIC AMBULANCE   **1982   US = 41 GB/US**
1. Red body, identical to Code Red version.
2. White body, orange trim, "Paramedics": 1984.

26-H   CABLE TRUCK   **1982   GB**
1. Light orange body, gray drums, black racks.
2. Yellow body, otherwise as type 1: 1983.
3. Red body, otherwise as type 1: 1984.

26-I   VOLVO COVERED TRUCK   **1984   GB**
1. blue body, yellow top, Fresh Fruit Co. logo.
2. Yellow body, otherwise as type 1, Ferrymasters logo: 1986.

27-H   JEEP CHEROKEE   **1986   GB/US**
1. White body, yellow-green-blue trim, "Quadtrak".

28-I   DODGE DAYTONA Z   **1983   GB/US**
1. Metallic maroon upper/silver gray lower body.
2. Silver gray upper/black lower body, Turbo Z logo: 1985.

29-F   SHOVEL NOSE TRACTOR   **1981   GB/US**
22. Yellow-orange body, black shovel, engine & trim, no emblem on roof: 1982.

30-G   ARTICULATED TRUCK   **1981   GB**
3. Blue cab, yellow semi, white grille, black "International": 1983.
4. Blue cab, yellow semi and grille, black "International": 1983.
5. Red cab, yellow semi, black "International": 1983.
6. Red cab, yellow semi, no logo: 1983.
7. Blue cab & semi, white or yellow grille, Pauls logo: 1984.

30-H   PETERBILT TIPPER TRUCK   **1982   US = 23 GB**
1. Yellow cab & chassis, gray tipper, Dirty Dumper logo.
2. Pace logo, otherwise as type 1: 1985.

30-I   MERCEDES-BENZ 280GE   **1985   GB**
1. White body, red roof, Rescue Unit logo.
2. White body & roof, checkered Polizei logo, used in TP117: 1987.

31-H   MAZDA RX7   **1982   GB/US**
1. Black body, gold sides, black "RX7", white "Mazda".
2. White body, red hood & Mazda logo, #7: 1986.

31-I   ROLLS-ROYCE SILVER CLOUD   **1986   GB = 62 US**
1. Silver body, gray interior, James Bond film promo.
2. Cream body, gray interior: 1986.

32-G   ATLAS EXCAVATOR   **1981   GB/US**
4. Yellow body, black arm, shovel, chassis, treads & stripes, no logo: 1983.

33-G   VW GOLF GTI   **1985   US = 56 GB**
1. Red body, black trim, small GTI logo.
2. Large GTI logo, otherwise as type 1: 1985.
3. White body, navy blue trim, Quantum logo, #66: 1987.

33-H   RENAULT 11 TURBO   **1986   GB = 43 US**
1. Metallic blue body, gray trim, white taxi sign & interior, James Bond film promo.
2. Black body, silver trim & "Turbo", tan interior: 1986.
3. Black body, no trim, tan interior: 1987.

34-G   CHEVY PRO STOCKER   **1981   GB/US**
4. Yellow body, blue & orange trim, #4: 1983.
5. White body, red-yellow-blue trim, Pepsi logo, #14: 1984.

34-H   FORD RS200   **1987   US**
1. White body, gray interior, blue trim, #7.

35-E   ZOO TRUCK   **1981   GB**
1. Red body, light blue cage, yellow lions.
2. Red body, silver gray cage, brown lions: 1983.
3. Red body, silver gray cage, blue lions: 1983?
4. Orange body, blue cage, yellow lions: 1983?

35-F   PONTIAC T-ROOF   **1982   US = 16 GB**
1. Black body, yellow emblem & lettering.
2. Black body, orange stripe Kellog logo: 1985.
3. Light gray body, red-orange-yellow trim: 1985.

35-G   PICKUP CAMPER   **1985   GB = 22 US**
1. White body, white camper, Aspen logo.

35-H   LAND ROVER 90   **1987   US**
1. Blue body, white roof, yellow & orange trim.

36-G REFUSE TRUCK   1980   GB/US
5. White body, blue rear, Metro DPW logo: 1984.
6. Green body, yellow-orange rear: 1987.

37-I MATRA RANCHO   1982   GB
1. Dark blue body & base, black interior, no trim.
2. Yellow body & base, black interior, red trim: 1982.

37-J JEEP 4x4   1985   US
1. Black body, red-orange-yellow trim.
2. White body, red-orange-blue trim: 1987.

37-K FORD ESCORT CABRIOLET   1986   GB = 17 US
1. White body, blue trim, gray interior.
2. Red body, Ford emblem, "XR3i", gray interior: 1986.

38-H MODEL A FORD TRUCK   1982   GB/US
1. Blue body, white roof, black chassis, Champion Spark Plugs logo.
2. White body, red roof, blue chassis, Matchbox USA logo: 1982.
3. White body, red roof, blue chassis, Pepsi-Cola logo: 1984.
4. Blue body, white roof, black chassis, Matchbox on the Move in '84 logo: 1984.
5. Red body, black roof & chassis, Arnotts Biscuits logo: 1984.
6. White body, red roof, dark blue chassis, Ben Franklin logo: 1984.
7. Blue body, white roof, black chassis, Kelloggs logo: 1984.
8. Gray body, brown roof & chassis, Tittensor First School logo: 1984.
9. Tan body, brown roof & chassis, Larklane Motor Museum logo: 1984.
10. Dark blue body, red roof, black chassis, Bass Museum & Shire Horse Stables logo: 1985.
11. Yellow body, green roof & chassis, Toy Collectors Pocket Guide logo: 1985.
12. Olive body, black roof & chassis, BBC 1925 logo: 1985.
13. Dark blue body, black roof & chassis, Matchbox Speed Shop logo: 1986.
14. Dark blue body, white roof, red chassis, Smiths Potato Crisps logo: 1986.
15. White body, black roof & chassis, Chesty Bonds logo: 1986.
16. Black body, red roof & chassis, Isle of Man TT86 logo: 1986.
17. White body, black roof & chassis, The Australian logo: 1986.
18. Dark green body, black chassis, Weet-Bix/Sanitarium logo: 1986.
19. Cream body, dark green chassis & roof, H.H. Brain Faggotts logo: 1986.
20. Yellow body, blue roof & chassis, Junior Matchbox Club logo: 1987.
21. Black body, roof & chassis, 2nd M.I.C.A. Convention logo: 1987.
22. Red body, black roof & chassis, Isle of Man Post Office logo: 1987.
23. Blue body, black roof & chassis, Silvo logo: 1987.
24. Red body, black roof & chassis, W.H. Smith & Son logo: 1987.
25. Red body, black roof & chassis, Dewhurst Butcher logo: 1987.
26. Red body, black roof & chassis, yellow emblem, Isle of Man TT87 logo: 1987.
27. Dark olive body, red roof & chassis, John West Salmon logo: 1987.

39-E ROLLS-ROYCE SILVER SHADOW II   1979   GB
5. Metallic tan body, white interior: 1982.
6. Plum body, white interior: 1983.

39-F TOYOTA SUPRA   1983   US = 60 GB
1. White body, red & black trim, #41.
2. White body, blue & gray trim, black hatch, white "Supra": 1985.

39-G BMW CABRIOLET   1985   GB/US
1. Metallic blue body & base, black "323i".
2. Red body & base, black trim: 1986.
3. White body, BMW emblem & "323i": 1986.

39-H FORD BRONCO II   1987   US
1. White body, red interior, red-orange-black trim.

40-F CHEVROLET CORVETTE T-TOP   1982   US = 62 GB
1. White body, orange & black trim, #09.
2. Dark blue body, red-yellow-white trim: 1985.
3. Yellow body, purple & blue trim: 1987.

40-G ROCKET TRANSPORTER   1985   US
1. White body & rockets, red NASA logo.

41-G KENWORTH CONVENTIONAL AERODYNE   1982   US
1. Red body, black & white trim.
2. Black body, orange-yellow-white trim: 1984.
3. Light gray body, red & blue trim: 1986.

41-H RACING PORSCHE 935   1983   GB = 55 US
1. Light blue body, blue-white-black trim, #71.
2. White body, purple Cadburys Buttons logo: 1985.
3. White body, red-orange-yellow trim, #10: 1986.

41-I JAGUAR XJ6   1987   US = 1 GB
1. Metallic red body, tan interior.

42-G 1957 FORD THUNDERBIRD   1982   GB/US
1. Red body, white interior.
2. Cream upper/red lower body, red interior: 1983.
3. Black body, red interior: 1986.

42-H MOBILE CRANE   1984   GB/US
1. Yellow body, black crane, red hook & logo.

43-G PETERBILT CONTINENTAL CAB   1982   US
1. Black body, red & white trim (single or double stripes).
2. Red body, black & white trim, "Super", as on CY3 Uniroyal: 1983.
3. Black body, brown & white trim, "Ace", as on CY5 Interstate: 1983.
4. Black body, red & yellow trim, as on CY7 Supergas: 1984.

43-H MERCEDES-BENZ AMG   1984   GB/US
1. White body, blue interior, gray trim, "AMG" on sides.
2. Red body, black trim & interior, "AMG" on sides: 1985.
3. White body, blue roof, red hood, #7: 1986.
4. White body, black interior, gray trim, "AMG" on hood & sides: 1986.
5. Black body, gold trim, "500SEC": 1987.
6. Red body, green & yellow stripes (no BP emblem): 1987.

43-I RENAULT 11 TURBO   1987   US = 33 GB
1. Metallic blue body, gray trim, white taxi sign & interior, James Bond film promo (1986 GB).
2. Black body, silver trim & "Turbo", tan interior: 1987.

44-G CHEVY 4x4 VAN   1982   US = 68 GB
1. Pearly silver body, red-blue-black Vanpire logo, black base: 1982.
2. Metallic green body, black & white Ridin' High logo: 1982.
3. Dark green body, otherwise as type 2: 1982.
4. Yellow body, Australian kangaroo logo: 1982.
5. White body, orange & red trim, Matchbox Racing logo: 1983.
6. White body, red-green-black Castrol GTX logo: 1984.

44-H CITROEN 15CV   1983   GB
1. Black body, tan interior.
2. Black body, white interior: 1983.
3. Dark blue body, white interior: 1986.

44-I SKODA LR130   1987   GB
1. White body, red trunk, black interior, #44.

45-F KENWORTH C.O.E. AERODYNE   1982   GB/US
1. White body, brown & blue trim.
2. Silver gray body, orange & purple trim, #45: 1984.
3. White body, red & green Chef Boyardee trim: 1985.
4. Red body, multicolored trim: 1986.

45-G FORD CARGO SKIP TRUCK   1987   GB?
1. Yellow body, gray bucket, orange trim.

46-H BIG BLUE   1983   US
1. Metallic blue raising body, red & yellow "Big Blue" & #39.
2. Nonmetallic dark blue body, otherwise as type 1: 1983.

46-I SAUBER GROUP C RACER   1984   GB = 66 US
1. Red body, white trim, black trim, #4.
2. White & red body Team Matchbox/Junior Collectors' Club logo: 1985.
3. White body, red & yellow trim & wing, #61: 1986.

46-J MISSION HELICOPTER   1985   US = 57 GB
1. Blue body, white tail & rotors, red trim.

2. Red body, white tail & rotors, red trim, Sheriff star: 1987.

47-G JAGUAR SS100   1982   GB/US
1. Red body, brown interior.
2. Blue body, light gray hood, white interior: 1987.

47-H SCHOOL BUS   1985   US
1. Yellow body, black logo & stripes, lower rear window cast in.
2. Lower rear window tampo-printed on, otherwise as type 1: 1986.

48-H MERCEDES-BENZ UNIMOG   1983   GB
1. Yellow body, black chassis, white top, Rescue logo.

48-I VAUXHALL ASTRA GTE   1986   GB
1. Red body, black "GTE" & stripe.
2. White body, red & blue trim, "AC Delco", #48: 1987.
3. Yellow body, black trim, Mobile Phone logo, in CY206 set: 1987.

49-F SAND DIGGER   1983   GB/US
1. Dark green body, red & yellow design.
2. Orange-red body, Dune Man logo: 1985.

49-G PEUGEOT QUASAR   1986   GB
1. White body, silver interior, red "Quasar".

50-G HARLEY-DAVIDSON   1980   GB/US
1. Metallic light tan body, no driver.
2. Metallic bronze body, red-brown driver: 1982.

50-H CHEVY BLAZER   1984   US
1. White & red body, Sheriff logo with star, chrome base & grille.
2. Black base & grille, otherwise as type 1: 1986?

51-F PONTIAC FIREBIRD RACER   1982   GB = 12 US
1. Black body, red trim, yellow interior: 1983. (Others listed under 12-H are also possible.)

51-I LONDON BUS   1985   US = 17 GB
See 17-G listing: types 2 and 17 have definitely been sold in the USA; others may have been.

51-J CAMARO IROC-Z   1986   US =68 GB
1. Blue body, gray interior, "IROC-Z" on sides only.
2. "IROC-Z" on hood and sides, wider stripes, otherwise as type 1: 1987.

52-F BMW M1   1983   GB/US
(plus rear wing, minus opening hood)
1. White body, black interior, #52.
2. Black body, red interior, #59: 1985.
3. Yellow body, black interior, #11: 1986.

53-G FLARESIDE PICKUP   1982   GB/US
1. Blue body, white interior, Baja Bouncer logo, #326.
2. Orange body, otherwise as type 1: 1983.
3. Yellow body, 2-tone blue trim, Ford 460 logo: 1986.

54-G NASA SPACE SHUTTLE COMMAND CENTER   1982   GB/US
1. White body, red door & interior, red & blue logo on roof & sides.
2. Logo on roof only, otherwise as type 1: 1986.

54-H AIRPORT FOAM PUMPER   1984   GB/US
1. Red body & nozzle, white roof & logo.
2. Yellow body, red nozzle, red & white trim: 1984.
3. Red body, red nozzle, yellow trim, red lettering: 1985.

55-J FORD SIERRA   1983   GB = 15 US
1. White upper/gray lower body, red interior.
2. Silver upper/gray lower body, "Ford Sport": 1984. (British-made models metallic silver; Macau pearly silver.)
3. Yellow upper/charcoal lower body, black "XR4x4": 1986.
4. Cream yellow upper/gray lower body, black "XR4x4" & trim, red #55: 1986.

55-K SUPER PORSCHE RACER   1983   US = 41 GB
1. Light blue body, blue-white-black trim, #71.
2. White body, purple Cadburys Buttons logo: 1985.
3. White body, red-orange-yellow-black trim, #10: 1986.

56-F MERCEDES-BENZ 450SEL   1979

4. White body, tan interior, green trim, Polizei logo: 1983.
5. White body, tan interior, no logo or rim: 1986.

56-G PETERBILT TANKER   1982   US = 5 5 GB
1. Black body, yellow tank, Supergas logo.
2. Blue body, white tank, red or white Milk logo: 1982.
3. Blue body, white tank, no logo: 1983?
4. Black body & tank, red & blue Amoco logo: 1985.
5. Black body, chrome tank, red & blue Amoco logo: 1985.
6. Red body, chrome tank, Getty logo: 1984.
7. Red body, chrome "Amoco" tank, "Getty" on doors: 1985.

56-H VW GOLF GTI   1985   GB = 33 US
1. White body, silver trim, small white GTI logo.
2. White body, black trim, large white GTI logo: 1985.
3. White body, navy blue trim, Quantum logo, #66: 1987.

57-G CARMICHAEL COMMANDO   1982   GB
1. White body, Police Rescue logo.
2. Red body, white trim, Fire logo: 1983.

57-H 4x4 MINI PICKUP TRUCK   1982   US
1. Orange-red body, black-white-silver trim.
2. Dark red body, black & white trim: 1982.
3. Blue body, Mountain Man logo: 1983.

57-I MISSION HELICOPTER   1985   GB = 46 US
1. Blue body, white tail & rotors, red trim.
2. Red body, white tail & rotors, red trim, "Sheriff" star: 1987.

58-G RUFF TREK PICKUP   1983   GB/US
1. Golden tan body, red & orange trim, Ruff Trek logo.
2. White body, red-yellow-blue trim, #217: 1985.

58-H MERCEDES-BENZ 300E   1987   US
1. Metallic light blue-gray body, blue interior.

59-G PORSCHE 928   1980   GB/US
29. Silver gray body, red interior, blue & black trim.

60-F PISTON POPPER   1982   US
1. Yellow body, blue trim, black lettering, #60.
2. Orange body, blue trim, Good Vibrations/Sunkist logo, unpainted grille & base: 1983.
3. Black grille & base, otherwise as type 2: 1986?

60-G TOYOTA SUPRA   1983   GB = 39 US
1. Red body & black trim, #41.
2. White body, blue & gray trim, black hatch, white "Supra": 1985.

60-H PONTIAC FIREBIRD RACER   1985   US = 12 GB
1. Yellow body, red-white-blue trim, "Son of a Gun", #55.
2. Yellow body, red & blue trim, Pirelli logo, #56: 1986.
3. White body, red-orange-blue trim, "Fast Eddie", #15: 1986.

60-I FORD TRANSIT   1987   GB
1. Red body, no logo.
2. Red body, orange & blue trim, Motorsport logo: 1987.
3. White body, red cross, Ambulance logo.
4. Yellow body, blue British Telecom logo, in CY206 set: 1987.
5. Red body, Australia Post logo: 1987.
6. White body, black & green UniChem logo: 1987.

61-E PETERBILT WRECK TRUCK   1982   GB/US
1. Orange-red body, black booms, black & white logo in pinkish-white square.
2. Logo without pinkish-white square, otherwise as type 1: 1982.
3. White body, black booms & trim, Police logo: 1984.
4. White body, black booms, blue trim, Police: 1984.
5. White body, blue booms and trim, Police: 1984.
6. White body, blue booms & trim, Police & Peterbilt: 1985.
7. White body, green booms, new Police logo: 1986.

62-G CHEVROLET CORVETTE   1979   GB/US = 40 US
11. Black body, orange & yellow trim, red base & pipes: 1983.

12. Black body, red & white trim, "The Force", #54: 1984.

62-H ROLLS-ROYCE SILVER CLOUD   1986   US = 31 GB
1. Silver gray body, gray interior, James Bond film promo (1985 GB).
2. Cream body, gray interior: 1986.

62-I VOLVO 760   1986?   GB
1. Silver gray body, black interior: 1987.

63-H SNORKEL FIRE ENGINE   1983   US = 13 GB
1. Red body, white snorkel, identical to Code Red version.
2. Red body, white snorkel, Metro logo: 1983.
3. Red body, white snorkel, shield emblem: 1987.

63-I 4x4 OPEN BACK PICKUP   1982   GB = 13 US
1. Orange body, black rack, black & orange trim, #24. (Sponsor names on types 1 & 2 vary.)
2. Dark yellow body, orange & black trim, black rack, #24: 1982.
3. White body, blue & red trim, red rack, #63: 1986.

64-F CATERPILLAR TRACTOR   1979   GB/US = 9 GB
10. Yellow body & blade, black cab, unpainted engine & chassis, Caterpillar emblem: 1982.
11. Tan cab, otherwise as type 10: 1982.
12. Black blade, otherwise as type 10 (or 11?): 1983.
13. Light gray engine & chassis, otherwise as type 10: 1986.

64-G DODGE CARAVAN   1983   GB = 68 US
1. Maroon body, sealed side door.
2. Maroon body, opening side door: 1983.
3. Silver body, black bottom stripe: 1984.
4. Black body, silver trim, red interior: 1984.
5. Black body, no trim: 1984.
6. Black body, silver & gold trim: 1985.
7. Black body, silver trim, Adidas logo: 1986.
8. White body, red-orange-blue-black trim, "Caravan": 1987.
9. Black body, green & yellow stripes (no BP emblem): 1987.

65-E AIRPORT COACH   1977   GB/US
20. Blue body, white roof, British logo: 1983.
21. White body & roof, Alitalia logo: 1984.
22. Red body, white roof, TWA logo: 1984 or earlier.
23. White body & roof, blue-yellow-black Stork S. B. logo: 1986.
24. Blue body, white roof, Australian logo: 1987.
25. Blue body, white roof, Girobank logo: 1987.
(Note: above variations are GB, not US.)

65-F TYRONE MALONE BANDAG BANDIT 1982   US
1. Black body, green & white trim, white lettering.
2. "Detroit Diesel" on roof, otherwise as type 1: 1983.

65-G STP INDY RACER   1985   US
1. Blue body, red driver & wings, STP logo, #20.
2. Yellow body, red driver & wings, Matchbox Racing logo, #5: 1986.

65-H AIRPLANE TRANSPORTER   1985   GB = 72 US
1. Yellow body, red "Rescue", plane with red wings, white fuselage.
2. Plane with white wings, red fuselage, otherwise as type 1: 1985.

65-I CADILLAC ALLANTE   1987   GB = 72 US
1. Silver gray body, gray interior.

66-G TYRONE MALONE SUPER BOSS   1982   GB/US
1. White body, red & blue trim.
2. "Detroit Diesel" on roof, otherwise as type 1: 1983.

66-H SAUBER GROUP C RACER   1984   US = 46 GB
1. Red body, white trim, black wing, BASF logo, #4.
2. White body, red & yellow Team Matchbox/Junior Collectors' club logo: 1984.
3. White body, black trim & wing, Castrol logo, #61: 1986.

66-I ROLLS-ROYCE SILVER SPIRIT 1987   GB/
1. Tan body and interior.

67-F IMSA MUSTANG   1983   GB = 11 US

1. Black body, red trim, white "Mustang".
2. Black body, green-yellow-white trim: 1986.

67-G FLAME OUT   1983   US
1. White body, red & orange trim, chrome engine, #48.

67-H LAMBORGHINI COUNTACH   1985   US = 11 GB
1. Red body & base, tan interior.
2. Black body, red-orange-white trim, #5: 1986.
3. Red body, green & yellow BP emblems, #15: 1987.

67-I IKARUS COACH   1986   GB
1. White body, orange roof and Voyager logo.
2. White body, red roof, Gibraltar logo: 1987.
3. Cream body & roof, orange & brown trim, Ikarus logo: 1987.

68-E CHEVY VAN   1979   US = 44 GB
21. Pearly silver body, red-blue-black Vanpire logo, black base.
22. Metallic green body, black & white Ridin' High logo: 1982.
23. Dark green body, otherwise as type 22: 1982.
24. Yellow body, Australian kangaroo logo: 1982.
25. White body, red & orange trim, Matchbox Racing logo: 1983.

68-F DODGE CARAVAN   1984   US = 64 GB
1. Maroon body, sealed side door.
2. maroon body, opening side door: 1984.
3. Silver body, black bottom stripe: 1984.
4. Black body, silver trim, red interior: 1984.
5. Black body, no trim: 1984.
6. Black body, silver & gold trim: 1985.
7. Black body, silver trim, Adidas logo: 1986.
8. White body, red-orange-blue-black trim, "Caravan": 1987.
9. Black body, green & yellow stripes (no BP emblem): 1987.

68-G CAMARO IROC-Z   1986   GB = 51 US
1. Lime green body, black & white trim.
2. Blue body, gray interior, IROC-Z logo on sides only: 1986.
3. IROC-Z logo on sides and hood, wider stripes, otherwise as type 2: 1987.

69-F WILLYS STREET ROD   1982   US
1. White body, red & orange trim, "White Heat", red #313.
2. Blue body, orange & white trim, "White Heat", white #313, pearly silver bumpers & base: 1983.
3. Black plastic bumpers & base, otherwise as type 2: 1985.

69-G 1983 CORVETTE   1983   GB = 14 US
1. Silver gray body, red & black trim, red interior.
2. Red upper/silver gray lower body, black interior: 1984.

70-F FERRARI 308GTB   1981   GB/US
1. Orange-red body & base, black interior.
2. Orange-red body, silver panels with Ferrari lettering: 1986.
3. Bright red body, otherwise as type 2: 1986.
4. Red & blue body, white interior, "Pioneer", #39: 1986.

71-G 1962 CORVETTE   1982   US
1. Blue body, white trim, chrome interior.
2. Blue body, white trim, light blue interior: 1982.
3. White body, red trim: 1982.
4. White body, red & blue trim, blue flame design, #39: 1983.
5. Red body, white trim, white #2: 1986.

71-H SCANIA T142 TRACTOR   1985   GB = 8 US
1. White body, red chassis, orange & yellow trim.
2. White body, black chassis, red-orange-yellow trim: 1987.

72-G DODGE DELIVERY TRUCK   1982   GB
1. Red body, white box, Pepsi-Cola logo.
2. Red body, white box, Smiths logo: 1983.
3. Red body, white box, Kelloggs logo: 1984.
4. Bright yellow body & box, black Hertz logo: 1985.
5. Pale yellow body & box, black Hertz logo: 1985.

Matchbox® Series

6. White body & box, blue & red Streets Ice Cream logo: 1985.
7. Red body & box, Royal Mail logo: 1985.
8. White body & box, Jetspress logo: 1986.
9. White body & box, red Kellogg's/blue Milch-Lait-Latte logo: 1986.
10. Blue body, otherwise as type 9: 1986.
11. Green cab, white box, Minties logo: 1987.
12. Dark yellow cab, yellow box, Risi logo: 1987.

72-H   SAND RACER (or SAND CAT)   **1984   US**
1. White body, black top & interior, #211.

72-I   PLANE TRANSPORTER   **1985   US = 65 GB**
1. Yellow body, red trim, "Rescue", plane with red wings & white fuselage.

2. Plane with white wings & red fuselage, otherwise as type 1: 1985.

72-J   FORD SUPERVAN II   **1986   GB = 6 US**
1. White body, dark blue Ford logo.
2. White body, bright blue Ford logo: 1987.

72-K   CADILLAC ALLANTE   **1987   US = 65 GB**
1. Silver gray body, red interior.

73-G   MODEL A FORD COUPE   **1979   GB/US**
10. Red body, black chassis: 1985.
11. Black body & chassis, flame design: 1986.

74-G   MUSTANG GT   **1984   US**
1. Orange body, yellow & blue trim.

2. Silver gray body, purple & yellow trim: 1986.

74-H   FIAT ABARTH   **1982   GB = 9 US**
1. White body, orange & maroon trim, Matchbox logo, #45.
2. White body, red & green trim, Alitalia logo, #3: 1984.

74-I   TOYOTA MR2   **1986   GB = 9 US**
1. White body, red & yellow trim, Pace Car logo.

75-G   HELICOPTER   **1982   GB/US**
3. White body, black Police logo" 1983.
4. White body, orange bottom & trim, "Rescue": 1984.

75-H   FERRARI TESTA ROSSA   **1986   GB/US**
1. Red body, black & yellow Ferrari emblems, black interior.

Dinky Toys

The manufacturers of Matchbox recently acquired the rights to the time-honored name of Dinky Toys, and have so far put six Matchbox castings on the market under the Dinky Toys name, which appears only on the bubblepacks (the backs of which proclaim their origin), while the models themselves are unchanged save for their finish. Their baseplates still bear the Matchbox name as well as "Made in Macau". Neither models nor bubblepack cards are numbered, so we shall list them here by their Matchbox numbers:

7 VW RABBIT
Black body, red & orange trim, #9, red interior, black base.
9 FIAT ABARTH:
White body, red-orange-yellow trim, red interior, black base.

44 CITROEN 15CV:
Dark green body, red interior, chrome base.
51 PONTIAC FIREBIRD:
Blue body, yellow and white trim, #18, red interior, light gray base.

60 TOYOTA SUPRA:
White body, red-yellow-blue trim, red interior, black hatch, wing and base.
69 1984 CORVETTE
Red upper/metallic gray lower body, blue and silver trim, black interior & base.

Superfast Specials

This series, replaced by the very similar Superfast Lasers in the 1987 catalog, appeared at the end of 1985 and was first shown in the 1986 catalog. All the models are regular Matchbox castings; only their color schemes are different, plus their use of special wheels—which is what gave the original Matchbox Superfast series its name these many years ago. The Lasers have new wheels with hologram hubs instead of spokes. All regular issues listed here exist with either wheel type unless otherwise noted. Three of the models have also appeared in Halley's Comet commemorative form.

SF1   MERCURY POLICE CAR   **1985**
1. Black body, Halley's Comet design, SF wheels: 1985.
2. White body, yellow and blue trim, State Police logo, SF wheels: 1985.
3. Pearly silver grille & base, Laser wheels, otherwise as type 2: 1987.

SF2   1982 PONTIAC FIREBIRD   **1985**

1. Black body, Halley's comet design, SF wheels: 1985.
2. Blue upper/white lower body, red-orange-yellow-white trim, SF wheels: 1986.
3. Black lower body, otherwise as type 2: 1986.
4. Metallic silver body, Laser wheels, otherwise as type 2: 1987.

SF3   PORSCHE 928   **1985**

1. Metallic blue & white body, red & orange trim, #28: 1985.

SF4   DAYTONA TURBO Z   **1985**
1. White & blue body, red & blue trim, Goodyear logo, #8: 1985.

SF5   MERCEDES-BENZ AMG   **1985**
1. Red body, yellow & white trim, AMG logo, SF wheels: 1985.

Superfast Specials

2. Metallic red body, Laser wheels, otherwise as type 1: 1987.
SF6   PORSCHE 935   1985
 1. Red body, blue & yellow trim, Auto Tech logo, #35, SF wheels: 1985.
 2. Metallic red body, Laser wheels, otherwise as type 1: 1987.
SF7   FORD SIERRA   1985
 1. Black upper/gray lower body, green & white trim, #85, SF wheels: 1985.
 2. Green body, white & orange trim, #85, Laser wheels: 1987.
SF8   '62 CORVETTE   1985
 1. Orange body & base, white & black trim, #11, SF wheels: 1985.
 2. Metallic gold body, Laser wheels, otherwise as type 1: 1987.
SF9   DATSUN 280ZX TURBO   1985
 1. Black body, orange-yellow-white trim, Turbo lettering: 1985.
SF10   TURBO VETTE   1985
 1. Black body, red-yellow-white trim, "Turbo Vette": 1985.
SF11   FERRARI 308GTB   1985
 1. Yellow upper/red lower body, red "Ferrari" & trim.
SF12   CHEVY STOCK CAR   1985
 1. Black body, Halley's Comet design, SF wheels: 1985.

2. White & orange body, yellow & white trim, #21: 1986.
SF13   '84 CORVETTE   1986
 1. White upper/red lower body, red & orange trim, #7: 1986.
SF14   BMW CABRIOLET   1986
 1. White body, black top, red-blue-black trim, "Alpina": 1986.
SF15   ESCORT CABRIOLET   1986
 1. White body, black top, orange trim, gray interior, #3, SF wheels: 1986.
 2. Blue body, orange & white trim, white interior, #3, Laser wheels: 1987.
SF16   SAUBER GROUP C   1986
 1. Yellow body, blue wing, orange & blue trim, #2: 1986.
 2. Black body, chartreuse-red-pink Cargantua logo: 1986, only in Cargantua set.
SF17   LAMBORGHINI COUNTACH   1986
 1. White body, wing & base, blue & pink trim, "LP500S", SF wheels: 1986.
 2. Metallic silver body, Laser wheels: 1987.
SF18   FIREBIRD RACER   1986
 1. Light blue body, dark blue base, dark blue & yellow trim, #10, SF wheels: 1986.
 2. Metallic dark blue body, light blue & yellow trim, #10, Laser wheels: 1987.
SF19   FIERO RACER   1987

1. Yellow upper/orange lower body, red trim, Protech logo, #16, SF wheels: 1987.
2. Metallic gold lower body, laser wheels, otherwise as type 1: 1987.
SF20 was not used; it was to have been a VW Golf.
SF21   NISSAN 300ZX TURBO   1987
 1. Red body, black base, tan interior, orange & yellow trim, SF wheels: 1987.
 2. Metallic red body, Laser wheels, otherwise as type 1: 1987.
SF22   CAMARO IROC-Z   1987
 1. Red body, black & white trim, "Carter", #12, SF wheels: 1987.
 2. Metallic red body, Laser wheels, otherwise as type 1: 1987.
SF23   TOYOTA MR2   1987
 1. Blue upper/white lower body & hood, red trim, SF wheels: 1987.
 2. Metallic blue upper body, Laser wheels, otherwise as type 1: 1987.
SF24   FERRARI TESTA ROSSA   1987
 1. Black body, interior & base, silver trim, red "Ferrari", SF wheels: 1987.
 2. Metallic silver body & base, gold trim, Laser wheels, otherwise as type 1: 1987.
SF25   PEUGEOT QUASAR   1987
 1. Blue body, rose trim, silver interior, white #9, SF wheels: 1987.
 2. Metallic blue body, Laser wheels, otherwise as type 1: 1987.

Matchmates

In 1984 the Matchmates were issued; they consist of bubble-packs holding two models of vehicles made by the same firm. The Matchmates models, shown in the 1984 and 1985 catalogs, were unchanged from their regular Matchbox Series forms.

M1   CITROEN   1984
 1. MB44 Citroen 15cv & MB12 Citroen Ambulance.
M2   Ford   1984
 1. MB73 Model A Coupe & MB38 Model A Van.
M3   JAGUAR   1984

1. MB47 Jaguar SS100 & MB22 XK120.
M4   JEEP   1984
 1. MB14 Laredo & MB5 Eagle 4x4.
M5   CORVETTE   1984
 1. MB62 Corvette (older type) & MB69 1983 Corvette.

2. MB62 Corvette T-Top & MB69 1983 Corvette: 1985.
M6   KENWORTH   1984
 1. MB41 Conventional & MB45 C-O-E Aerodyne.
 2. Colors may have been changed in 1985.

Twin Packs

A new series of Twin Packs appeared in the 1984 catalog, replacing the older one-and two-digit types listed fully in MATCHBOX CARS. The new series uses three-digit catalog numbers. There are undoubtedly variations, but my data on them are so limited that I can list only the types shown in the yearly Matchbox catalogs, above and beyond those in my collection.

Twin Packs

TP102 Ford Escort & Glider Trailer   1984
  1. Green car and trailer, white glider.
TP103 Cattle Truck & Trailer   1984
  1. Yellow truck and trailer, brown stakes.
  2. Light blue truck and trailer, brown stakes: 1987.
TP104 apparently not used.
TP105 Datsun & Boat Trailer   ?
TP106 Renault 5 & Motorcycle Trailer   1984
  1. White (or black?) car, yellow trailer, red cycles.
  2. Light gray & black car, orange hood, "Scrambler" logo, light gray trailer, black cycles: 1987.
TP107 Datsun 260Z & Caravan Trailer   1984
  1. Silver gray car, blue trim, white trailer, brown door.
TP108 Farm Tractor & Trailer   1984

  1. Blue tractor, red trailer, black stakes.
  2. Yellow-orange tractor and trailer, black stakes: 1987.
TP109 Citroen Ambulance & Police Boat   1984
  1. White ambulance, blue trim, white & blue boat, blue trailer.
TP110 Matra Rancho & Lifeboat   1984
  1. Dark blue car, orange & white boat, black trailer.
  2. Orange car, white & blue trim, black boat, white trailer 1987.
TP111 Ford Cortina & Horse Box   1984
  1. Red car, yellow trailer, white horses.
TP112 Unimog & Alpine Rescue Trailer   1984
  1. Yellow truck & trailer, white tops, red "Alpine Rescue" logo.
  2. Red truck & trailer, white tops, "Unfall Rettung" logo: 1987.
TP113 Porsche & Caravan Trailer   1985
  1. Black car, gold trim, white trailer, brown door.

TP114 VW Golf & Horse Box   1985
  1. Black car, yellow trailer, "Silver Shoes" logo.
TP115 Ford Escort & Boat Trailer   1987
  1. White car & boat, blue trim, black trailer.
TP116 Jeep Cherokee & Caravan   1987
  1. Tan & black car, tan trailer, green & red trim.
TP117 Mercedes G-Wagon & Horse Box   1987
  1. White car & trailer, red & black trim, Polizei logo.
TP118 BMW Cabriolet & Glider Trailer   1987
  1. Red car & trailer, white glider & trim, Gliding Club logo.
TP119 Flareside & Seafire Boat   1987
  1. Yellow truck & boat, two-tone blue trim, black trailer.

Models of Yesteryear

This popular series has grown to a total of thirty regularly issued models, and several of them have been made in a variety of logo types, as well as being used for numerous promotional models which will not be listed here. And for the past few years, several Limited Edition models have been offered in short runs, and Special Editions, either of regular Yesteryears or of castings made especially for this purpose, have been put on the market for the Christmas season. Some of their catalog numbers duplicate those of regular Yesteryears. The Special Editions are one-shot issues, and at least one of the special castings was made in soft dies that could be used only for limited production before deteriorating. Through it all, the Yesteryears have remained second in popularity only to the regular Matchbox Series—and to many of us, definitely first in terms of beauty and charm.

Y1-C JAGUAR 1936 SS-100   1977
  8. Metallic light blue body & chassis, black interior: 1979.
  9. Dark green body, black interior: 1981.
  10. Dark yellow body and chassis, black interior, with diorama: 1987.
Y2-D BENTLEY 1930 4.5 LITER   1985
  1. Green body and chassis, light brown interior.
Y3-D MODEL T FORD 1912 TANKER   1982
  1. Green body, black chassis, white roof, red tank, BP logo.
  2. Cream body & roof, dark red chassis & tank, Carnation logo: 1983.
  3. Green body & tank, black chassis, white roof, Zerolene logo: 1983.
  4. Blue body & tank, black chassis, white roof, Express Dairy logo: 1983.
  5. Red & blue body, black chassis, blue tank & roof, Mobiloil logo: 1985 Limited Edition.
  6. Green body & tank, black chassis, white roof, Castrol logo: 1986.
  7. Red body, roof & tank, black chassis, Red Crown logo: 1987 Special Edition.
Y4-D DUESENBERG 1930 MODEL J   1976
  4. Brown and tan body, brown chassis, tan roof & interior: 1983.
  5. Silver body, dark blue chassis & trim, black roof & interior: 1986.
Y5-D TALBOT 1927 VAN   1978
  18. Light blue body, black chassis, gray roof, Nestle's logo: 1981.
  19. Dark brown body, tan chassis & roof, Wrights Soap logo: 1982 Limited Edition.

  20. Blue body, black chassis, white roof, EverReady logo: 1983.
  21. Black body & chassis, yellow roof, Dunlop logo: 1984 Limited Edition.
  22. Cream roof, green chassis & roof, Rose's logo: 1984.
  23. Brown body, tan chassis & roof, Speelgoed Otten logo: 1985, available in The Netherlands and Germany.
Y6-D ROLLS-ROYCE 1920 FIRE ENGINE   1977
  8. Red body & chassis, black interior, white ladder: 1983.
  9. Red body, black chassis & interior, white ladder: 1984.
Y7-D FORD 1913 BREAKDOWN TRUCK   1985
  1. Orange body, gray chassis & roof, green boom, Barlow logo.
Y8-D MG 1945 TC   1978
  7. Blue body & chassis, tan top, black interior: 1983.
  8. Cream body, brown chassis, tan top & interior: 1984.
Y8-E YORKSHIRE 1897 STEAM WAGON   1987
  1. Red body, gray roof, tan canopy, black chassis & interior, Johnnie Walker logo.
Y9-B SIMPLEX 1912   1968
  9. Yellow body, black top & chassis, light brown interior, diorama: 1986.
Y9-C LEYLAND LORRY   1986
  1. Dark green body, red chassis, tan interior, A. Luff & Sons logo: 1986 Special Edition.
Y10-C ROLLS-ROYCE 1906 SILVER GHOST   1969
  7. Silver body & chassis, maroon interior: 1982.

Y10-D MASERATI 1957 250F   1986
  1. Red body, black seat, silver gray exhaust, #12.
Y11-C LAGONDA 1938 DROPHEAD COUPE   1972
  7. Plum body & chassis: 1985 Limited Edition.
Y11-D BUGATTI 1932 TYPE 51   1986
  1. Blue body, brown interior, gray exhaust, #4.
Y12-C MODEL T FORD 1912 VAN   1979
  13. Blue body, white chassis, black chassis, Smiths Crisps logo: 1981.
  14. Light green body, green chassis, light gray roof, Yesteryear 25th Anniversary logo: 1981 Limited Edition.
  15. Red body, black roof & chassis, Arnotts logo: 1982 Limited Edition.
  16. Yellow body, black roof & chassis, Sunlight logo: 1982 Limited Edition.
  17. Green body, tan roof, black chassis, Harrods logo: 1982.
  18. Blue body, white roof, black chassis, Cerebos logo: 1982.
  19. Black body, black chassis, white roof, Captain Morgan logo: 1983.
  20. Red body, black roof & chassis, Royal Mail logo: 1983.
  21. White body, red roof, blue chassis, Pepsi-Cola logo: 1984.
  22. Orange body, black roof & chassis, Hoover logo: 1984 Limited Edition.
  23. Metallic tan body, dark brown roof & chassis, Motor 100 logo: 1985 Limited Edition.
  24. Ivory body & roof, green chassis & pickle on roof, H. J. Heinz logo: 1986 Limited Edition.

Models of Yesteryear

25. Blue body, yellow roof, black chassis, Rosella logo: 1987 Limited Edition.

Y12-D MODEL T FORD 1912 PICKUP   1986
1. Blue body, black chassis, Imbach logo: Special Edition.

Y12-E STEPHENSON'S ROCKET 1829   1987
1. Yellow bodies, black trim, white stack: Special Edition.

Y13-C CROSSLEY 1918 TRUCK   1973
9. Cream body, pale green roof & top, Carlsberg logo: 1983.
10. Green body, white roof & top, black chassis, Waring's logo: 1985.
11. Green body, cream roof & top, black chassis, Waring's logo: 1985.

Y14-C STUTZ 1931 BEARCAT   1973
8. Blue body, charcoal chassis, tan interior: 1985 Limited Edition.

Y14-D E.R.A. 1936   1986
1. Black body, tan seat, gray exhaust, #7.

Y15-B PACKARD 1930 VICTORIA   1969
14. Light tan body, brown chassis & top, tan interior: 1984.

Y15-C LONDON TRAMCAR   1987
1. Red body, white windows, gray roof & chassis, Swan Vestas logo.

Y16-B MERCEDES 1928 SS COUPE   1972
8. Red body, silver chassis, black interior, folded top: 1985 Limited Edition.

Y16-C FERRARI 1960 FORMULA I   1986
1. Red body, black seat, gray exhaust, #17.

Y17-A HISPANO-SUIZA 1938   1975
7. Two-tone blue body, black chassis, roof & interior: 1982.
8. Green body, dark green chassis, black roof & interior, diorama: 1986.

Y18-B ATKINSON STEAM WAGON   1985
1. Green body, red chassis, Sand & Gravel logo; Special Edition.
2. Dark yellow body, black chassis, Blue Circle Portland Cement logo: 1986.
3. Dark blue body, black chassis, dark brown barrels, Bass & Co. logo: 1987 Special Edition.

Y19-A AUBURN 1936 SPEEDSTER   1980
5. Cream body, black chassis, red interior & wheels: 1983.
6. White body & chassis, blue trim & interior: 1985 Limited Edition.

Y19-B FOWLER 1905 SHOWMAN'S ENGINE   1987
1. Dark blue body, white roof, black boiler & stack: Special Edition.

Y19-C MORRIS 1929 VAN   1987
1. Blue body, white roof, black chassis, Brasso logo.

Y20-A MERCEDES-BENZ 1937 540K   1980
1. Silver gray body, black chassis, red interior.
2. White body & chassis, red interior & trim: 1985.   3. Red body & chassis, light brown interior, diorama: 1987.

Y21-A MODEL A FORD 1927 WOODY   1981
1. Yellow body, brown chassis, 2-tone brown body, black roof, no logo.
2. Two-tone brown body, metallic red hood, brown chassis, black roof, A. & J. Box logo: 1983.
3. Navy blue & cream body, blue hood, black roof & chassis, Carter's logo: 1983.

Y21-B AVELING-PORTER 1894 STEAM ROLLER   1987
1. Green body, gray roof & rollers, black stack, James Young & Sons logo: 1987 Special Edition.

Y22-A MODEL A FORD 1930 VAN   1982
1. Red body, black chassis & roof, Oxo logo.
2. Cream body, red roof & chassis, Palm Toffee logo: 1984 Limited Edition.
3. Tan body, red roof, brown chassis, Toblerone logo: 1984 Limted Edition.
4. Dark yellow body, red roof, black chassis, Maggi Soup logo: 1983 Limited Edition.
5. Red body, black roof & chassis, Postes Canada Post logo: 1984 Limited Edition.
6. Red-brown body, white roof, brown chassis, Spratts logo: 1986 Limited Edition.
7. Dark blue body, white roof, black chassis, Lyons Tea logo: 1987.

Y23-A AEC OMNIBUS   1982
1. Red body, black chassis, tan interior, Schweppes logo on white background.
2. New Schweppes logo on yellow background, otherwise as type 1: 1983.
3. Red body, black chassis, tan interior, R.A.C. logo: 1985.
4. Red body, black chassis, tan interior, Maples logo: 1985 Limited Edition.
5. Cream upper-brown body, brown interior, Haig logo: 1986.

Y24-A BUGATTI 1927 T44   1983
1. Black and yellow body, black chassis.
2. Light gray and red body, red chassis, diorama: 1987.

Y25-A RENAULT 1910 AG VAN   1983
1. Green body & chassis, white roof, Perrier logo: 1983.

2. Yellow body, blue chassis, white roof, James Neale logo: 1985 Limited Edition.
3. Silver body, blue chassis, white roof, Duckhams Oils logo: 1985 Limited Edition.
4. Light blue body, dark blue chassis, white roof, Eagle Pencil logo: 1985.
5. Olive body & roof, black chassis, red cross, St. John Ambulance logo: 1986 Special Edition.
6. Red body, black chassis, white roof, T. Tunnock logo: 1987 Limited Edition.
7. Green body, black chassis, white roof, Delhaize & Co. logo: 1987.

Y26-A CROSSLEY 1918 LORRY   1984
1. light blue body, black chassis, tan top, brown barrels, Löwenbräu logo.
2. Black body & top, red-brown chassis, brown barrels, Romford Brewery logo: 1986 Limited Edition.
3. White body, black chassis, maroon top, brown barrels, Gonzalez Byass logo: 1987.

Y27-A FODEN 1922 STEAM LORRY   1984
1. Blue body, red chassis, pale gray roof & top, Pickfords logo.
2. Brown body, black chassis, tan roof & top, Hovis logo: 1985 Limited Edition.
3. Golden brown body, black chassis, roof & top, Tate & Lyle logo: 1986.
4. Cream body, green chassis, dark green roof, tan load of bags, Spillers logo: 1987 Limited Edition.

Y27-B FODEN STEAM WAGON & TRAILER   1986
1. Green bodies, white cab & canopies, red chassis, Frasers' House Furnishers logo: 1986 Special Edition.

Y28-A UNIC 1907 TAXI   1984
1. Red body, black top & chassis.
2. Blue body, black top & chassis: 1987.

Y29-A WALKER ELECTRIC VAN   1985
1. Olive body & chassis, cream top, tan interior, Harrods; Limited Edition.
2. Green body & roof, charcoal chassis, Joseph Lucas logo: 1986 Limited Edition.

Y30-A MACK 1920 TRUCK   1985
1. Light blue body, dark blue chassis, gray roofs, Acorn Storage logo: 1985.
2. Yellow body, tan top, maroon interior, Consolidated Motor Lines logo: 1985 Special Edition.
3. Cream body, green chassis, tan roof, Arctic Ice Cream logo: 1986 Limited Edition.

Convoy

The Convoy line of semi-trailer trucks in more-or-less Matchbox scale first appeared in 1982 and is still on the market. It offers models of large vehicles that could not be included in the Matchbox Series because of their size and expense, and includes a number of colorful logo types and loads. Convoy and Matchbox models have been included in a small number of Convoy Action Packs since 1985. Many variations exist, and the reader is urged to consult MATCHBOX USA for full details. Cabs include MB6 Scania, 41 Kenworth Conventional Aerodyne, 43 Peterbilt Conventional, and 45 Kenworth C.O.E. Aerodyne, plus a DAF unit made especially for this series.

CY-1A KENWORTH CAR TRANSPORTER   1982
1. Red 45 cab & semi, white upper deck.

CY-2A KENWORTH ROCKET TRANSPORTER   1982
1. Silver 45 cab and semi, white rocket.
2. White 45 cab. Note: rockets come in two sizes.)

CY-3A PETERBILT DOUBLE CONTAINER TRUCK   1982
1. Red 43 cab, white semi, Uniroyal logo.
2. Red 43 cab, white semi, Uniroyal logo.
3. White 43 cab & semi, tan containers, Federal Express logo: 1984.
4. White 43 cab, black semi, tan containers, Federal Express logo.

5. White 43 cab, black semi, cream containers, Pepsi-Cola logo: 1986.

CY-3B KENWORTH BOX TRUCK   1987
1. Red 45 cab & box, yellow semi & roof, Linfox logo.

CY-4A KENWORTH BOAT TRANSPORTER   1982
1. Red or orange 41 cab, silver semi, orange & white boat.

Convoy

CY-4B SCANIA BOX TRUCK   1987
1. White 6 cab & box, black semi, Ansett Freight Express logo.

CY-5A PETERBILT COVERED TRUCK   1982
1. White 43 cab & semi, green cover, Inter-State Trucking logo.
2. Yellow 43 cab & cover, gray semi, dark blue sides, Michelin logo: 1985.

CY-6A KENWORTH HORSE TRANSPORTER   1982
1. Green 41 cab, cream semi, green roof, Blue Grass Farms logo.
2. No logo, otherwise as type 1: 198.

CY-7A PETERBILT TANKER   1982
1. Black 41 cab & semi chassis, dark yellow tank, Supergas logo.
2. Red 41 cab, gray semi, chrome tank, Getty logo: 1984.

CY-8A KENWORTH SEMI   1982
1. White 45 cab, red & white semi, Redcap logo.
2. Black 45 cab & semi, Matchbox Moving in New Directions logo: 1986.
3. Silver 45 gray & blue cab & semi, Matchbox Showliner logo: 1986.
4. White 45 cab & semi, black semi chassis, K-Line logo: 1986.
5. White 45 cab & semi, blue chassis, red-yellow-blue trim, Matchbox logo: 1987.

CY-9A KENWORTH SEMI   1982
1. Black 41 cab & semi, Midnight Xpress logo.
2. Black 45 cab, otherwise as type 1: 198.
3. Black 41 cab & semi, yellow box, Stanley logo: 1986.
4. Dark blue DAF cab, box & semi, Crookes Healthcare logo: 1987. (Officially this is not CY9 but CY102.)
5. Dark yellow DAF cab & semi, black trim & IPEC logo: 1987.

CY-10A KENWORTH TYRONE MALONE TRANSPORTER   1983
1. White body, red & blue trim, carrying MB66 truck.

CY-11A KENWORTH HELICOPTER TRANSPORTER   1983
1. Silver 45 cab & semi, orange MB75 copter.
2. Black 45 cab, silver semi, black & white copter: 1985.

CY-12A KENWORTH AIRCRAFT TRANSPORTER   1984
1. White 45 cab & semi, blue plane, white "Darts" logo.

CY-13A PETERBILT FIRE ENGINE   1984
1. Red 43 cab & semi, white ladder.
2. Modified cab without sleeper and second rear axle, otherwise as type 1: 1985. (Note: catalog numbers are as given above, but my CY12 bubblepack contains the Fire Engine and CY13 the Aircraft Transporter.)

CY-14A KENWORTH POWERBOAT TRANSPORTER   1985
1. White 45 cab, silver semi, white boat, brown rack.

CY-15A PETERBILT TRACKING VEHICLE   1985
1. White 43 cab & semi, blue rocket, red & blue NASA logo.
2. Yellow 43 cab & semi, blue British Telecom logo, in CY206: 1987.

CY-16A SCANIA BOX TRUCK   1985
1. White 6 cab & semi, blue box, Duckhams logo.
2. White & green 6 cab, black semi, white box, 7UP logo: 1985 Promo.
3. Purple 6 cab & semi, white box, Edwin Shirley/Sealink logo: 1987.
4. White 6 cab, red chassis & semi, Heinz Ketchup logo: 1987.
5. Red 6 cab & box, white chassis & trim, Kentucky Fried Chicken logo: 1987.
6. White 6 cab & box, blue chassis, Signal Toothpaste logo: 1987.

7. Yellow 6 cab & box, white & red chassis, Weetabix logo: 1987.
8. White 6 cab & box, black chassis, red trim, Wimpy logo: 1987.
9. Blue 6 cab, box & chassis, orange & white trim & Matey Bubble Bath logo: 1987.

CY-17A SCANIA PETROL TANKER   1985
1. White 6 cab & tank, blue semi chassis, Amoco logo.
2. Red 6 cab & tank, orange semi chassis, Tizer logo: 1987.
3. White 6 cab & tank, green chassis, Diet 7Up logo: 1987.

CY-18A SCANIA DOUBLE CONTAINER TRUCK   1986
1. Blue 6 cab & containers, yellow semi, Varta logo.
2. White 6 cab & containers, blue chassis & semi, Wall's Ice Cream logo: 1987.
3. Red 6 cab, semi & containers, Kit Kat logo: 1987.
4. Orange 6 cab & boxes, brown chassis, Rowntrees Breakaway logo: 1987.

CY-19A PETERBILT BOX TRUCK   1986
1. White 43 cab & semi, Ansett Wridgways logo.

CY-20A KENWORTH/SCANIA TIPPER   1986
1. Yellow Kenworth 45 cab & semi, Taylor Woodrow logo.
2. Pink Scania 6 cab & semi, Readymix logo: 1986.
3. Yellow Kenworth 45 cab & semi, Eurobran logo; in CY205: 1987.

CY-21A DAF AIRCRAFT TRANSPORTER   1987
1. White DAF cab, black semi, orange plane.

CY-22A DAF POWER LAUNCH TRANSPORTER   1987
1. White DAF cab, blue chassis & semi, white & red boat, Lakeside logo.

Convoy Action Packs

CY-201 FIRE RESCUE SET   1985
1. CY13 Fire Engine, MB54 Airport Foam Pumper, special version of MB75 Helicopter (Fire Dept. logo).

CY-202 POLICE SET   1985
1. CY11 Helicopter Transporter, MB10 Police Car, MB61 Peterbilt Wrecker.

CY-203 CONSTRUCTION SET   1985
1. CY-type Low Loader with MB32 Excavator, MB23 Peterbilt Tipper, MB29 Shovel Tractor.

CY-204 NASA SET   1986
1. CY2 Rocket Transporter, MB54 Tracking Vehicle, special version of MB75 Helicopter (NASA logo).

CY-205 FARM SET   1987
1. CY20 Tipper, MB46 Tractor & Harrow, MB51 Combine.

CY-206 BRITISH TELECOM SET   1987
1. CY15 Tracking Vehicle, MB48 Vauxhall Astra, MB60 Ford Transit.

Team Matchbox

These colorful racing sets are composed of the CY10 flatbed truck, a Matchbox stock car and team van or pickup, each set in the colors of a racing team. There have been eight different types since the series was introduced in 1985, but only four have been on the market in one country at any one time.

TM-1A PEPSI TEAM   1985
1. Yellow truck, white MB34 Chevy Pro Stocker, yellow MB68 Chevy Van, with red-white-blue Pepsi logo, #14.

TM-2A SUPER STAR TEAM   1985
1. White truck, white MB34 Chevy Pro Stocker, white MB58 Ruff Trek pickup, with red-yellow-blue trim, #217.

TM-3A DR. PEPPER TEAM   1985
1. White truck, dark red MB9 AMX, white MB68 Chevy Van, with red & white or red & brown Dr. Pepper logo, #4.

122

Team Matchbox®

Super Kings

The Super Kings (originally King Size) range has existed for many years. As before, it is presently composed of a variety of cars, trucks and other vehicles in scales generally larger than the Matchbox Series. Though the Super Kings often duplicate Matchbox models in terms of subject matter, in scale they are more akin to the 1/43 scale models made by many other firms. The Kings have never ranked among the most popular Matchbox lines, probably because their size made them incompatible with the smaller Matchbox cars. The manufacturers have tried in a variety of ways to make the Super Kings more popular. Several models have been issued in German, French, Danish and other national versions during the Eighties, and recently such refinements as flashing lights and steering have been offered. So the Super Kings, which many collectors thought (and some, perhaps, hoped) would fade out of sight within a few years of Matchbox's sale to Universal, have remained in production and offered a wide variety of new models, logo types and innovations. As before in this book, only new models and major variations will be listed, which means that many numbers will not appear.

123

Super Kings

K84-A   PEUGEOT 305   1981
  4. Metallic blue body, off-white interior, Elf/Canon logo, #5: 1984.
  5. White body with mud, blue & red trim, #10: 1986.
K86-A   VW GOLF 7 GAS PUMP   1982
  1. Black body, white interior, red-orange-yellow trim, white pump.
  2. Yellow body, ADAC Strassenwacht logo, white interior & pump: 1983.
  3. White body, red & white trim, red interior, white pump: 1985.
K87-A   TRACTOR & ROTARY RAKE/STAKE TRAILER   1982
  1. Red tractor body, white roof, orange rake frame, yellow rakes.
  2. Red-white-silver tractor, red trailer, silver chassis, tan stakes: 1983.
K88-A   MONEY BOX SECURITY VAN   1981
  1. White cab & body, blue roof, Volksbank Raiffeisenbank logo: 1981.
  2. Orange cab & roof, cream body, Caisse d'Epargne logo: 1982.
  3. Red cab, white body, blue roof, Matchbox logo: 1984.
K90-A   MATRA RANCHO   1982
  1. Red body, white hood & roof, Trans Globe Couriers logo.
  2. Yellow body, black & red trim: 1985.
K92-A   HELICOPTER TRANSPORTER   1982
  1. Yellow cab, green chassis & semi, white & green copter, Heli-Hire logo.
K95-A   AUDI QUATTRO   1982
  1. Silver gray body, red & black trim, Audi logo, #1.
  2. White body, red-yellow-brown trim, Pace logo, #10: 1984.
  3. White body, red-blue-black trim, #17: 1986.
K96-A   VOLVO AMBULANCE   1983
  1. White body, orange roof & interior, red trim.
K97-A   POLICE RANGE ROVER & MOTORCYCLES   1983
  1. White body, orange trim, white & black cycles.
K98-B   PORSCHE 944   1983
  1. Silver gray body, black hatch, 2-tone blue & black trim.
  2. Golden brown body, black hatch, red & black trim: 1985.
  3. Red body, black hatch, white trim & lettering: 1987.
K99-B   DODGE POLICE VAN   1983
  1. Silver body, orange & black trim?
  2. White body, green roof & Polizei logo: 1984.
K100-A   FORD SIERRA XR4i   1983
  1. White upper/gray lower body & interior, white or gray hatch.
  2. Silver upper body, otherwise as type 1: 1983.
  3. Metallic red upper/gray lower body: 1984.
  4. Black upper/gray lower body: 1986.
K101-A   RACING PORSCHE   1983
  1. Gold body, red-yellow-black trim.
  2. Red body & interior, black chassis, yellow & black Sunoco logo, #16.
K102-A   RACE SUPPORT SET   1983
  1. Yellow Team Porsche van, black roof 7 rack, white #9 Porsche.
K103-A   PETERBILT TANKER   1983
  1. Silver gray body, blue chassis, Comet logo.
  2. White body, otherwise as type 1: 1984.
K104-A   RANCHO RESCUE SET   1983
  1. White & black wagon & boat, red trailer, Coast Guard logo.
K105-A   PETERBILT TIPPER   1984
  1. White cab, red tipper & trim.
  2. Yellow cab & tipper, Taylor Woodrow logo: 1985.

K106-A   AIRCRAFT TRANSPORTER   1984
  1. Red cab, silver semi, red plane.
K107-A   POWERBOAT TRANSPORTER   1984
  1. White truck & boat, blue chassis & trim, Spearhead logo.
K108-A   DIGGER & TRANSPORTER   1984
  1. Yellow digger & cab, black chassis & semi, red shovel, Avro logo.
K109-A   PETROL TANKER   1984
  1. Yellow cab, white roof & tank, gray chassis, Shell logo.
K110-A   FIRE ENGINE   1984
  1. Red body, white chassis & interior, gray ladder.
K111-A   REFUSE TRUCK   1985
  1. Orange cab, body & rear, Waste-Beater logo.
K112-A   FIRE SPOTTER TRANSPORTER   1985
  1. Red cab & semi, red & white airplane.
K113-A   GARAGE TRANSPORTER   1985
  1. Yellow cab, red chassis & semi, white airscreen, Shell garage, yellow tarp.
  2. White tarp, otherwise as type 1: 1985.
K114-A   MOBILE CRANE   1985
  1. Yellow truck, cabin & lower boom, black upper boom, Taylor Woodrow logo.
K115-A   MERCEDES-BENZ 190E   1985
  1. White body, black interior. 2. Silver gray body, black interior: 1987.
K116-A   RACING CAR TRANSPORTER   1985
  1. Red truck with airscreen, Ferrari logo, two racers.
K117-A   BULLDOZER TRANSPORTER   1985
  1. Yellow & black cab & dozer, black semi.
K118-A   ROAD CONSTRUCTION SET   1985
  1. Tao trucks, two trailers, figures, road signs.
K119-A   FIRE RESCUE SET   1985
  1. K110 Fire Engine, Unimog, trailer, figures.
K120-A   CAR TRANSPORTER   1986
  (ex-K10)
  1. White cab & semi, black chassis, Carrier logo.
K121-A   PETERBILT WRECKER   1986
  (ex-K20)
  1. Navy blue cab, black booms, white rear & chassis, Highway Patrol/City Police
     logo, steering.
K122-A   DAF ROAD TRAIN   1986
  (ex-K21)
  1. White truck & trailer, Eurotrans logo, steering.
K123-A   LEYLAND CEMENT TRUCK   1986
  (ex-K26)
  1. Yellow cab & rear, black chassis, steering.
K124-A   MERCEDES CONTAINER TRUCK   1986
  (ex-K31)
  1. White cab & container, gray chassis, 7-Up logo, steering.
K125-A   BEDFORD VAN   1986
  1. Steering, no other data.
K126-A   HELICOPTER TRANSPORTER   1986
  (ex-K92)
  1. Blue DAF cab & semi, blue & orange copter, Royal Navy logo, steering.
K127-A   PETERBILT TANKER   1986
  (ex-K103)

  1. White cab & tank, red chassis, Total logo, steering.
K128-A   AIRCRAFT TRANSPORTER   1986
  (ex-K106)
  1. Red cab & semi, tan plane, steering.
K129-A   MERCEDES POWER LAUNCH TRANSPORTER   1986
  (ex-K107)
  1. Dark blue cab, light blue chassis, gray semi, tan & white boat, Krüger Boots logo,
     steering.
K130-A   DIGGER TRANSPORTER   1986
  (ex-K108)
  1. Yellow cab & digger, brown chassis & semi, steering.
K131-A   PETROL TANKER   1986
  (ex-K109)
  1. Orange cab, white tank, black & gray chassis, Shell logo, steering.
  2. Red cab & tank, black & gray chassis, Texaco logo: 1986.
K132-A   FIRE ENGINE   1986
  (ex-K110)
  1. Red body, white chassis, gray ladder, steering.
  2. White ladder, otherwise as type 1: 1986.
K133-A   IVECO REFUSE TRUCK   1986
  (revised K111, new cab)
  1. Maroon cab & rear body, white chassis, steering.
K134-A   FIRE SPOTTER TRANSPORTER   1986
  (ex-K112)
  1. Red cab, white chassis, red semi & plane, silver wings, steering.
K135-A   MERCEDES GARAGE TRANSPORTER   1986
  (ex-K113)
  1. Yellow cab, orange tarp, red chassis & semi, steering.
K136-A   FERRARI RACING TRANSPORTER   1986
  (ex-K116)
  1. Red cab & semi, white chassis, Ferrari logo, steering.
K137-A   ROAD CONSTRUCTION SET   1986
  (ex-K116)
  1. Yellow trucks & trailers, black chassis, steering.
K138-A   FIRE RESCUE SET   1986
  (ex-K118)
  1. Red & white trucks, red trailer, steering.
K139-A   IVECO TIPPER TRUCK   1987
  1. Yellow cab & tipper, black chassis, Wimpey logo.
K140-A   LEYLAND CAR RECOVERY VEHICLE   1987
  1. White cab & body, blue chassis, operating ramp.
K141-A   LEYLAND TIPPER TRUCK   1987
  1. Red cab, gray tipper, black chassis, yellow ECD logo.
K142-A   BMW POLICE CAR   1987
  1. White body, yellow stripe, black checker design, Police logo, flashing rear sign.
  2. White body, green doors & hood, Polizei logo, flashing rear sign.
K143-A   BEDFORD AMBULANCE   1987
  1. White body, orange-red cross & stripe, blue Ambulance logo, flashing signs.
K144-A   AIRPORT LAND ROVER   1987
  1. Yellow body, Frankfurt Flughafen logo, flashing signs.
  2. Yellow body, Heathrow Airport logo, flashing signs.

Specials

In 1984 this new series of large-scale competition cars was put on the market. It has since grown to include fourteen models, though only seven castings have been used, with each car offered in two racing versions.

SP1 KREMER PORSCHE CK5 — 1984
1. White body, red trim, Grand Prix/Kremer logo, #22.
2. White body, two-tone blue trim, kremer logo, #35: 1985.

SP2 KREMER PORSCHE CK5 TURBO — 1984
1. White body, silver & other trim, Shell logo, #19.
2. White body, green & other trim, Shell logo, #2: 1987.

SP3 PIONEER FERRARI 512BB — 1984
1. Blue body, white trim, Pioneer logo, #71.
2. Yellow body, red & green trim, Ferrari logo, #147: 1987.

SP4 RJ RACING FERRARI 512BB — 1984
1. Red body, European University logo, #46.
2. Black body, red-orange-yellow trim, RJ Racing logo, #88: 1986.

SP5 AUTO SYSTEMS LANCIA RALLY — 1984
1. Yellow body, red trim, Auto Systems logo, #102.
2. Dark green body, yellow trim, Pirelli logo, 116: 1986.

SP6 MARTINI LANCIA RALLY — 1984
1. White body, red & blue trim, Martini logo, no number.

SP7 ZAKSPEED FORD MUSTANG — 1984
1. White body, blue & black trim, Ford logo, #16.
2. Dark blue body, yellow trim, Duckhams logo, #38: 1987.

SP8 ZAKSPEED MUSTANG TURBO — 1984
1. White body, no other data.
2. Black body, red-white-yellow trim, Avon logo, #83: 1986.

SP9 N.G.K. CHEVY PRO STOCKER — 1984
1. Yellow body, black trim, NGK logo, #12.

SP10 HEUER CHEVY PRO STOCKER — 1984

1. Metallic blue body, yellow trim, Mambo Racing logo.
2. Dark green body, red & white trim, Thrush logo, #9: 1985.

SP11 GOODYEAR CHEVROLET CAMARO — 1984
1. White body, green trim, Goodyear logo, #18.
2. White body, red & gray trim, Total logo, #7: 1986?

SP12 CHEVROLET CAMARO TURBO — 1984
1. Red body, white & black trim, #56.
2. White body, yellow and blue trim, Bosch logo, #3: 1987. (1987 catalog shows SP12-1 as SP11 and SP11-2 as SP12!)

SP13 PORSCHE 959 ED RACING — 1986
1. Red body, yellow trim, ED Racing logo, #44.

SP14 PORSCHE TURBO 959 — 1986
1. White body, red-yellow-blue trim, #53.

Turbo Specials

This small series of large-scale competition cars came on the market in 1985. Like the Specials, which they much resemble, they are finished in bright-colored racing liveries; unlike them, these cars have two-speed pullback motors. The first four models issued were numbered; eight subsequent models apparently were not, and in the 1987 catalog the first four are no longer numbered.

TS1 FIRESTONE CHEVROLET CAMARO — 1985
1. White body, red & blue trim, Firestone logo, #4

TS3 ZAKSPEED FORD MUSTANG — 1985
1. Yellow body, red & black trim, Michelin logo, #20.

TS3 MICHELIN KREMER PORSCHE — 1985
1. Red body, orange-yellow-black trim, Michelin logo, #15.

TS4 GOODYEAR PRO STOCKER TURBO — 1985
1. White body, silver & black trim, Momo logo, #5.

1985 Unnumbered Series

TS KREMER PORSCHE — 1985
1. White body, two-tone blue trim, Kremer logo, #35.

TS CHEVROLET CAMARO — 1985

1. White body, red-silver-black trim, Total logo, #7.

TS CHEVY PRO STOCKER — 1985
1. Dark green body, red-white-silver-black trim, Thrush logo, #9.

TS ZAKSPEED MUSTANG — 1985
1. Black body, red-yellow-white trim, Avon logo, #83. (Note: these four finishes are identical to the corresponding Specials.)

125

1987 Unnumbered Series

1987   1. White body, red & blue trim, #48.
         TS KREMER PORSCHE CK5 TURBO   1987
1987   1. Red body, yellow & black trim, #70.

TS PORSCHE 959   1987
  1. White body, yellow-green-black trim, #27.

Turbo Two

The 1987 Matchbox catalog includes this new series of cars and vans with two-speed pullback motors. They bear some resemblance to the regular Matchbox series, but their proportions are affected at times by the need for enough space to house their motors, making some of them look shorter or higher than normal. I have not seen this series and can only list what is in the catalog:

AM2601 Pontiac Fiero, yellow.
AM2602 Peugeot 205 Turbo, silver.
AM2603 Ford Supoervan II: orange.
AM2604 Racing Porsche: orange.

AM2605 Toyota MR2: red.
AM2606 Group C Racer: blue.
AM2607 Pontiac Fiero: white.
AM2608 Peugeot 205 Turbo: yellow.

AM2609 Ford Supervan II: white.
AM2610 Racing Porsche: red.
AM2611 Toyota MR2: yellow.
AM2612 Group C Racer: white.

(Note that each casting is used twice.)

Other series of toy cars, such as the Lock-Ups, Hot Rod Racers, Speed Riders, Trick Shifters, Burning Key Cars, etc., have not been listed here, nor have the Skybusters, Battle Kings, Sea Kings and character car series shown in MATCHBOX TOYS. The collector is urged to consult the yearly Matchbox catalogs and the collectors' journals for information on them.

Gift Sets

For many years Matchbox has offered gift sets comprising a variety of Matchbox, King Size and Yesteryear models. This practice continues, though the number of gift sets offered in recent years has not been great. On the other hand, the Gift Sets as such have recently been augmented by the offering of various other play sets and accessories. There are numerous items which could have been listed, but we have to stop somewhere, so the Gift Sets will conclude the Matchbox portion of the book. Since the 1983 Matchbox catalog does not show any Gift Sets, the data presented here are less than complete.

Gift Sets

G1   CAR TRANSPORTER PACK   1984 or before.
  1. Blue K10 transporter and five cars.
  2. White transporter and five cars: 1986.
G2-A   CONVOY ACTION PACK   1984 or before.
  1. Three Convoy trucks, truck cab, police car.
G2-B   CAR TRANSPORTER PACK   1987
  1. White K10 transporter and five cars (renumbered G1).
G4   CONVOY ACTION SET   1985
  1. Three Convoy trucks, truck cab, police car (renumbered G2-A).

  2. New colors, new truck cab: 1987.
G5-A   CONSTRUCTION SET   1982
  1. Five vehicles plus accessories.
G5-B   FEDERAL EXPRESS PACK   1987
  1. Two covered trucks, one Ford Transit Van, one VW Golf, one jet plane.
G6   VIRGIN ATLANTIC SET   1987
  1. Airliner, Helicopter, Airport Bus, Dodge Caravan and Ford Sierra.
G7   EMERGENCY ACTION PACK   1984
  1. Five emergency vehicles, buildings.

G8   TURBOCHARGED ACTION PACK   1984
  1. Four cars, one van, launcher.
G9?
G10   PAN AM ACTION PACK   1986
  1. Airliner, Foam Pumper, Airport Bus, Dodge Caravan, Police Car.
G11   LUFTHANSA ACTION PACK   1986
  1. Airliner, Foam Pumper, Airport Bus, Mercedes G-Wagon, Porsche 928.

As has been stated in the Introduction in another context, the fact that some items are listed here and others are not is NOT to be taken as a value judgment of what is worth collecting and what is not. That decision rightly belongs to each individual collector. So enjoy your hobby in your own way!

Introduction
Lledo™ *Series*

The firm of Lledo (London) Ltd. was founded in 1982 by John. W. Odell, who named his new company by spelling his own name backwards—a habit he picked up during his World War II service when he couldn't remember code names and persuaded his superiors to give him one he couldn't forget. Jack Odell is the reason why Lledo models have become so dear to the hearts of many Matchbox collectors, for he was, almost from the beginning of Lesney Products, one of the partners in that distinguished and now lamented firm. After financial problems caused the manufacturers of Matchbox cars to sell out, Jack Odell sought a new outlet for his time, energy, expertise and creative talents. His heart had always been especially close to the Models of Yesteryear, and he decided to produce similar models himself. Thus he recruited several ex-Matchbox employees, founded the firm of Lledo, and set to work.

In April of 1963 the first six Lledo "Models of Days Gone" appeared on the market. Believing that there was an unfulfilled demand for models of horsedrawn vehicles, Mr. Odell had planned and produced five of them: DG001 Tram, 002 Milk Float, 003 Delivery Van, 004 Omnibus and 005 Fire Engine, the last two particularly in the style of early Models of Yesteryear. The sixth model issued in 1963 was the DG006 Model T Ford Van, and it, rather than the horsedrawn vehicles, was to be Lledo's first big success. It soon appeared in a wide variety of colorful logo types, attracted many orders for promotional models—a trend which had not been anticipated but which was to prove profitable to Lledo, if frustrating to collectors—, and showed Mr. Odell once and for all that the market for high-quality miniature trucks, complete with logo, far exceeded that for models of horsedrawn vehicles.

Now the pattern became clear: in addition to the regular Models of Days Gone, the firm would also produce promotional models using the same castings. The first few promotionals did not differ from the Days Gone issues except in their finish; the castings were exactly the same, as were the boxes they were packaged in. But as the production of the promotionals increased, it was realized that the two lines of models needed to be kept separate in ways that could be seen by the buyer. So the baseplates of the models were adapted to take either of two inserts, one with the Days Gone name and the other lettered "Lledo Promotional Model". New boxes for the promotionals were also made, and it was hoped that the two streams of models would thereby be separated once and for all.

For the most part, they have. Questions still arise about some of the earliest promotional models, produced before the new-type bases were in production, about a few models privately painted and lettered, but utilizing the castings of Days Gone issues, and about some models assembled by an inexperienced work force at a time of rapid expansion and production. But though the last-named situation produced some unusual combinations of castings for both regular and promotional issues, it is now known by most collectors just which items were Models of Days Gone and which were Lledo Promotional Models.

The models can also be classified by the system already in use when Lledo products first came on the market. It had been popularized by Ray Bush for use in his U. K. Matchbox club, so that when Mr. Bush established the International Specialist Days Gone Collectors Club (and adopted Jack Odell's wartime "Lledo Calling" code as the title of the club's journal), his system of codes was already at hand:

Code One models are those wholly produced by Lledo, including paint and logo.

Code Two models are those manufactured by Lledo and sold to a second party who finishes them (by applying adhesive labels, for instance) in a way already known and agreed to by Lledo.

Code Three models are those adapted in some way by other parties without Lledo's knowledge and consent: by putting on a new logo over or in place of the original one, stripping and refinishing the model, chopping the casting into another type of vehicle, etc.

The two main courses of Lledo production became clearly defined during 1964, and the first six models were joined by another seven in that year: DG007 Ford Woody Wagon, DG008 Model T Ford Tanker, DG009 Model A Ford Car (a touring car with top down), DG010 Albion Single Decker Coach, DG011 Large Horse Drawn Van, DG012 Fire Engine, and DG013 Model A Ford Van. Once again it was the last model in the year's production that became the most frequently used; though it lacked the picturesque charm of the Model T, the Model A shared its potential for bearing an advertising logo, and even exceeded it when a roof blade was mounted diagonally on its top.

1984 was also the last year in which a horsedrawn vehicle was introduced. It was now clear that, for all their oldtime appeal, the horsedrawn models just could not complete with the motor trucks, so DG011 became the last Days Gone model of the type, and by the end of 1985 production of the horsedrawn models had nearly ceased except for an occasional promotional or special order.

Six new models were introduced in 1985: DG014 Model A Ford Car (the same basic vehicle as DG009, but now with top up), DG015 AEC Double Deck Bus, DG016 Heavy Goods Van, DG017 Long Distance Coach, DG018 Packard Van (originally issued as an ambulance), and DG019 Rolls Royce Car (a Phantom II, in fact).

Some new trends made themselves known here, chiefly toward more buses—for there must be almost as many model bus collectors as model truck collectors, and both groups want a wide variety not only of basic models but of logo types. In addition, the Rolls-Royce joined the Model A Ford to represent essentially non-commercial vehicles, and the Packard, in its original form as an ambulance, offered something new to collectors of emergency vehicles, who were to enjoy another treat when the DG012 Fire Engine was offered with a removable wheeled fire escape ladder.

In 1986 three new models appeared: DG020 Model A Ford Stake Truck, DG021 Chevrolet Van, and DG022 Packard Town Van. One other model, the DG023 Scenicruiser Bus, was to join them just after the year's end, its issue delayed by production problems. 1986 was basically a year of settling down into new full production and preparing for what 1987 would bring. In addition to the DG023 Scenicruiser, two new Rolls-Royce cars appeared early in the year: DG024 Playboy Convertible Coupe and DG025 Silver Ghost Tourer. A series of interesting trucks had been announced early in the year, and at summer's end the first of them, DG026 Chevrolet Bottle Truck, made its appearance. The DG027 Mack Breakdown Truck and DG028 Mack Canvas Back Truck should be the next two Models of Days Gone.

In addition, 1987 has brought the first of Lledo's Marathon series of modern vehicles. The first four models in this series are all buses and have already appeared in a variety of logo types.

The fine quality, colorful charm and reasonable prices of the series have endeared them to many collectors all over the world. As Ray Bush has often pointed out in the pages of "Lledo Calling", each individual hobbyist is free to decide what he or she wants to collect. There are several possibilities: Days Gone basic models only, Days Gone variations (for there have been casting changes in the majority of the models), Days Gone plus other Code One items, such as the set of light gray models made as specimens for prospective customers, and any of the above plus promotionals, not to mention some Code 3 items that cannot properly be called Lledo Promotional Models. Some collectors, knowing they will never get all the existing promotionals, have given up trying to collect them at all, while others have accepted the situation as it is and collect whatever they can get. This writer knows at least one fellow hobbyist whose Lledo collection numbers over nine hundred, and what with all the variations in existence, it must now be possible to assemble over a thousand different Lledo models.

Granted, they may not all differ markedly, and some of their differences may strike one as rather boring. For example, all the models using the chassis casting first used on the DG10 Albion can be found with either thick or thin rear edges of their front fenders, and all DG21 Chevrolet Vans exist with casting number 1 or 2 under their chassis. In such cases two casting types were used

simultaneously, one of each coming out of the dies together, whereas other casting changes are chronological in nature, resulting from changes made in the dies, usually to strengthen or adapt them.

We must also note several small families of Lledo models that have been prepared for special markets. Lledo's U.S. importer, Hartoy, commissioned a "Fantastic Set o' Wheels" set meant to sell at low prices in supermarkets, drugstores and the like, but they did not sell well and the last of them, we hear, have been sold back to Britain, where they will either join or compete with the series made for sale in the Tesco supermarket chain. The Tesco series are Days Gone models, sometimes with slight variations, and so, with more latitude in logo and color variations, are the Edocar series issued in The Netherlands. Most recently, Britain has seen the appearance of an array of View Vans, these being Model T or Model A Ford vans showing scenes from tourist attractions and made for sale as souvenirs.

So there is plenty to collect; the next question, once one decides what to collect, is where one can get the models. And here the situation differs from the usual one, simply because there aren't many shops (at least in America) that carry any Lledo models, much less a large assortment of them. It is necessary to be in contact with dealers to build up a big Lledo collection. The more dealers you know, and the more sources your dealers buy from, the more Lledo models you are going to obtain.

What one pays for the models depends on whether they are Days Gone, which generally sell for $3 to $5 when current, or Lledo Promotionals, which start at $7 to $10 and go up, in some cases quite high. They are joined at the top by a few Days Gone rarities issued in limited numbers. Prices of the rarest Lledo models usually stop at $50 to $80, but occasionally one will be offered for as much as $125, though whether anyone buys them at those prices is questionable.

What the collector needs, besides access to the models and money to buy them, is information, and the best sources of information are the collectors' club journals. By far the most informative for the Models of Days Gone is the British club's "Lledo Calling". Mr. Bush stresses that the organization is strictly a Days Gone club, and mentions promotionals only when misunderstandings about the actual status of a model need to be cleared up. In America, "Lledo U.S.A.", published by Charles Mack (like Ray Bush the director of a Matchbox collectors' club), publishes black-and-white photos and brief descriptions of all issues, Days Gone and Promotionals alike. "Lledo U.S.A." is the only source of specific data on the Lledo Promotionals, which have also been listed in chronological order, though not described, in Ray Dowding's "Lledo Collectors Guide", printed in Britain and updated at times. There are also Lledo clubs in Australia and other countries, but this writer has no information on their publications.

Having tracked down the models we want to collect, let's have a look at them. Each model is partly diecast metal and partly plastic. Generally the body and chassis are metal, and the interior, base and other parts are plastic. The horsedrawn models are mostly or all metal except for their black, dark brown, light brown or tan horses. Grilles and windshields are either silver or gold—or, if you prefer, chrome or brass plating over plastic. Wheels are either 12-spoke metal or a variety of spoked or solid plastic types; tires are plastic and either black, white (cream, to be more precise), or very rarely gray or tan. In the early days each Days Gone model came with a set of plastic figures. When the DG015 Double Decker Bus was introduced in 1985, the practice of issuing sets of figures was discontinued for all models.

The logo of a Days Gone model is invariably tampo-printed with paint—or is there one odd exception to this rule? But a number (not all) of the promotional and Code 3 models have adhesive labels or decals—one way to recognize them for what they are. The exact mixture of paint and the pressure of the tampo printer can result in varying shades of paint, but most collectors and chroniclers agree that these are not worth trying to list unless the difference between two varieties is easy to see. In describing the colors of the models and their components, I have had to use rather simple terminology: blue, for example, means any shade of blue too dark to be called light and too light to be called dark. There are several shades of cream involved, and I gave up trying to differentiate among them, though if I had it to do over, I might well call the lightest cream ivory; it is certainly lighter than the darkest cream, which is in turn lighter than light tan.

Even the boxes the models come in vary considerably. A box may be one of the usual Days Gone or Lledo Promotional types or, in some cases, one of those prepared especially for one model or series. A good example would be the Hamleys boxes containing the Days Gone issues bearing the name of, and made to be sold by, Hamleys, the great London toyshop. And we must not forget that some models have been issued with certificates attesting to their promotional or commemorative use, and often bearing serial numbers. These certificates have become a part of Lledo collecting.

Before we look at individual issues and their variations, it would be well to list the basic models by name and number. "Lledo Calling" lists the Models of Days Gone by the numbers assigned at the Lledo factory, while both Ray Dowding and Charles Mack list Lledo Promotionals in more or less chronological order. In addition, such series as the Edocars and the "Fantastic Set o' Wheels" can be listed easily. These lists are quite all right as far as they go, but it may well be easier for the all-out Lledo collector to have all the models using the same casting, of whatever origin, listed together. This is why I have developed the system of numbers and letters you will find (and probably tear your hair over) in the main listing. The first two numbers will indicate the basic casting, the next three letters will try to indicate the name on the logo (or the main color of the model if it has no logo), and the last two digits will be either DG for Days Gone, LP for Lledo Promotional, or an indication of some other origin.

The details given in the listings will be as thorough as possible under the circumstances. Some of the terminology deserves a brief comment. A transverse signboard at the front of a roof is a header, while a diagonal or longitudinal type is a roof blade. A frame is what I call a line, sometimes plain and sometimes fancy, surrounding a logo or portion thereof. The "gunmetal" color of some wheels is a metallic blue-black or brown-black quite different from gloss black. The rest of the terms should be clear enough.

There remains that horror of collectors, the price guide, which we include solely because many people who buy the book will want it. As in my earlier Corgi Toys book, two values, a low and a high, will be listed—and no doubt some of the high values will have become too low by the time the book is in print! But such is life in our hobby. I can only hope that the financial considerations will be of lesser importance to you than the fun you get out of collecting.

The illustrations will show as many Lledo products as I have been able to assemble for photographing, and the listings will include as much information as I have. I would like to thank Ray Bush of "Lledo Calling" for his kind permission to include information from his club's journal, including much data on Days Gone variations and his Days Gone numbering system—the hyphenated six-digit number given after the name of each Days Gone model. Thanks also to Charles Mack of "Lledo U.S.A." for basic information on rare models shown in that journal, and to Mark Henderson and Fred Clausen for the information derived from their Lledo Promotional lists. I have seen other lists, but they have not aded any information to this book.

And now to the listings and the photos, beginning with some general lists, then the very specific lists of all Lledo models—including a few Code Three items that purists will say I should not have included. I put them in because I thought some of you might like to see what a few creative idividuals have done with Lledo models. I hope you will find this book informative and interesting, and that it will help to enrich your hobby. Happy collecting to you all!

Numerical Lists of Lledo™ *Models*

1. Models of Days Gone, with official factory numbers as cited in "Lledo Calling".

001 Horse Drawn Tram 1983
   001 Westminster 1983
   002 Main Street 1983
   003 National Tramway Museum 1984
   004 Downtown 1984
002 Horse Drawn Milk Float 1983
   001 Express Dairy 1983
   002 Chambourcy Yogurt 1984
   003 Clifford Dairies 1984
   004 Celtic Dairies 1984
003 Horse Drawm Delivery Van 1983
   001 Windmill Bakery 1983
   002 Pepperidge Farm 1983
   003 Stafford County Show 1984
   004 Matthew Norman 1984

005 Fine Lady Bakeries 1984
006 Robertsons Jams 1984
007 LSWR Parcels 1984
008 Hamleys 1984
009 Tri-Sum Potato Chips 1984
010 Coca-Cola 1985
011 Royal Mail 1985
012 Lledo Club Member 1987
004 Horse Drawn Omnibus 1983
   001 Lipton's/Victoria-King's Cross 1983
   002 Lipton's/Bowery-Broadway 1983
   003 Oakeys/Putney 1984
   004 Pears Soap/Victoria-King's Cross 1984
   005 Madame Tussaud's 1984
   006 Hamleys 1984

007 Mason's Pantry 1985
008 High Chapparal 1986
005 Horse Drawn Fire Engine 1983
   001 London Fire Brigade 1983
   002 Chicago Fire Brigade 1983
   003 Guildford Fire Brigade 1983
   004 Hong Kong Fire Brigade 1984
   005 Great Western Railway 1984
   006 Philadelphia Bureau of Fire 1984
   007 Bifbac II Convention 1984
   008 Lake City 1984
006 Model T Ford Van 1983
   001 Ovaltine 1983
   002 Yorkshire Post 1983
   003 Cookie Coach Co. 1984
   004 British Meat 1984
   005 Marcol Products 1984
   006 City of London Police Ambulance 1984
   007 Aeroplane Jelly 1984
   008 I.P.M.S. 21st Anniversary 1984
   009 Illinois Toy Show 1984
   010 International Garden Festival 1984
   011 Stretton Spring Water 1984
   012 Yorkshire Evening Post 1984
   013 Coca-Cola at Soda Fountains 1984
   014 Coca-Cola Every Bottle Sterilized 1984
   015 British Bacon 1984
   016 Days Gone Collectors Club 1984
   017 Yorkshire Biscuits 1984
   018 Wonder Bread 1984
   019 Railway Express Agency 1984
   020 Philadelphia Fire Rescue 1984
   021 Philadelphia Fire Ambulance 1984
   022 Harry Ramsden's Fish & Chips 1984
   023 Auto-Model Exchange 1984
   024 Daily/Sunday Express 1984

   025 Perrier-Jouet 1984
   026 Marks & Spencer 1984
   027 Hamleys 1984
   028 Magasin du Nord 1984
   029 Echo Centenary 1984
   030 Murphy's Crisps 1984
   031 Ovaltine 75th Anniversary 1985
   032 Home Ales 1985
   033 Barclay's Bank 1985
   034 Kodak Film 1985
   035 Chocolat Lindt 1985
   036 Wells Drinks 1985
   037 Australian Days Gone Club 1985
   038 Alton Towers 1985
   039 Evening Chronicle Centenary 1985
   040 Woodward Department Store 1985
   041 Royal Mail 350 Years 1985
   042 John Smith's Tadcaster Brewery 1986
   043 Cwm Dale Spring Water 1986
   044 Northern Daily Mail 1985
   045 Days Gone Toy Fairs 1986 1986
   046 Cadbury Cocoa-Bournville 1986
   047 Tizer 1986
   048 Hardware Journal 1986
   049 Hershey's-Reese's Pieces 1986
   050 Coca-Cola red 1986
   051 Coca-Cola green 1986
   052 Bay to Birdwood 1986
   053 Canadian Craft & Hobby Show 1986
   054 Canadian Premium Incentive Show 1986
   055 Cadbury's Drinking Chocolate 1986
   056 Days Gone Toy Fairs 1987 1987
   057 Hedges & Butler 1987
   058 Wells Black Velvit 1987
   059 Fairy Soap 1987
   060 Rose & Crown 1987

061 Royal Air Force 1987
007 Ford Woody Wagon 1984
  001 Pat's Poodle Parlour 1984
  002 Coca-Cola 1984
  003 Ford Sales & Service 1984
  004 West Point Toy Show 1984
  005 Hamleys 1984
  006 Godfrey Davis Ford 1985
  007 Chocolates by Della 1986
  008 Commonwealth Games 1986
008 Model T Ford Tanker 1984
  001 Esso 1984
  002 Coca-Cola 1984
  003 Philadelphia Bureau of Fire 1984
  004 Hofmeister Lager 1985
  005 Castrol 1985
  006 Pennzoil 1985
  007 Blue Mountain Bush Fire Brigade 1986
  008 Hershey's Chocolate Milk 1986
  009 Crow Carrying Co. 1987
  010 Water Works 1987
009 Model A Ford Car (top down) 1984
  001 Police 1984
  002 New York to Rio 1984
  003 Philadelphia Bureau of Fire 1984
  004 15 Millionth Ford 1985
010 Albion Single Decker Motor Bus 1984
  001 Brighton Belle 1984
  002 Union School Bus 1984
  003 Tillingbourne Valley 1984
  004 Potteries 1984
  005 Southern Vectis 1984
  006 Hamleys 1984
  007 Barton 1985
  008 Tartan Tours 1985
  009 Great Western Railway 1985

  010 Trailways 1985
  011 Imperial Airways 1986
  012 Redburns Motor Services 1986
  013 Hershey's Chocolate 1986
  014 Commonwealth Games 1986
  015 London Country 1986
  016 Silver Service 1987
011 Large Horse Drawn Van 1984
  001 Turnbull & Co. 1984
  002 Big Top 1985
  003 Abels of East Anglia 1985
  004 Staffordshire County Show 1985
  005 Williams Griffin 1985
  006 Royal Mail 1985
  007 MacCosham's 1986
  008 Coca-Cola 1986
012 Dennis Fire Engine 1984
  001 Luckhurst County 1984
  002 Cardiff City 1985
  003 Bermuda 1985
  004 London (LCC) 1986
  005 Chelmsford Town 1986
  006 Auxiliary Fire Service 1987
  007 Essex County 1987
013 Model A Ford Van 1984
  001 Evening News 1984
  002 Royal Mail 1984
  003 Mary Ann Brewery 1984
  004 Hamleys 1984
  005 Jersey Evening Post 1985
  006 Coca-Cola at Soda Fountains 1985
  007 Basildon Bond 1985
  008 Michelin 1985
  009 Stroh's Beer 1985
  010 Coca-Cola Every Bottle Sterilized 1985
  011 Festival Gardens 1985

012 Tucher Brau 1985
013 Evening Sentinel 1985
014 Royal Mail 350 Years 1985
015 Robinson's Squashes 1986
016 Camp Coffee 1986
017 Mitre 10 1986
018 Hershey's Kisses 1986
019 Hershey's Sweets & Treats 1986
020 Coca-Cola Seven Million 1986
021 F. D. B. 1986
022 Ryder Rental 1986
023 H. P. Sauce 1987
014 Model A Ford Car (top up) 1985
001 San Diego Fire Chief 1985
002 Taxi 1985
003 Acme Office Cleaning 1986
004 Grand Hotel 1986
005 Hamleys 1986
006 State Penitentiary 1987
015 Double Decker Bus 1985
001 Hall's Wine/General 1985
002 Coca-Cola/Chicago 1985
003 Festival Gardens 1985
004 Hamleys 1985
005 Cinzano/London Transport 1985
006 Castlemaine Corporation 1985
007 Evening Argus 1986
008 Royal Wedding 1986
009 Commonwealth Games 1986
010 Swan Vestas/Southdown 1986
011 Madame Tussaud's 1987
016 Heavy Goods Van 1985
001 Mayflower 1985
002 Croft Original 1985
003 Royal Mail 1986
004 Bushell's Tea 1986

005 Trebor Peppermints 1986
006 LNER Express Parcels Service 1986
007 Hamleys 1986
008 Hershey's Krackel 1986
009 Hershey's Mr. Goodbar 1986
010 Coca-Cola 1986
011 Kiwi Polishes 1986
012 Fyffes 1986
013 Cadbury's Milk Chocolate 1987
017 Single Decker Coach 1985
001 Southend Corporation 1985
002 BOAC Corporation Transport 1985
003 Eurotour Cruises 1985
004 London Transport 1986
005 Commonwealth Games 1986
006 Stratford Blue 1986
007 Morell's/Oxford 1986
008 Hamleys 1986
009 Big Top 1986
010 Burnley Corporation 1987
011 Pennine 1987
018 Packard Van 1985
001 Ambulance (circled crosses) 1985
002 Ambulance (plain crosses) 1985
003 Rapid Cash Transport 1986
004 Commonwealth Games 1986
005 Firestone 1986
006 Camperdown Children's Hospital 1986
007 White Star 1987
008 Colman's Mustard 1987
019 Rolls Royce Car 1986
001 Burgundy & Black 1986
002 Cream 1986
003 Yellow & Tan 1986
004 Olive Tan & Yellow 1986
005 Gold & White 1987

020 Ford Stake Truck 1986
  001 Eagle Ales 1986
  002 Coca-Cola 1986
  003 Whitbread 1986
  004 Goodrich 1986
  005 Stroh's Beer 1987
  006 Uniroyal 1987
021 Chevrolet Van 1986
  001 Sharp's Toffees 1986
  002 Leicester Mercury 1986
  003 Coca-Cola 1986
  004 Hostess Cakes 1986
  005 Lledo Club Member 1987
  006 Dr. Pepper 1987
022 Packard Town Van 1986
  001 Stag Whisky 1986
  002 Lord Ted Cigars 1986
  003 F. T. D. Say It With Flowers 1987

  004 Lledo Club Member 1986/87 1987
  005 Whitman's Chocolate 1987
023 Scenicruiser 1987
  001 Greyhound 1987
  002 Golden West Tours 1987
  003 Buffalo Luxury Travel 1987
024 Rolls Royce Playboy 1987
  001 Yellow/black 1987
  002 Metallic lilac/purple 1987
025 Rolls Royce Silver Ghost 1987
  001 Dark blue/black 1987
  002 Silver/blue 1987
  003 White/black 1987
026 Chevrolet Soft Drink Van 1987
  001 Schweppes 1987
027 Mack Breakdown Truck
  001 A1 24 Hour Recovery 1987

2. Fantastic Set o' Wheels, marketed by Hartoys, 1985.

006 Model T Ford Van: Malibu or Bust
007 Ford Woody Wagon: Ford Tri-State Dealer
008 Model T Ford Tanker: Liquoid Bubble
010 Single Decker Bus: Oak Ridge School Bus

012 Dennis Fire Engine: Boston Fire Dept.
013 Model A Ford Van: Jolly Time Ice Cream
014 Model A Ford Car: San Diego Fire Chief
014 Model A Ford Car: Taxi

3. Edocars, marketed in The Netherlands by Edor B. V., 1986

A-1 (008) Model T Ford Tanker, no logo.
A-2 (012) Dennis Fire Engine, no logo.
A-3 (014) Model A Ford Car, Taxi.
A-4 (016) Heavy Goods Van: Humbrol/Airfix.

A-5 (017) Single Decker Coach, no logo.
A-6 (018) Packard Van, Ambulance.
A-7 (019) Rolls Royce, black/silver.
A-8 (021) Chevrolet Van, Edocar.

4. Tesco Vintage Champions, marketed in Britain, 1986.

008 Model T Ford Tanker, Hofmeister.
010 Single Decker Bus, Tartan Tours.
012 Dennis Fire Engine, Luckhurst County.
013 Model A Ford Van, Robinsons Squashes.
014 Model A Ford Car, San Diego Fire Chief.
015 Double Decker Bus, Halls Wine.

016 Heavy goods Van, Trebor Peppermints.
017 Single Decker Coach, Southend Corporation.
018 Packard Van, Ambulance.
019 Rolls Royce, yellow/tan.
Variations that differ from regular Days Gone issues will be found in the list of variations.

5. View Vans, marketed in Britain and elsewhere, 1987.

006 Blackpool, green.
006 Canterbury Cathedral, ?
006 Carlisle, green.
006 Chester, maroon.
013 Chester, brown.
013 Dunster Yarn Market, brown.
013 Edinburgh, cream.
013 Gettysburg, cream.
013 Guernsey, brown.
013 Isle of Wight, brown: 2 types.
013 Jersey, brown: 2 types.
006 Kings College, Cambridge, green.
013 Lincoln, brown.

013 Llangollen, brown.
006 London: 2 maroon types, one green.
013 London, cream: 2 types.
013 Margate, brown.
013 The Peaks, brown.
013 Plymouth Flag Officer/Royal Marines, cream.
006 Scarborough, green.
013 Stirling, cream.
013 Stratford-upon-Avon, 2 types.
013 Windermere, cream.
006 Windsor, maroon.
013 Windsor, brown.
013 Wye College, brown.

For lists of Lledo Promotional Models, the reader is referred to those included in "Lledo U.S.A." and the "Lledo Collectors Guide", which could not be printed here as they are copyrighted. The two lists are not identical, and the collector may find it interesting to compare them.

Lledo™ Models & Variations

This listing, by basic model number and then alphabetical code, will include all the models of Lledo manufacture known to this writer as of completion of the manuscript. The first digits in the code will be the number of the basic model; the next three letters will represent the name of the individual item, and the last two digits will indicate the model's classification as follows:

C3: Code 3: models made privately without the knowledge and consent of Lledo.

DG: Days Gone: models made for regular retail sale as part of the Models of Days Gone series.

EC: Edocar: models made for sale by Lledo's agents in The Netherlands.

FS: Fantastic Set o' Wheels: made for saly by Hartoy in the United States.

LP: Lledo Promotional: models wholly or partially made by Lledo for promotional use.

MA: Marathons: models of modern-day commercial vehicles.

SP: Special models made and used by Lledo but not classified as Models of Days Gone.

VV: View Vans: Models made for sale as souvenirs.

The parts of the body described below will include:

The BODY and CHASSIS, usually made of metal. When there are two body parts, the front one will be called the CAB, the rear one the BODY.

The ROOF, either metal or plastic, sometimes including a HEADER signboard across the front, or a roof BLADE, either longitudinal or diagonal.

The raised TOP of a touring car, the INTERIOR including the seats,

the FLOOR if separate from the seats, the TRUNK if separate from the body casting, and the rear-mounted SPARE WHEEL are of plastic.

The WINDOWS are usually a plastic piece that forms the window frames and surrounding area of a bus. In the Scenicruiser and the Marathon buses, the windows are the actual window panes, either tinted and opaque or clear and transparent.

The GRILLE, usually including headlights and front bumper, and the WINDSHIELD, which can include side lights and ladder rack, are of plastic, usually gold (actually brass) or silver (actually chrome) plated.

The HITCH of a horsedrawn vehicle is a cast metal part which holds the horse(s) and the front axle.

The BASE is almost always of black plastic and bears identifying lettering.

The WHEELS of some horsedrawn vehicles comprise both wheels and tires and are made of metal; otherwise the wheels are the hubs on which the tires are mounted; 12-spoke wheels are always metal 20-spoke or the unspoked types (6-bolt, disc, etc.) are always plastic, so the material, being obvious, will not be listed. The TIRES are made of plastic and are either white (actually cream), black, gray or brown.

Lledo™ Models

001 HORSE DRAWN TRAM   118mm 1983
Metal body, roof, pillars, domes, hitch; plastic seats and horse; small cream plastic flanged wheels, bottom of casting lettered "DAYS GONE/DG 1/MADE IN/ENGLAND/by Lledo.
Castings:
  A. Plain hitch, plain end panel.
  B. Hitch with horizontal bar, plain end panel.
  C. Hitch with horizontal bar, brace on end panel.
  D. Hitch with horizontal bar and brace, brace on end panel.

01-DOW-DG DOWNTOWN   #001-004 1984
Cream body, roof, silver pillars, gold domes and hitch, green seats, cream wheels, black horse. Logo: white or cream "3 DOWNTOWN 3" on roof signs, plus red and gold crest on front and back body panels. Casting D.
  1. White main logo.
  2. Cream main

01-MAI-DG MAIN STREET   #001-002 1983
Green or brown body, light gray roof, cream pillars, gold domes and hitch, reddish seats, cream wheels, black horse. Logo: red & green "MAIN STREET" on white background on roof signs, plus white crest on front and back body panels. Casting D.
  1. Green body, black horse.
  2. Green body, dark brown horse.
  3. Brown body, black horse.
  4. Brown body, dark brown horse.

01-MAN-LP/C3 MANLY JAZZ FESTIVAL   1984
Green body, light gray roof, cream pillars, gold domes and hitch, reddish seats, cream wheels, dark brown horse. Logo: orange "Manly jazz festival" on off-white background on roof signs, plus orange & white "MANLY/HORSE TRAMWAY 1903 / 292" and design on front and rear or only on rear body panel(s). Casting D.
  1. Front and rear logo: code 2 promotional.
  2. Rear logo only: code 3.
  3. Brown body, privately made from Main Street version: code 3.

01-NAT-DG NATIONAL TRAMWAY MUSEUM   #001-003 1984
Blue body, cream roof and pillars, gold domes and hitch, light brown seats, cream wheels, dark brown horse. Logo: red "THE NATIONAL TRAMWAY MUSEUM/CRICH, DERBYSHIRE, AUGUST 1984" in black frame on cream background on roof signs, plus white or cream "GRAND TRANSPORT/ extravaganza" and frame on front and rear body panels. Casting D.
  1. Cream front and rear logo.
  2. White front and rear logo.

01-WES-DG WESTMINSTER   #001-001 1983
Green body, light gray roof, cream pillars, gold domes and hitch, reddish seats, cream wheels, dark brown or black horse. Logo: red & green "WESTMINSTER" on light gray roof panels, plus yellow, cream or white crest on front and back body panels. Castings A, B, C, D.
  1. Casting A, yellow crest, black horse.

2. Casting A, yellow crest, dark brown horse.
3. Casting A, cream crest, dark brown horse.
4. Casting B, yellow crest, black horse.
5. Casting B, yellow crest, dark brown horse.
6. Casting B, cream crest, black horse.
7. Casting B, cream crest, dark brown horse.
8. Casting C, white crest, black horse.
9. Casting C, white crest, dark brown horse.
10. Casting D, white crest, black horse.
11. Casting D, white crest, dark brown horse.

002 HORSE DRAWN MILK FLOAT   91mm 1983
Metal body, chassis, hitch and rear axle mount, plastic roof and horse, 12-spoke metal wheels, "DG2-DG3" on bottom of hitch, "DAYS GONE" on chassis, "MADE IN/ENGLAND/by Lledo" on axle mount. Castings:
  A. Horizontal bar across each side of body.
  B. No bar.

02-CEL-DG CELTIC DAIRIES   002-004 1984
Cream body, red roof, chassis, hitch and axle mount, gold wheels, white tires, tan horse. Logo: Green "CELTIC/DAIRIES" above and below black and gold prince's plumes and motto "ICH DIEN". Casting B. 1. As above.

02-CHA-DG CHAMBOURCY   002-002 1984
Cream body, light blue or turquoise roof, blue chassis, hitch and axle mount, gold wheels, white tires, dark brown horse. Logo: blue "chambourcy" and design, red & green fruit design, blue "REAL FRUIT YOGHURT". Casting B.
  1. Light blue roof.
  2. Turquoise roof.
  3. Darker blue chassis.

02-CLI-DG W. CLIFFORD & SONS   002-003 1984
Red body, white roof, yellow chassis, hitch and axle mount, gold wheels, black horse. Logo: Yellow "W. CLIFFORD/&/SONS/DAIRYMEN/31 CROSS LANCES Rd./HOUNSLOW", horizontal line and telephone number. Casting B.
  1. As above.

02-EXP-DG EXPRESS DAIRY   002-001 1983
Dark blue body, white roof, medium blue chassis, hitch and axle mount, gold wheels, black tires, black or dark brown horse. Logo: White "EXPRESS/DAIRY/20" and frame. Casting A.
  1. Dark brown horse.
  2. Black horse.

02-GRY-SP GRAY   1987?
Gray body, chassis, hitch and axle mount, blue roof, 20-spoke cream wheels, black tires, black horse. No logo. DG bBase Specimen.

003 HORSE DRAWN DELIVERY VAN   93mm 1983
Metal body, chassis, hitch and rear axle mount, plastic roof and horse, 12-spoke metal wheels (except on Royal Mail, which has solid plastic wheels, and Club Member model, which has 20-spoke plastic wheels). "DG2-DG3" on bottom of hitch, "DAYS

GONE" on chassis, "MADE IN/ENGLAND"/by Lledo" on axle mount (Phoenix Dye House and some Royal Mail models lack some lettering, and Club Member model has "DG3" on main base).

03-CAR-C3 THEOPHILUS CARTLIDGE   year?
Dark olive green body, dark brown roof, chassis, hitch and axle mount, gold wheels, black tires, black horse. Logo: Yellow "THEOPHILUS/CARTLIDGE/NURSERY & SEEDSMAN" in frame; "FINNEY", "GARDENS", "HANLEY" in frames on panels below; "GARDENS/PICNIC" and "OPEN FOR/PARTIES" in frames on rear doors. Logo consists of decals, also small white number decal on bottom of hitch.
  1. As above.

03-COC-DG COCA-COLA   003-010 1985
Dark yellow body, black roof, chassis, hitch and axle mount, gold wheels, black tires, black horse. Logo: red "The/Coca-Cola/Co." in black frame, plus 3 black frames on panels below.
  1. As above.

03-CRU-C3 EBENEZER CRUICKSHANK   year?
Dark orange body, black roof, dark brown chassis, hitch and axle mount, gold wheels, black tires, black horse. Logo: black "Ebenezer/Cruickshank" and "Gutta Percha . Merchant" in yellow scroll frames; black "Ruislem", "and", & "Hanley" in yellow scroll frames on panels below. Logo consists of decals, also small white number decal on bottom of hitch.
  1. As above.

03-FIN-DG FINE LADY BAKERIES   003-005 1984
Light tan body, chassis, hitch and axle mount, light brown roof, gold wheels, black tires, dark brown horse. Logo: red "Fine Lady Bakeries Ltd." and brown figures in brown frame; red "Southam Rd.", "Banbury" and "Oxon" in brown frames on panels below.
  1. As above.

03-GRY-SP GRAY   year?
Gray body, chassis, hitch and axle mount, black roof, 20-spoke cream wheels, black tires, black horse. No logo. DG base Specimen.
  1. As above.

03-HAM-DG HAMLEYS   003-008 1984
Dark blue body, chassis, hitch and axle mount, black roof, gold wheels, black tires, black horse. Logo: White "HAMLEYS", underline and "REGENT STREET . LONDON" in gold frame; three white toy designs in gold frames on panels below.
  1. As above.

03-LCM-DG LLEDO CLUB MEMBER   003-012 1987
Red body, black roof, chassis, hitch and axle mount, red 20-spoke white tires, black horse. Logo: yellow and black Lledo emblem, black "Club Member Edition Spring 1987", yellow frames. "DAYS GONE" lettering on main base instead of hitch. Special box.
  1. As above.

03-LEA-C3 ELIAS LEAR   year?
Dark tan body, dark brown roof, chassis, hitch and axle mount, gold wheels, black tires, black horse. Logo: black-outlined yellow "ELIAS LEAR"/black "MANU-

Lledo™ Models

FACTURER OF"/black-outlined yellow "POTTERS' LATHES" in yellow frame; black "DAISY", "BANK" and "LONGTON" in yellow frames on panels below. Logo consists of decals, also small white number decal on bottom of hitch.
1. As above.

03-LSW-DG L. S. W. R. PARCELS　　　003-007 1984
Salmon pink body, dark brown roof, chassis, hitch and axle mount, gold wheels, black tires, black horse. Logo: brown "L. S. W. R.", design and lines, and "PARCELS ROPLEY"; brown frames on panels below.
1. As above.

03-NOR-DG MATTHEW NORMAN　　　003-004 1984
Dark green body, chassis, hitch and axle mounts, black roof, gold wheels, black tires, black horse. Logo: Yellow "MATTHEW NORMAN"/carriage design/"Fine Carriage Clocks"; yellow "LONDON", "BASLE" and "NEW/YORK" in frames on panels below.
1. As above.

03-PEP-DG PEPPERIDGE FARM　　　003-002 1983
White body, light tan chsssis, hitch and axle mount, light brown roof, gold wheels, black tires, light or dark brown horse. Logo: white "PEPPERIDGE FARM" in red-orange-black design; orange frames on panels below.
1. Light brown horse.
2. Dark brown horse.

03-PHO-LP PHOENIX STEAM DYE HOUSE　　　1985
Dark blue body, black roof, chassis, hitch and axle mount, gold wheels, black tires, dark brown horse. Logo: gold "Phoenix/Steam Dye House" in frame; gold "12-18/Southport/Avenue", "Chicago" and "Tel./No. 1434" in frames on panels below. No lettering on hitch or chassis.
1. As above.

03-ROB-DG ROBERTSON'S SILVER SHRED　　　003-006 1984
Dark green body, cream chassis, hitch and axle mount, yellow roof, gold wheels, black tires, dark brown horse. Logo: yellow "ROBERTSON'S/SILVER SHRED/ MARMALADE" and lines; yellow-gold-light green-white designs with green "THE", "WORLD'S" and "BEST" on panels below.
1. As above.

03-ROY-DG ROYAL MAIL　　　003-011 1985
Red body, black roof, chassis, hitch and axle mount, red 6-bolt plastic wheels, black tires, black horse. Logo: black-outlined "GR" crest and "Royal Mail"; black frames on panels below. Special box.
1. Complete lettering on bottom.
2. No lettering on hitch.
3. No lettering on base.
4. No lettering on hitch or base.

03-STA-DG STAFFORDSHIRE COUNTY SHOW　　　003-003 1984
Pale or lime green body, light tan roof, chassis, hitch and axle mount, gold wheels, black tires, black horse. Logo: Red "Staffordshire/Agricultural Society", black "COUNTY SHOW" with red wreath; red "MAY/23rd 24th", black rope design & red "1984" on panels below.
1. Pale green body.
2. Lime green body (darker than type 1).

03-TIR-C3 J. TIRRELL　　　year?
Very dark blue body, black roof, chassis, hitch and axle mount, gold wheels, black tires, black horse. Logo: yellow "J. TIRRELL/HOMOEOPATHIC/CHEMIST / MARKET SQUARE, HANLEY" in frame; yellow "ICELAND/MOSS/1/4", "FINEST/ROCK/1/2" and "TARIXACUM/1/6" in frames on panels below. Logo consists of decals, also small white number decal on bottom of hitch.
1. As above.

03-TRI-DG TRI-SUM POTATO CHIPS　　　003-009 1984
Red body, black roof, chassis, hitch and axle mount, gold wheels, black tires, dark brown horse. Logo: Red "Tri-Sum/Potato Chips" on white panel; red "ENJOYED". "SINCE" and "1908" and scrolls on white panel below.
1. As above.

03-WIN-DG WINDMILL BAKERY　　　003-001 1983
Yellow body, light tan chassis, cream or light tan hitch, tan axle mount, light brown roof, gold wheels, black tires, tan, light brown or dark brown horse. Shade of yellow body may vary. Logo: brown "WINDMILL BAKERY" and arc, tan windmill design on white semicircle with brown figures; brown frames on panels below.
1. Cream hitch, tan horse.
2. Cream hitch, light brown horse.
3. Tan hitch, light brown horse.
4. Tan hitch, dark brown horse.

004 HORSE DRAWN OMNIBUS　　　108mm 1983
Metal body, rear steps and hitch; plastic upper floor and seats, two horses; all-metal 12-spoke front and larger 16-spoke rear wheels; "DG4/DAYS GONE" on bottom of body (except Bridlington model); "MADE IN / ENGLAND/LLEDO" on bottom of rear platform. Castings:
A. Body tapers in sharply just above rear platform.
B. Body tapers out slightly just above rear platform.
C. Signboards under central windows, otherwise as type B.

04-BAL-DG BALMORAL　　　004-　1987
Light orange body and hitch, red seats, dark brown horses, gold wheels. Upper logo: red "BALMORAL", green "TOURS". Lower logo: brown "ABERDEEN" on green background on new panel, green lines and "BEN NEVIS BALMORAL LOCH NESS". Casting C. Special box, part of Ruby Wedding set. DG base.
1. As above.

04-BRI-LP BRIDLINGTON　　　1986
Red body, steps and hitch, green seats, black wheels, black horses. Logo: white-outlined orange "Bridlington" on blue background above; white "HARBOUR TO PRIORY/VIA QUAY ROAD" below. No lettering on bottom of body. Casting B.
1. As above.

04-EXC-LP EXCHANGE AND MART　　　1987
Dark green body, steps and hitch, red seats, gold wheels, dark brown horses. Logo: white "Exchange and Mart" and other lettering, white and green emblems, red frames above; green "PICCADILLY" on white signboard, green "2d" on white oval, white lettering. Casting C, special box.
1. As above.

04-GRY-SP GRAY　　　year?
Light gray body, steps and hitch, red seats, gold wheels, tan horses. Logo: none. Factory specimen. Casting B.
1. As above.

04-HAM-DG HAMLEYS　　　004-006 1984
Red body, steps and hitch, green seats, gold wheels, black horses. Logo: yellow underlined "HAMLEYS" on blue background above; white "THE WORLD'S FINEST TOYSHOP/REGENT STREET, LONDON" below. In special Hamleys box or gift set. Casting B.
1. As above.

04-HIC-DG HIGH CHAPPARAL　　　004-008 1986
Tan body, steps and hitch, red seats, gold wheels, black horses. Logo: red "HIGH/CHAPPARAL" and red-white-black-tan figures on white background in red frame above; black "VASTERNSTADEN" on white background on signboard, red "WILDA WESTERN I SVERIGE" and partial frame below. Casting C.
1. As above.

04-LBR-DG LIPTON'S/BOWERY-BROADWAY　　　004-002 1983
Red or green body, steps and hitch, green or light brown seats, black, brown, orange-brown or gold wheels, dark brown or black horses. Logo: white "LIPTON'S TEAS / LARGEST SALES IN THE WORLD" on green background above; yellow "FIFTH AVENUE COACH COMPANY/BOWERY BROADWAY" below. Casting B.
1. Red body, light brown seats, black wheels, black horses.
2. Red body, light brown seats, black wheels, dark brown horses.
3. Red body, green seats, black wheels, black horses.
4. Red body, red-brown seats, black wheels, black horses.

5. Red body, red-brown seats, black wheels, black horses.
6. Green body, green seats, brown wheels, black horses.
7. Green body, red-brown seats, brown wheels, black horses.
8. Green body, red-brown seats, black wheels, dark brown horses.
9. Green body, red-brown seats, orange-brown wheels, black horses.
10. Green body, red-brown seats, orange-brown wheels, dark brown horses.
11. Pale dark green body, light brown seats, gold wheels, dark brown horses.
12. Dark green body, red-brown seats, gold wheels, dark brown horses.
13. Dark green body, red-brown seats, gold wheels, dark brown horses.

04-LVK-DG LIPTON'S/VICTORIA & KING'S CROSS　　　004-001 1983
Red body, steps and hitch, green or light brown seats, black wheels, dark brown or black horses. Logo: green or white "LIPTON'S TEAS/LARGEST SALES IN THE WORLD" on white or green background above; yellow "LONDON GENERAL OMNIBUS COMPANY LIMITED/VICTORIA & KING'S CROSS" in partial frame below. Casting A or B.
1. Casting A, green logo on cream background, dark green seats, black horses.
2. Casting A, green logo on cream background, dark green seats, dark brown horses.
3. Casting B, green logo on white background, dark green seats, black horses.
4. Casting B, green logo on white background, dark green seats, dark brown horses.
5. Casting B, white logo on green background, dark green seats, dark brown horses.
6. Casting B, white logo on green background, bright green seats, dark brown horses.
7. Casting B, white logo on green background, light green seats, dark brown horses.
8. Casting B, white logo on green background, red-brown seats, dark brown horses.

04-MAD-DG MADAME TUSSAUD'S　　　004-005 1984
Yellow body, steps and hitch, red seats, red or black wheels, dark brown horses. Logo: red "MADAME TUSSAUD'S/EXHIBITION" above; green "LONDON GENERAL OMNIBUS COMPANY LIMITED/green-outlined yellow "FAVORITE" in partial green frame. Shades of upper logo vary. Casting B or C.
1. Casting B, red wheels.
2. Casting C, "FAVORITE" on new panel, red wheels.
3. Casting C, "FAVORITE" on new panel, black wheels.

04-MAS-DG MASON'S PANTRY　　　004-007 1985
Dark brown body, steps and hitch, red seats, gold wheels, tan horses. Logo: brown-outlined yellow "MASON'S PANTRY" above, brown-outlined yellow "Mrs. Beaton's" and arched yellow "FOODS OF CHARACTER" below. Casting B.
1. "FOODS OF CHARACTER" over rear wheels.
2. "FOODS OF CHARACTER" over front wheels.

04-OAK-DG/LP OAKEY'S/PUTNEY　　　004-003 1984
White body, steps and hitch, red seats, red wheels, dark brown horses. Logo: blue-outlined cream "OAKEY'S"/white "KNIFE POLISH" on blue background above, white-outlined black "PUTNEY" in frame below. Casting B.
1. As above: DG issue.
2. Decals added on front and back of body and on stairs: Code 2 (or 3?).

04-PVK-DG PEARS/VICTORIA & KING'S CROSS　　　004-004 1984
Light tan body, steps and hitch, red seats, gold wheels, dark brown horses. Logo: red "KING/OF/SOAPS" at left, large "PEARS" in center, "SOAP/OF/KINGS" at right, on yellow background above, brown "LONDON GENERAL OMNIBUS COMPANY LIMITED"/VICTORIA & KING'S CROSS" in partial frame below, or "VICTORIA" on new panel; no "King's Cross". Casting B or C. In Collector Pack or singly.
1. Casting B, "VICTORIA & KING'S CROSS".
2. Casting C, "VICTORIA" on new panel.

005 HORSE DRAWN FIRE ENGINE　　　106mm 1983
Metal body, chassis, boiler, hitch; two plastic horses; all-metal 12-spoke front and larger 16-spoke rear wheels; lettered "DG5" on bottom of central chassis, "MADE IN" and "ENGLAND" on rear sides and "DAYS GONE/BY LLEDO" at rear. Castings:
A. No braces.
B. Brace at base of footrest.

Lledo™ Models

C. Braces at base of footrest and on bottom ahead of rivets.
D. No figure pins, otherwise as type C.

05-BIF-DG BIFBAC II **005-007 1984**
Maroon body, chassis and hitch, gold boiler and wheels, tan horses. Logo: gold "BIFBAC II/CONVENTION", number 84 and frames. Casting C.
1. As above.

05-CHI-DG/SP CHICAGO FIRE BRIGADE **005-002 1983**
Red body, chassis and hitch, gold boiler, black (gloss or gunmetal) wheels, black or dark brown horses. Logo: yellow "CHICAGO/FIRE BRIGADE", number 27 and frame. Casting A, B or C.
1. Casting A, black horses.
2. Casting A, brown horses.
3. Casting B, black horses.
4. Casting B, lighter red body, gloss black wheels.
5. Casting C, tan horses, brass wheels? Special issue for Lledo use.

05-COV-LP COVENTRY **1986**
Red body, chassis and hitch, gold boiler, gunmetal wheels, black horses. Logo: gold "COVENTRY" in frame. Casting A. Standard base lettering. Certificate.
1. As above.

05-GRY-SP GRAY **year?**
Gray body, chassis and hitch, copper boiler, gold wheels, tan horses. No logo. DG base. Specimen.
1. As above.

05-GUI-DG/LP GUILDFORD FIRE BRIGADE **005-003 1983**
Dark green body, dark green or black chassis and hitch, gold or black boiler, gold or red wheels, black or dark brown horses. Logo: yellow or white "GUILDFORD/FIRE BRIGADE", number 15 and frames. Casting B or C.
1. Black boiler, green chassis, yellow logo, gold wheels, black horses, casting B: DG.
2. Black boiler, green chassis, yellow logo, gold wheels, black horses, casting B: DG.
3. Gold boiler, green chassis, yellow logo, gold wheels, black horses, casting C: DG.
4. Gold boiler, green chassis, yellow logo, gold wheels, black horses, casting C: DG.
5. Gold boiler, darker green body and chassis, yellow logo, gold wheels, black horses, casting C: DG.
6. Gold boiler, black chassis, white wheels, white logo, dark brown horses: DG.

05-GWR-DG G. W. R. FIRE BRIGADE **005-005 1984**
Dark brown body, chassis and hitch, gold boiler, dark brown or gold wheels, tan or black horses. Logo: gold "G. W. R./FIRE BRIGADE/SWINDON" in frame; number 1 in circle. Issued in regular box or on plinth in special box. Casting C.
1. Brown wheels, tan horses.
2. Brown wheels, black horses.
3. Gold wheels, black horses.
4. Gold wheels, tan horses, on plinth.

05-HKF-DG HONG KONG FIRE BRIGADE **005-004 1984**
Cream body, chassis and hitch, gold or red boiler, red wheels, black horses. Logo: red or maroon "H KFB", number 2 and frames. Casting B or C.
1. Red boiler, red logo, casting B.
2. Red boiler, red logo, casting C.
3. Gold boiler, red logo, casting B.
4. Gold boiler, red logo, casting C.
5. Gold boiler, maroon logo, casting C.

05-HUL-LP HULL POLICE FIRE BRIGADE **1986**
Blue body, chassis and hitch, gold boiler and wheels, dark brown horses. Logo: red-outlined silver "HULL POLICE FIRE BRIGADE" and number 4, red and silver frames. Casting C.
1. As above.

05-LAK-DG LAKE CITY **005-008 1984**
Dark yellow body, chassis and hitch, red boiler, black wheels, black horses. Logo: green "LAKE CITY", number 5 and frames. Casting C.
1. As above.

05-LON-DG LONDON FIRE BRIGADE **005-001 1983**

Red body, chassis and hitch, gold or unpainted boiler, gunmetal wheels, black or dark brown horses. Logo: yellow "LONDON/FIRE BRIGADE", number 27 and frame. Casting A, B or D.
1. Gold boiler, black horses, casting A.
2. Gold boiler, black horses, casting B.
3. Gold boiler, dark brown horses, casting B.
4. Unpainted boiler, black horses, casting B. (Note: the unpainted boiler has been called "chromed".)
5. Bright gold boiler, black horses, casting D.

05-MET-LP METROPOLITAN FIRE BRIGADE **1986**
Red body, brown chassis and hitch, copper boiler, gunmetal wheels, dark brown horses. Logo: black-outlined number 8 and "METROPOLITAN", gold "FIRE BRIGADE", black and gold frames. Casting C.
1. As above.

05-PHI-DG PHILADELPHIA BUREAU OF FIRE **005-004 1984**
Red body, chassis and hitch, gold boiler and wheels, tan wheels. Logo: gold "P. B. F." and number 5, black frames. Casting C.
1. As above. The American and British issues are said to have different shades of red.

06 MODEL T FORD VAN **70mm 1983**
Metal body and chassis; plastic roof, windshield and grille; roof includes header board on all models; 12-spoke metal or 20-spoke plastic wheels. Castings:
A. DG chassis numbered "DG6-DG"; body with full door lines.
B. DG chassis numbered "DG6-DG8"; body with full door lines.
C. DG chassis numbered "DG6-8"; body with full door lines.
D. DG chassis numbered "DG6-8"; body almost entirely lacking door lines.
E. Lledo Promotional chassis; body with full door lines.
F. Lledo Promotional chassis; body almost entirely lacking door lines.
G. Chassis lettered "MADE IN ENGLAND/by Lledo"; body with complete door lines. Used for Fantastic Set o' Wheels.

06-AER-DG AEROPLANE JELLY **006-007 1984**
Blue body, white roof, red chassis, gold grille and windshield, 12-spoke gold wheels, black tires. Logo: yellow "Aeroplane/Jelly Co.", red and white emblem, white music with yellow "I like Aeroplane Jelly", white "12 mph" and frame. Header: blue music and "Aeroplane/Jelly Co." DG6-DG8 base, door lines.
1. As above.

06-ALL-? ALLINSON **1986**
No data.
1. As above.

06-ALT-DG ALTON TOWERS **006-038 1985**
Dark brown body, cream roof and chassis, gold grille and windshield, 12-spoke gold metal wheels, black tires. Logo: off-white or light yellow "Alton/Towers/Europe's Premier / Leisure Park" and frame, gold and yellow door emblem. Header: brown "Alton Towers". DG6-8 base, with or without door lines. Special box.
1. Door lines.
2. No door lines.

06-ANM-LP ANDERSON & McAULEY **1986**
Maroon body, black roof and chassis, 12-spoke gold wheels, black tires. Logo: gold "Anderson/& McAuley" and frames. No header logo. LP base, no door lines.
1. As above.

06-AUC-LP AUTOMOTIVE COMMERCIAL **1986**
No data.
1. As above.

06-AUE-DG AUTOMODEL EXCHANGE **006-023 1984**
Maroon body, tan roof, black chassis, gold grille and windshield, 12-spoke gold wheels, black tires. Logo: gold "the/Automodel/Exchange, black "DAYS GONE SPECIALISTS" on black-rimmed gold bar, gold "SYDNEY/AUSTRALIA", gold and black map and kangaroo; gold "think/of the/future" and "collect/Lledo/now" on rear doors. Header: black "collect Lledo". DG6-DG8 base, door lines.

06-AUS-DG AUSTRALIAN DAYS GONE CLUB **006-037 1985**

Tan body, light or dark brown roof, dark brown chassis, gold grille and windshield, 12-spoke gold wheels, black tires. Logo: red "AUSTRALIAN/COLLECTOR'S/CLUB" and boomerang pattern, brown and tan "DAYS GONE" in brown frame, brown and dark tan animal figures, brown decorative frame. Header: pale green or dark brown boomerang with dark or light brown (roof color) "FOUNDED 1984". DG6-DG8 or DG6-8 base, door lines.
1. Dark brown roof, pale green header boomerang, dark red logo lettering, DG6-DG8 base.
2. Same details as type 1, DG6-8 base.
3. Light brown roof, dark brown header boomerang, orange logo lettering, DG6-DG8 base.
4. Same details as type 3, DG6-8 base.

06-AVO-LP AVON ROAD RESCUE **1985**
No data.
1. As above

06-BAR-DG BARCLAY'S BANK **006-033 1985**
Blue body, cream roof and chassis, gold or silver grille and windshield, black 12-spoke or 20-spoke wheels, white tires. Logo: black eagle emblem and blue "Barclays" on white panels, white "54 Lombard Street, London" and "FOUNDED/1896", black frame. Header: blue "BARCLAYS" and eagle in frames, or cream "BARCLAYS" and eagle on blue panels. Sold singly or in gift set. DG6-DG8 or DG6-8 base, with or without door lines.
1. DG6-DG8 base, blue header lettering, metal wheels, gold grille.
2. DG6-8 base, blue header lettering, metal wheels, gold grille.
3. DG6-8 base, blue header lettering, plastic wheels, gold grille.
4. DG6-8 base, cream header lettering, metal wheels, gold grille.
5. DG6-8 base, cream header lettering, plastic wheels, gold grille.
6. DG6-8 base, no door lines, cream header lettering, plastic wheels, gold grille.
7. DG6-8 base, no door lines, cream header lettering, plastic wheels, silver grille.

06-BAS-DG BASSETT'S LIQUORICE **1987**
Black body, roof and chassis, gold grille and windshield, 12-spoke gold wheels, black tires. Logo: White "Bassett's" and "ALLSORTS", red apostrophe and "LIQUORICE", red-white-yellow-black candy box design, yellow "THE ORIGINAL ALLSORTS", WHITE "ESTAB. A842". Header: White "Bassett's" with red apostrophe. LP base, no door lines.
1. As above.

06-BAY-DG BAY TO BIRDWOOD RUN **006-052 1986**
Black body, roof and chassis, gold grille and windshield, 12-spoke gold wheels, black tires. Logo: gold-outlined red "BAY to/BIRDWOOD/RUN", black "AUSTRALIA'S PREMIER/HISTORIC MOTORING EVENT" ON GOLD STRIPES, GOLD "ADELAIDE/AUSTRALIA", designs and frame. Header: gold "BAY to/BIRDWOOD RUN". DG6-8 base, door lines.
1. As above.

06-BBB-LP ...BETTER BIT OF BUTTER... **1987**
Cream body, brown roof and chassis, gold grille and windshield, 20-spoke cream wheels, black tires. Logo: yellow and brown figures, brown "You'll never put a better bit of butter on your knife". Header: white "COUNTRY LIFE/ENGLISH BUTTER". LP base, no door lines.
1. As above.

06-BEA-LP BEAMISH **1987**
Plum body, cream roof and chassis, gold grille and windshield, gold 12-spoke wheels. Logo: black-outlined gold "B.E.A.M.I.S.H", plum "The Great Northern Experience" on black-outlined gold bar, gold telephone number, "BEAMISH", design and frames. Header: red "BEAMISH". LP base, no door lines. Certificate.
1. As above.

06-BEU-LP BEAULIEU MOTOR MUSEUM **1985**
Dary yellow body, black roof and chassis, gold grille and windshield, gold 12-spoke wheels, black tires. Logo: red "Beaulieu/The National Motor Museum/Palace House and Gardens/Beaulieu Abbey and Exhibition/Bucklers Hard" and black car design, on adhesive label or tampo-printed. Header: none. Sometimes referred to as "Beaulieu

Autojumble" model. LP base. With or without door lines.
1. Door lines, adhesive labels: original issue.
2. No door lines, tampo-printed logo: 1987 reissue.

06-BKP-VV BLACKPOOL 1987
Dark green body, bright green roof, black chassis, gold grille and windshield, 12-spoke gold wheels, black tires. Logo: picture of city and tower, gold camera and frames. Header: gold "BLACKPOOL". View Vans box. LP base, no door lines.
1. As above.

06-BRB-DG BRITISH BACON 006-015 1983
Light blue body, medium blue roof, black chassis, gold grille and windshield, 12-spoke gold wheels, black tires. Logo: blue "BRITISH", stripe and "Bring home the best", red "BACON", red and white emblem with blue and white ribbon. Header: white "BRITISH BACON". DG6-DG8 base, door lines.
1. As above.

06-BRD-LP BRIDLINGTON 1985
Blue body and chassis, white roof, gold grille and windshield, 12-spoke gold wheels, black tires. Logo: white-outlined red "Bridlington", white "For Funshine Holidays". No header. LP base, door lines.

06-BRH-LP BRITISH HOVERCRAFT 1986
Ivory body, red roof, blue chassis, gold grille and windshield, 12-spoke gold wheels, black tires. Logo: black "BRITISH HOVERCRAFT CORPORATION", design and "GOING PLACES", red-white-blue-black hovercraft design in black oval, black and white emblem, blue frame. Header: black "EAST/COWES", emblem and "ISLE/OF WIGHT". LP base, no door lines. Certificate.

06-BRM-DG BRITISH MEAT 006-004 1983
Cream body, brown or black chassis, gold grille and windshield, 12-spoke gold wheels, black tires. Logo: red and blue "BRITISH MEAT" in blue fork-plate-knife frame, blue "SMITHFIELD/LONDON", "IT'S BEST", "12 MPH" and frames. Sometimes black "PRIME/TASTY/FRESH" and "BEEF/LAMB/PORK" and frames on rear doors. Header: white "BRITISH MEAT"; two sizes of header and lettering. DG6-DG or DG6-DG8 base, door lines.
1. Brown roof and chassis, small header with letters of uniform size, DG6-DG base.
2. Same details as type 1, DG6-DG8 base.
3. Black roof and chassis, small header with letters of uniform size, DG6-DG8 base.
4. Brown roof and chassis, large header with letters largest in middle, logo on rear doors, DG6-DG8 base.

06-BRT-LP BRIT TYRES 1986
Red body, black roof and chassis, gold grille and windshield, 12-spoke gold wheels, black tires. Logo: black-outlined "Brit Tyres", white "Quality tyre fitting service/...at your home", white "Rix Road, Stoneferry, Hull" on black music, black-outlined white telephone number, red-white-blue Union Jack, white flagpole, on adhesive label. Header: white "Brit Tyres Sales" on adhesive label. LP base, door lines.

06-CAA-LP CADA TOYS 1986
Light orange body, black roof and chassis, silver grille and windshield, 20-spoke red wheels, black tires. Logo: black and red "Cada Toys" on white panel in black frame, black "1965-1986" and "No. 1/WHOLESALER", white "55A-57 BAKER STREET/READING/TEL 507122: on black panel, red stripe, plus black "BERKSHIRES/LEADING/WHOLESALER" on rear doors. Header: white "DEAL WITH THE BEST". LP base.
1. As above.

06-CAB-DG CADBURY'S COCOA/BOURNVILLE 006-046 1986
Dark red or maroon body, cream roof and chassis, gold grille and windshield, 20-spoke gold wheels, white tires. Logo: brown-outlined gold "Cadbury's", brown "COCOA" on gold, white "BOURNVILLE" and cup design, gold frame. No header. DG6-8 base, with or without door lines. Certificate.
1. Dark red body, door lines.
2. Maroon body, no door lines.

06-CAC-DG CADBURY'S DRINKING CHOCOLATE 006-055 1986
Maroon body, cream roof and chassis, gold grille and windshield, 20-spoke red or 12-spoke gold wheels. Logo: gold and white "CADBURY'S", gold "Drinking/Chocolate" and frame, white cup design. Header: cream "CADBURY" on dark red background. DG6-8 base, with or without door lines. Special box.
1. 20-spoke red wheels, door lines.
2. 20-spoke red wheels, no door lines.
3. 12-spoke gold wheels, darker body, lighter roof and chassis, no door lines, 1987.

06-CAD-LP CADBURY 1987
Purple body, cream roof, maroon chassis, 12-spoke gold wheels, black tires. No other data.
1. As above.

06-CAM-VV CAMBRIDGE 1987
Green body, light green roof, black chassis, gold grille, 12-spoke gold wheels, black tires. Logo: picture of King's College, gold camera and frames. Header: gold "CAMBRIDGE". View Vans box. LP base, no door lines.
1. As above.

06-CAN-DG CANADIAN PREMIUM/INCENTIVE 006-054 1986
White body, orange roof and chassis, gold grille and windshield, 12-spoke gold wheels, white tires. Logo: black "TORONTO /September 3, 4, 5, 1986 /13th Annual", orange "CANADIAN PREMIUM//INCENTIVE TRAVEL/SHOW & BUSINESS/GIFT EXPOSITION" and frame, black "Franklin's Diecast Miniatures Inc.". telephone number and "COLLECT LLEDO". Header: black "Metro Toronto/Convention Centre". DG6-8 base, with or without door lines.
1. Door lines.
2. No door lines.

06-CAP-LP CANADIAN PREMIUM/INCENTIVE 1987
Details same as 1986 issue above except for black "September 9, 10, 11 1987/14th Annual" at top of logo. LP base with door lines.

06-CAR-VV CARLISLE 1987
Dark green body, bright green roof, black chassis, gold grille and windshield, 12-spoke gold wheels, black tires. Logo: picture of Carlisle Cathedral, gold camera and frames. View Vans box. LP base, no door lines.

06-CAS-LP WAKEFIELD CASTROL 1986
Dark green body, white or black roof, black chassis, gold grille and windshield, 12-spoke gold wheels, black tires. Logo: White-outlined red "Castrol", gold "WAKEFIELD", "MOTOR/OIL" and "Est'd /1899", plus white-outlined red "Castrol" and gold "Always ask for" and "by Name" on rear doors. No header. LP base, door lines.
1. White roof.
2. Black roof.

06-CAT-VV CANTERBURY CATHEDRAL 1987
No data.
1. As above.

06-CHA-LP CHAMPION SPARK PLUGS 1987
Yellow-orange body, black chassis and roof, gold grille and windshield, 12-spoke gold wheels, black tires. Logo: white "CHAMPION" on blue, blue "DOUBLE RIBBED/SPARK PLUGS", red arrows, red and blue frames. Header: white "CHAMPION" and frame. LP base, no door lines. Special box.

06-CHE-VV CHESTER 1987
Maroon body, dark red roof, black chassis, gold grille and windshield, 12-spoke gold wheels, black tires. Logo: picture of clock tower, gold camera and frames. View Vans box. LP base, no door lines.
1. As above.

06-CHN-LP CHANNEL 4 (4-TEL) 1986?
Blue body and chassis, light blue wheels, 20-spoke light blue wheels, black tires. No other data.

06-CLA-DG CITY OF LONDON POLICE AMBULANCE 006-006 1984
Cream body, white roof, black chassis, gold grille and windshield, 12-spoke gold wheels, black tires. Logo: red cross, red and black coat of arms, "City of London/POLICE AMBULANCE" and other lettering, plus red crosses on rear doors. Header: red "POLICE/AMBULANCE". Limited issue. DG6-DG8 base, door lines.
1. As above.

06-CLF-LP W. CLIFFORD & SONS 1987
Tangerine red body, white roof, black chassis, gold grille and radiator, 12-spoke gold wheels. Logo: yellow "W. CLIFFORD/&/SONS/DAIRYMEN/31 CROSS LANCES ROAD/HOUNSLOW/line, telephone number and frames. Header: black "W. CLIFFORD/& SONS". LP base, no door lines.
1. As above.

06-CLP-LP CLARKSON PUCKLE 1986
Red body and chassis, black roof, gold grille and windshield, 12-spoke gold wheels, black tires. Logo: white "Clarkson Puckle/FOR/AGREED VALUE/INSURANCE", red and white emblem. No header. LP base, door lines.
1. As above.

06-COA-LP/DG COCA-COLA 006-013 1983-84
Yellow or yellow-orange body, black roof and chassis, gold grille and windshield, 12-spoke gold wheels, black tires. Logo: red "Coca-Cola/AT SODA FOUNTAINS". No header. DG6-DG8 base, door lines.
1. Yellow body, smaller logo lettering, code 2.
2. Yellow-orange body, larger and slightly darker logo lettering, regular DG issue.

06-COB-DG COCA-COLA 006-014 1984
Yellow-orange body, black roof and chassis, gold grille and windshield, 12-spoke gold wheels, black tires. Logo: red "The/Coca-Cola/Co.", black "EVERY BOTTLE STERILIZED" and frames. No header. DG6-DG8 base, door lines.
1. As above.

06-COC-DG COCA-COLA 006-050 1986
Tangerine red body, black roof and chassis, silver or gold grille and windshield, 20-spoke gold wheels, black tires. Logo: white "DRINK", white "Coca-Cola", logo "IN STERILIZED BOTTLES" and frame, white squares and "SALES/and/ADVERTISING". Header: white "Coca-Cola". DG6-8 base, with or without door lines.
1. Door lines, silver grille and windshield.
2. No door lines, gold grille and windshield, 1987.

06-COD-DG COCA-COLA 006-051 1986
Green body, roof and chassis, gold grille and windshield, 12-spoke gold wheels, black tires. Logo: white "Drink/Coca-Cola/DELICIOUS/AND/REFRESHING" on red panel with yellow frame, white "SALES/and/ADVERTISING" in yellow frame. Header: white "Coca-Cola". DG6-8 base, with or without door lines.
1. Door lines.
2. No door lines, 1987.

06-COH-LP COOK & HICKMAN 1987
Red body, black chassis and roof, gold grille and windshield, 20-spoke red wheels, black tires. Logo: gold "COOK/&/HICKMAN/SOLICITORS/PURVEYORS OF LEGAL SERVICES", address and frame, black underlines. Header: gold "COOK &/HICKMAN". LP base, no door lines.
1. As above.

06-CON-LP CONESTOGA COUNTRY CLUB 1986
White body, green roof and chassis, gold grille and windshield, 12-spoke gold metal wheels, black tires. Logo: green "CONESTOGA/COUNTRY CLUB", address, telephone number and "TENNIS/&/GOLF", brown covered wagon design in circle. No header. LP base, door lines.
1. As above.

06-COO-DG COOKIE COACH CO. 006-003 1983
Orange body, black roof and chassis, gold grille and windshield, 12-spoke gold wheels, black tires. Logo: yellow or white "COOKIE/COACH/COMPANY", gold or yellow ovals and frames. Header: white "COOKIE COACH/COMPANY". DG6-

Lledo™ Models

DG8 or DG6-8 base, with or without door lines.
1. Yellow lettering, gold ovals ansd frames, DG6-DG8 base, door lines.
2. White lettering, yellow ovals and frames, DG6-DG8 base, door lines.
3. White lettering, yellow ovals and frames, DG6-8 base, door lines.
4. No door lines, otherwise as type 3.

06-COU-LP   COUTURE DESIGNER   1986
No data.
1. As above.

06-CRA-DG   CRAFT & HOBBY SHOWCASE   006-053 1986
White body, blue roof and chassis, gold grille and windshield, 12-spoke gold wheels, black tires. Logo: blue maple leaf design, "CRAFT & HOBBY SHOWCASE/ AUGUST 10, 11, 1986/Franklin's Diecast Miniatures Inc.", telephone number and frame. Header: white "collect Lledo". DG6-8 base, with or without door lines.
1. Door lines.
2. No door lines.

06-CUM-LP   CUMBERLAND NEWS   1987
Red body and roof, black chassis, gold grille and windshield, 12-spoke gold wheels, black tires. Logo: black-outlined gold "Cumberland News", black-white-gold newspaper design. Header: black "Cumberland". LP base. No door lines.
1. As above.

06-CWM-DG   CWM DALE SPRING   006-043 1986
White body and roof, blue or red chassis, gold grille and windshield, 12-spoke gold or 20-spoke black wheels, white or black tires. Logo: blue pring design, red "CWM DALE/SPRING", blue "Wells/Drinks/Ltd.", red and blue frames. Header: red "MINERAL WATER". DG6-8 or LP base, with or without door lines.
1. Blue chassis, black 12-spoke metal wheels, white tires, DG6-8 base, door lines.
2. Blue chassis, black 20-spoke plastic wheels, white tires, DG6-8 base, door lines.
3. Red chassis, gold 12-spoke metal wheels, white tires, DG6-8 base, door lines.
4. LP base, door lines, other details not known.
5. DG6-8 base, no door lines, black 20-spoke wheels.

06-CWR-LP   CASTROL WORLD RALLY   1987
No data.
1. As above.

06-DAI-DG   DAILY EXPRESS/SUNDAY EXPRESS 006-024 1984
Green body, black roof and chassis, gold grille and windshield, 12-spoke gold wheels, black tires. Logo: cream "DAILY EXPRESS/SUNDAY EXPRESS" and line, black disc. No header. In Collector Pack 1. DG6-DG8 base, door lines.
1. As above.

06-DAS-DG   DAYS GONE COLLECTORS CLUB   006-016 1984
Black body, roof and chassis, gold grille and windshield, 12-spoke gold wheels, white tires. Logo: cream "Models of/DAYS GONE/COLLECTORS/CLUB/ COMMEMORATING THE 1st. MILLION MODELS/by Lledo" and "FOUNDED/1984/12 mph" in gold frames. Header: cream "BEAUTIFUL DIECAST MODELS". DG6-DG8 base, door lines.
1. As above.

06-DAY-DG   DAYS GONE TOY FAIRS   006-045 & 056 1986-87
Dark red or maroon body, cream roof and chassis, gold grille and windshield, 20-spoke black wheels, white tires. Logo: silver "Models of/DAYS GONE/1986/ TOY FAIRS", names of 8 locations, "by Lledo", "No. 1" and "12 MPH", gold frames. Header: red "collect Lledo". DG6-8 base, with or without door lines.
1. Dark red body, one fair location misspelled "Harrowgate", door lines.
2. Dark red body, correct "Harrogate", door lines.
3. Maroon body, year changed to "1987" in logo, no door lines.

06-DEL-LP   DELTIC PRESERVATION SOCIETY   1987
Dark blue body, yellow-orange roof, black chassis, gold grille and windshield, 12-spoke gold wheels, black tires. Logo: black-outlined gold "DELTIC/PRESERVATION SOCIETY", emblem and "1977-10th ANNIVERSARY-1987", black "1977 D.P.S. 1987"; both are adhesive labels. LP base, no door lines.
1. As above.

06-DHT-LP   DH-TRANS BV   1986

Cream body, black roof and chassis, gold grille and windshield, 12-spoke gold wheels, black tires. Logo: black "24 UUR SERVICE" on orange panel, black "INT. EXPEDITIE EN TRANSPORTSBEDRIJF/DH-TRANS BV", black and orange emblem, orange stripe, also black and orange emblem and orange panel with black "24 UUR SERVICE" on rear doors. Header: black "DH-TRANS expres" on orange background. LP base, door lines.
1. As above.

06-ECH-DG   SOUTH WALES ECHO CENTENARY   006-029 1984
Cream body, blue roof and chassis, gold grille and windshield, 12-spoke gold wheels, white or black tires. Logo: black-outlined white "1884-1984", blue-gold-black-white emblem with white "South Wales/Echo" and gold "Centenary", black "100/Years" and frame. Header: white "South/Wales Echo". DG6-DG8 base, door lines.
1. White tires.
2. Black tires.

06-EDP-LP   EASTERN DAILY PRESS   1987
Yellow body, black roof and chassis, gold grille and windshield, 12-spoke gold wheels, black tires. Logo: blue "Eastern/Daily Press", black "Your complete/morning newspaper" and "EST./1870" in oval. No header. LP base, no door lines.
1. As above.

06-EPS-LP   EPSOM STAMP CO.   1986
Cream body, brown roof and chassis, gold grille and windshield, 20-spoke cream wheels, black tires. Logo: brown "Epsom Stamp Co." telephone number, lines and frame, on adhesive label. Header: cream "Epsom Stamp Co." on brown adhesive label. LP base, no door lines. Certificate.
1. As above.

06-EVC-DG   EVENING CHRONICLE CENTENARY   006-039 1985
Red body and roof, black chassis, gold grille and windshield, 12-spoke gold wheels, black tires. Logo: black-gold-cream emblem with black-outlined white "1885-1985", black "Evening/Chronicle" and red "Centenary", black-outlined cream panel with black "ALL THE/LATEST/NEWS". Shade of emblem oval may vary from off-white to light yellow. Header: cream "EVENING/CHRONICLE". DG6-DG8 or DG6-8 base, door lines.
1. DG6-DG8 base.
2. DG6-8 base.

06-EVF-LP   EVERTON FOOTBALL CLUB   1987
Dark blue body, black chassis and roof, gold grille and windshield, 12-spoke gold wheels, black tires. Logo: white & blue emblem, white "1986/87/EVERTON F. C./DIVISION 1/ CHAMPIONS". Header: white "EVERTON F. C." DG6-DG8 base, door lines. In DG box.
1. As above.

06-EXC-LP   EXCHANGE & MART   early 1986
Red body and chassis, black roof, gold grille and windshield, 12-spoke gold wheels, black tires. Logo: red-white-black emblem with black-outlined white "Exchange/& Mart", black "1986/MOTORING EVENTS" and red "Hagley Hall". No header. LP base, door lines. Special box.
1. As above.

06-EXM-LP   EXCHANGE & MART   late 1986
Tan body, brown roof and chassis, gold grille and windshield, 12-spoke gold wheels, black tires. Logo: brown-tan-red-gold emblems with red initials, tan "The Bazaar/Exchange/and Mart/Journal of the Household", brown lettering, and gold "Every/Thursday/2d", in brown frames. Header: Gold "Est. 1868". Special box. LP base, no door lines.
1. As above.

06-FAC-LP   FARROW OF CHELTENHAM   1986
No data.
1. As above.

06-FAI-DG   FAIRY SOAP   006-059? 1987
White body, jade green roof, dark green chassis, gold grille and windshield, 12-spoke gold wheels, black tires. Logo: 2-tone green "Fairy" and design, red "so mild and so pure/for all the family" and "Fairy". No header. DG6-8 base, no door lines.

1. As above.

06-FAM-LP   FAMOUS MENSWEAR/BOYSWEAR   1986
Dark brown body, black roof and chassis, gold grille and windshield, 20-spoke cream wheels, black tires. Logo: cream "the Famous/of Cheltenham/MENSWEAR/ BOYSWEAR", "208/HIGH/STREET" and frames, red-cream-blue "18/CENTENARY 86/19". Header: cream "the Famous/of Cheltenham". LP base, door lines.
1. As above.

06-FAR-LP   FARNHAM MALTINGS   1985 1985
Black body, roof and chassis, gold grille and windshield, 12-spoke gold wheels, black tires. Logo: gold "FARNHAM/MALTINGS" and frame, light green "10th March 1985", oval and "the south's best/swapmeet". No header. DG6-DG8 base, door lines.
1. As above.

06-FAS-LP   FARNHAM MALTINGS   1987 1987
Yellow body, black roof and chassis, 12-spoke gold wheels. No other data.
1. As above.

06-FAV-VV   FARNHAM MALTINGS   1987
Green or maroon body and roof, black chassis,... grille and windshield, 12-spoke gold wheels, black tires. Logo: ...
1. Green body and roof.
2. Maroon body and roof.

06-FIS-LP   FISHERMAN'S FRIEND   1985
Tan body, brown roof and chassis, gold grille and windshield, 12-spoke gold wheels, black tires. Logo: black "Lofthouse's original", orange "FISHERMAN'S FRIEND", tan "extra strong throat and chest lozenges" on black stripe, black and orange fishing boat design, black emblem, on adhesive label. No header. LP base, door lines.
1. As above.
2. Different logo?

06-FOT-LP   FOTORAMA   1985
White or silver body, red roof and chassis, gold grille and windshield, 12-spoke gold or 20-spoke red wheels, black tires. Logo: on white body: red F, blue "OTORAMA/A World of Colour" and frame; on silver body: blue-red-yellow "FOTORAMA", blue "A WORLD OF COLOUR" and frames, red F. No header. DG or LP base, with or without door lines.
1. White body, red-blue logo, DG base (not sure which).
2. White body, red-blue logo, LP base, door lines.
3. Silver body, red-yellow-blue logo, LP base. no door lines, 1987.

06-FPA-LP   FRANKLIN CHARITY PRO-AM   1986-87
Maroon or dark green body, black roof and chassis, gold grille and windshield, 12-spoke gold wheels, black tires. Logo: of 1986 issue: gold steam engine design, "1986 FRANKLIN/CHARITY PRO-AM/TUESDAY SEPTEMBER 16, 1986", "2nd/Annual" and frames. LP base, no door lines.
1. Maroon body, logo as above.
2. Dark green body, logo changed to "1987", "WEDNESDAY JULY 22, 1987" and "3rd/Annual".

06-FUR-LP   FURNISS OF TRURO   1987
Yellow body, black roof and chassis, gold grille and windshield, 12-spoke gold wheels, black tires. Logo: red and white "FURNISS OF TRURO", red "ESTABLISHED 1886" and "FAMOUS FOR BISCUITS AND FUDGE," blue and yellow background, white frames, blue lettering on sides and rear doors. Header: white "Furniss of Truro". LP base, no door lines. Certificate.
1. As above.

06-GAR-LP   GARDNER MERCHANT CATERING   1985
Tan body, light or reddish brown roof, dark brown chassis, gold grille and windshield, 12-spoke gold wheels, black tires. Logo: brown-outlined gold "Gardner/Merchant/A Century of Catering Service" and "100", brown frames. No header. LP base, door lines.
1. Light brown roof
2. Reddish brown roof.

06-GAS-LP   GARDNER MERCHANT SITE SERVICES   1985

Lledo™ Models

Tan body, light or reddish brown roof, dark brown chassis, gold grille and windshield, 12-spoke gold wheels, black tires. No other data.
1. Light brown roof.
2. Reddish brown roof.

06-GRY-SP GRAY   1986 or earlier
Light gray body and chassis, light cream roof, gold grille and windshield, 20-spoke light cream wheels, black tires. No logo or header. DG6-8 base, door lines. Factory specimen.
1. As above.

06-HAJ-DG HARDWARE JOURNAL   006-048 1986
Dark blue body, cream roof, light cream chassis, gold grille and windshield, 12-spoke gold wheels, black tires. Logo: white "Australian/Hardware/Journal", "1886/1986" and frame, and black emblem with black-outlined gold "100" and black lettering. DG6-8 base, door lines.
1. As above.

06-HAM-DG HAMLEYS   006-027 1984
Dark green body, light green roof, red chassis, gold grille and windshield, 12-spoke gold wheels, black tires. Logo: white "HAMLEYS" and underline, "REGENT STREET LONDON/THE WORLD'S FINEST TOYSHOP", gold frames. Header: white "HAMLEYS" and underline. DG6-DG8 or DG6-8 base, door lines. Special box.
1. DG6-DG8 base. Sold singly.
2. DG6-8 base. Sold in gift set.

06-HAT-DG HATFIELDS   1986
White body, black roof, chassis and lower body panels, gold grille and windshield, 20-spoke black wheels, black tires. Logo: black "Hatfields", underline and "Established 1886" on white upper body, gold "Furnishers of distinction for over a century", emblem and frames on black lower panels. Header: gold "Hatfields". LP base, no door lines.
1. As above.

06-HAY-LP W. HAYDON   1986
Black body, roof and chassis, gold grille and windshield, 12-spoke gold wheels, black tires. Logo: black-outlined white "W. HAYDON", gold "FURNISHING. IRONMONGERY/FRISTER & ROSSMANN'S/SEWING MACHINES/GUNS & AMMUNITION" and frames. DG6-DG8 or LP base, door lines. Boxed or on plinth.
1. DG6-DG8 base, on plinth (or boxed?).
2. LP base, boxed.

06-HED-DG HEDGES & BUTLER   006-056? 1987
Green body, tan roof, cream chassis, gold grille and windshield, 20-spoke black wheels, white tires. Logo: gold "Hedges/& Butler/Limited/WINE MERCHANTS SINCE 1667" and emblem. No header. DG6=8 base, no door lines.
1. As above.

06-HER LP HERITAGE HOMES   1986
Dark brown body and roof, black chassis, gold grille and windshield, 12-spoke gold wheels, white tires. Logo: orange and black butterfly and "Heritage", black "HOMES IN A CLASS OF THEIR OWN", cream background and frame, black "Cecil M. Yuill/Limited", other lettering and butterfly on tan oval. Header: white "Heritage Homes". DG6-8 base, no door lines.
1. As above.

06-HLC-LP HERTS LLEDO COLLECTORS   1984
Cream body, light brown roof, dark brown chassis, gold grille and windshield, 12-spoke gold wheels, black tires. Logo: cream "HERTS" and "COLLECTORS ASSOCIATION" on black ribbons, black "LLEDO", "1984", number 1 and frames with dots. Header: light brown "H.L.C.A." on black background. Logo and header decals. DG6-DG8 base, door lines. Certificate.
1. As above.

06-HME-LP HENDY MOTOR ENGINEERS   1985
Dark green body, black roof, gold grille and windshield, 12-spoke gold wheels, black tires. Logo: black Ford emblem, HENDY/MOTOR ENGINEERS" on

light green background, and light green "Southampton" and telephone number on black background adhesive label. No header. DG6-DG8 base, door lines.
1. As above.

06-HRA-DG HARRY RAMSDEN'S   006-022 1984
Cream body, red roof and chassis, gold grille and windshield, 12-spoke gold wheels, black tires. Logo: blue "Harry/Ramsden's" and lines, black fish design, "the most famous Fish & Chip Shop in the world", and "12 MPH". No header. DG6-DG8 base, door lines.
1. As above.

06-HOM-DG HOME ALES   006-032 1984
Green (2 shades) body and (2 shades) roof, black chassis, gold grille and windshield, 12-spoke gold wheels, black tires. Logo: green figure on white background, black-outlined gold "HOME ALES", gold "NOTTINGHAM" and "EST./1878", black frames, plus green figure on white background and white "FINE/ALES" on rear doors. Header: gold "HOME ALES". DG6-DG8 base, door lines.
1. Darker green body and roof (same shade).
2. Lighter green body and roof (body lighter than roof).

06-HOR-LP HORNBY RAILWAYS   1985
Dark red body, black roof and chassis, gold grille and windshield, gold grille and windshield, 12-spoke gold wheels, black tires. Logo: yellow "HORNBY RAILWAYS", "No. 1" and frames. Header: yellow "HORNBY" and frame. LP base, door lines.
1. As above.

06-HUD-LP HUDDERSFIELD DAILY EXAMINER   1987
Orange or yellow body, black chassis and roof, gold grille and windshield, 12-spoke gold wheels, black tires. Logo: black-outlined gold "HUDDERSFIELD/DAILY/EXAMINER", black frames, black "YOUR LOCAL PAPER" on rear doors. Header: gold "THE EXAMINER". LP base, no door lines.
1. Orange body.
2. Yellow body.

06-HUM-LP HUMI-SERV   1987
Dark green body, black roof and chassis, gold grille and windshield, 12-spoke gold wheels, black tires. Logo: gold "Humi/Serv" in circle and Cheltenham telephone number, on adhesive label. No header. LP base, no door lines.
1. As above.

06-IGF-DG INTERNATIONAL GARDEN FESTIVAL   006-010 1984
Cream body, green roof, black chassis, gold grille and windshield, 12-spoke gold wheels, black tires. Logo: black "2nd May/14th Oct./International/Garden/Festival/LIVERPOOL "84", green and black figures. Header: white "LIVERPOOL '84", or no header lettering. DG6-DG8 base, door lines.
1. Header lettering.
2. No header lettering.

06-ILL-DG 2nd ILLINOIS MINIATURE TOY SHOW   006-009 1984
Yellow body, light brown roof, dark brown chassis, gold grille and windshield, 12-spoke gold wheels, white tires. Logo: brown car design and "2nd Illinois Miniature Toy Show". No header. DG6-DG8 base, door lines.
1. As above.

06-IPM-DG IPMS 21st ANNIVERSARY   006-008 1984
Cream body, blue roof and chassis, gold grille and windshield, 12-spoke gold wheels, black tires. Logo: blue globe, "21st ANNIVERSARY/IPMS", "1984/12 MPH" and frames. Header: white (U.K.) REGION". DG6-DG8 base, door lines.
1. As above.

06-JON-LP T. JONES   1987
Green body, black chassis and roof, gold grille and windshield, 12-spoke gold wheels, black tires. Logo: white "T. Jones/The Finest Quality Meats", black "Family/Butcher" and other lettering and frames. Header: white "T. Jones". LP base. no door lines. Fuji box.
1. As above.

06-JST-DG JOHN SMITH'S TADCASTER BREWERY   006-042 1986
Dark green body, light red roof, black chassis, gold grille and windshield, 12-spoke

gold wheels, black tires. Logo: red-outlined yellow "JOHN/SMITH'S" and frames, red and white magnet, white "ESTd 1758" and "TADCASTER/BREWERY". Header: yellow "MAGNET ALES". DG6-8 base, door lines.
1. Bright yellow logo color.
2. Yellow-green logo color.
3. "Shredded Wheat" on header.

06-JWM-LP JUWELIER WAGNER MADLER   1987
Magenta body, black roof and chassis, gold grille and windshield, 12-spoke gold wheels, black tires. Logo: gold gem design and "JUWELIER/WAGNER/MADLER/AM BRAND 4-6/65 MAINZ/TEL. 231877". No header. LP base, no door lines.
1. As above.

06-KIT-LP KIT KAT   1987
Red body, white roof and chassis, gold grille and windshield, 20-spoke red wheels, black tires. Logo: white "1937-1987", "50 years" and emblem, black-outlined white "KitKat". No header. LP base, no door lines.
1. As above.

06-KOD-DG KODAK FILM   006-034 1985
Orange body, black roof and chassis, gold grille and windshield, 12-spoke gold or 20-spoke white wheels, black tires. Logo: black-outlined red "Kodak" twice, red "film" twice, red and black film box design and frames. Header: yellow-outlined black "Kodak". DG6-DG8 base with, gold wheels, varying shades of red in logo.
1. DG6-DG8 base, gold wheels, varying shades of red in logo.
2. DG6-8 base, gold wheels, no door lines.
3. DG6-8 base, white wheels, no door lines.

06-KOY-LP KOYANAGI   1986
White body, light green roof and chassis, gold grille and windshield, 12-spoke gold wheels, black tires. Logo: blue and gold-outlined green Japanese lettering, blue telephone number. Header: gold Japanese lettering. DG6-8 or LP base, door lines.
1. DG6-8 base.
2. LP base.

06-KRO-LP KRONDORF AUSTRALIAN WINE   1987
Yellow-orange body, black roof and chassis, gold grille and windshield, 12-spoke gold wheels, black tires. Logo: black "Krondorf" and "PREMIUM/AUSTRALIAN WINES", green vine design and frame. No header. Adhesive labels. LP base, no door lines.
1. As above.

06-LAN-LP LANCASHIRE EVENING POST   1985
Brown or magenta body, black roof and chassis, gold grille and windshield, 12-spoke gold metal wheels, black tires. Logo: white "Lancashire", Established 1886", emblem and frame, orange stripes, black-outlined white "Evening/Post", on adhesive label. Two white emblem labels on rear doors. No header. LP base, door lines.
1. Brown body.
2. Magenta body, 1986.

06-LEG-LP LEGAL AND GENERAL   1985
White body, red roof, red chassis, gold grille and windshield, 12-spoke gold wheels, black tires. Logo: black "Legal &/General" and "EST. 1836", red-blue-yellow-green-black umbrella, blue frames. Header: black "Legal &/General". LP base, door lines.
1. As above.

06-LIN-DG CHOCOLAT LINDT   006-035 1985
Light blue body, light or medium blue roof, medium blue chassis, gold grille and windshield, gold metal wheels, white tires. Logo: white emblem and "Chocolat Lindt" monogram, gold "Lindt/OF SWITZERLAND LTD." Header: gold "Lindt". DG6-DG8 or DG6-8 base, door lines.
1. DG6-DG8 base, light blue roof (matches body).
2. DG6-DG8 base, medium blue roof.
3. DG6-8 base, light blue roof (matches body).
4. DG6-8 base, medium blue roof.

06-LON-VV LONDON   1987
Maroon or dark green body, dark red or medium green roof, black chassis, gold grille

and windshield, 12-spoke gold wheels, black tires. Logo: London picture (see below), gold camera emblem and frames. Header: gold "LONDON". View Vans box. LP base, no door lines.

1. Maroon body, red roof, Tower of London picture.
2. Maroon body, red roof, guardsman picture.
3. Green body and roof, Big Ben tower picture.

06-LSE-LP   LINCOLNSHIRE ECHO   1987
Red body, black roof and chassis, 12-spoke gold wheels, black tires, no other data.
1. As above.

06-MAG-DG   MAGASIN   DU NORD   006-028   1984
Green (shades vary) body, black roof and chassis, gold grille and windshield, 12-spoke gold wheels, black tires. Logo: gold "MAGASIN/du/NORD", "A/3/WESSEL/& VETT" and frames. Header: gold or white "A/S WESSEL & VETT". DG6-DG8 base, door lines.
1. White header lettering.
2. Gold header lettering.

06-MAL-FS   MALIBU OR BUST   1985
Yellow body, light brown roof, dark brown chassis, gold grille and windshield, 12-spoke gold wheels, black tires. Logo: red-orange-green-white-black desert scene, white-outlined red "Malibu or Bust!", black "GONE FISHING" on black-rimmed orange sign, brown fishing pole, green tackle box. No header. Casting G.
1. As above.

06-MAR-DG   MARCOL PRODUCT   006-005   1984
Tan or yellow body, black or light brown roof, maroon or dark brown chassis, gold grille and windshield, 12-spoke gold wheels, black tires. Logo: maroon emblem with red dragon, maroon-outlined tan or yellow (body color) "MARCOL" and maroon "PRODUCT" and "SEAL OF QUALITY", maroon "EST. 1900" and "BRIDGE/STREET/CARDIFF", and frame, plus sometimes red dragon and "Wales" on rear doors. Header: yellow or gold "M. A, RAPPORT/Co. Ltd." DG6-DG8 base, door lines.
1. Tan body, black roof, maroon chassis, gold header lettering, no rear logo, maroon logo appears darker.
2. Yellow body, light brown roof, dark brown chassis, yellow header lettering, no rear logo, maroon logo appears brighter.
3. Rear door logo, otherwise as type 2.
4. There may be a version with maroon rather than bright red dragon on logo.

06-MAS-DG   MARKS & SPENCER   006-026   1984
Dark green body, light green roof, black chassis, gold grille and windshield, 12-spoke gold wheels, black tires. Logo: gold circles with "MARKS & SPENCER/1884-1984/CENTENARY YEAR" and design on gold background, gold "FOUNDED/1884". "12 mph" and frames, plus "PENNY/BAZAARS" on rear doors. Header: black "MARKS & SPENCER". DG6-DG8 or DG6-8 base, door lines.
1. DG6-8 base.
2. DG6-8 base.
3. LP base?

06-MFF-LP   MASTIFF ASSOCIATION   1987
Black body, light brown roof, brown chassis, gold grille and windshield, 12-spoke gold wheels, black tires. Logo: gold circles with "MASTIFF ASSOCIATION" and dog"s head. No header. LP base, no door lines.
1. As above.

06-MIL-LP   MILLER OF NOTTINGHAM   1986
Dark yellow body, black roof and chassis, gold grille and windshield, 12-spoke gold wheels, black tires. Logo: black-outlined green "MILLER", black "of Nottingham Limited/Nationwide Painting Contractors/Industrial Commercial & Domestic", Nottingham telephone number and three emblems, green windmill design and frames, plus two green windmills on rear doors. Header: white "DECADE/YEAR" and "1976/1986". LP base, door lines.
1. As above.

06-MIT-LP   MITRE 10   1985
Light brown body, black roof, 12-spoke gold

metal wheels, black tires. Logo: black-white-yellow "MITRE 10" emblem, red and yellow stripes, black "THE MIGHTY AUSTRALIANS", line and "Australia's biggest hardware specialists". Header: black-white-yellow "MITRE 10" emblem, red and yellow stripes. LP base, door lines.
1. As above.

06-MKD-LP   MILTON KEYNES DIGITAL TYPE   1985
White body, blue roof and chassis, 12-spoke black wheels, white tires, Logo: "Digital Type Suppliers/Milton Keynes". Mounted on plinth. No other data.
1. As above.

06-MOO-LP   MOORSIDE SCHOOL   1987
Yellow-orange body, black roof and chassis, gold grille and windshield, 12-spoke gold wheels, black tires. Logo: black emblem with "MOORSIDE/SCHOOL/STAFFORDSHIRE", Wetley Rocks telephone number and frames. No header. LP base, no door lines.
1. As above.

06-MUR-DG   MURPHYS CRISPS   006-030   1985
Yellow-orange body, red roof and chassis, gold grille and windshield, 12-spoke gold metal wheels, black tires. Logo: red-outlined "MURPHYS" on white panel, blue "CRISPS &/SNACKS" on white panel, white and blue border, blue "12 MPH". Header: white "MURPHYS/crisps". DG6-DG8 base, door lines.
1. As above.

06-MUS-LP   THE MUSTARD SHOP   1987
Tan body, dark brown roof and chassis, gold grille and windshield, 12-spoke gold wheels, black tires. Logo: dark brown design, "THE/MUSTARD SHOP/3 Bridewell Alley, Norwich" and frame. Header: white "THE/MUSTARD SHOP". LP base, no door lines.
1. As above.

06-NCH-LP   NATIONAL CHILDREN'S HOME   1985
White body, red roof and chassis, gold grille and windshield, 12-spoke gold wheels, black tires. Logo: black-circled pink disc with red-outlined white number "75" and black "YEARS IN WALES" and frames. Header: white "NATIONAL CHILDREN'S HOME/1911-1986". LP base, door lines. Certificate.
1. As above.

06-NCJ-LP   N. C. JEWELLERY   1986
Black body, roof and chassis, gold grille and windshield, 12-spoke gold wheels, black tires. Logo: gold "N C", wreath, "Jewellery Pty. Ltd./SYDNEY/MANUFACTURERS & IMPORTERS/STERLING SILVER &/GOLD SPECIALISTS/RINGS CHAINS", "SINCE/1972" and partial frame. Header: gold "N C". LP base, door lines.
1. As above.

06-NDM-DG   NORTHERN DAILY MAIL   006-044   1985
Green body, tan roof, black chassis, gold grille and windshield, 12-spoke gold wheels, black tires. Logo: tan "THE NORTHERN DAILY" on white background with tan partial frame, tan-outlined white "Mail", green "WEST/HARTLEPOOL" on white background with gold partial frame, white telephone number and "12 MPH" in gold frame. Header: green "THE NORTHERN DAILY/MAIL". DG6-8 base, door lines.
1. As above.

06-NEL-LP   NEWBURY STEAM LAUNDRY   1986
Red body, black roof and chassis, 12-spoke gold wheels, black tires. Logo: Newbury/Sanitary Steam Laundry". No other data.
1. As above.

06-NGF-LP   NATIONAL GARDEN FESTIVAL   1986
Green body, white roof, red chassis, gold grille and windshield, 12-spoke gold wheels, black tires. Logo: red-white-green emblem with green "NATIONAL GARDEN" and red "FESTIVAL", white "STOKE-ON-TRENT/1986" and frame. Header: green "N.G.F. '86". LP base, door lines. Special box.
1. As above.

06-NRF-LP   NORFOLK 5th SWAPMEET   1986
Dark red body, tan roof, black chassis, gold grille and windshield, 12-spoke gold wheels, black tires. Logo: white "NORFOLK/5th/SWAPMEET/ST. ANDREWS

HALL/NORWICH/ORGANISED BY/THE EAST ANGLIAN/DIECAST MODEL CLUB". Header: white "MAY 25th 1986". Code 3? DG6-DG8 base, door lines.
1. As above.

06-NRS-C3   NORFOLK 7th SWAPMEET   1987
Cream body, blue roof and chassis, gold grille and windshield, 12-spoke gold wheels, white tires. Logo: blue "THE SEVENTH" and frame, other cream lettering on blue panels. Header: gold "4 MAY 1987". DG6-DG8 base, door lines. With figures.
1. As above.

06-ODD-LP   ODD FELLOWS   1987
Maroon body, black chassis and roof, 12-spoke gold wheels, black tires. Logo: emblem, "Independent Order/of Odd Fellows" & other lettering. No other data.
1. As above.

06-OTT-LP   THE OTTAWA CITIZEN   1986
Yellow body, black roof and chassis, gold grille and windshield, 12-spoke gold wheels, black tires. Logo: black "the Ottawa/Citizen/Since 1843/12 MPH" and frame. LP base, no door lines.
1. As above.

06-OVA-DG   OVALTINE   006-001   1983
Dark orange body, light brown roof, dark brown chassis, gold or silver grille and windshield, 12-spoke gold wheels, black tires. Logo: blue "OVALTINE", orange and brown design on dark cream or yellow disc, black circled number 10 and "12 mph". No header. DG6-DG, DG6-DG8 or DG6-8 base, with or without door lines.
1. DG6-DG base, gold grille, tan logo disc.
2. DG6 DG8, gold grille, tan logo disc.
3. Silver grille, other details not known.
4. DG6-8 base, gold grille, yellow logo disc.
5. DG6-8 base, no door lines, matt or gloss finish.

06-OVE-DG   OVALTINE 75 YEARS   006-031   1985
Dark orange body, tan roof, dark brown chassis, gold grille and windshield, 12-spoke gold wheels, black tires. Logo: blue "OVALTINE/75/YEARS" and wheat design, orange and brown central design on light tan disc, black circled number 10 and "12 MPH". Header: blue "OVALTINE". DG6-DG8 or DG6-8 base, door lines. Sometimes in special box.
1. DG6-DG8 base.
2. DG6-8 base.
3. Is there a version with light brown roof?

06-OVR-LP   OVERDRIVE   1985
White body, green roof and chassis, gold grille and windshield, 12-spoke gold wheels, black tires. Logo: red "Salterns", gold "The World's Finest Transport Operation", black frames. No other data. Has been called "Overdrive Manpower", "Overdrive Transport" and "Salterns".
1. As above.

06-PEJ-DG   PERRIER-JOUET   006-025   1984
Ivory body, green roof, black chassis, gold grille and windshield, 12-spoke gold wheels, white tires. Logo: pink-green-gold flower design, green-outlined gold "PERRIER-JOUET", gold "CHAMPAGNE" and "EPERNAY". Header: gold "PERRIER-JOUET". DG6-DG8 or DG6-8 base, with or without door lines.
1. DG6-DG8 base, door lines, lighter green roof.
2. DG6-8 base, door lines, lighter green roof.
3. DG6-8 base, door lines, darker green roof.
4. DG6-8 base, no door lines, darker green roof.

06-PER-LP   PERSIL   1987
Dark green body, red roof, black chassis, gold grille and windshield, 20-spoke red plastic wheels, black tires. Logo: black-outlined white "Persil" in red circle with white rim, white "WASHES WHITER" and lines. Header: white "Persil". LP base, no door lines. Special box. One of four Persil models.
1. As above.

06-PHA-DG   PHILADELPHIA FIRE AMBULANCE   006-021   1984 145

Lledo™ Models

Cream body and chassis (shades vary), black roof, gold grille and windshield, 12-spoke metal wheels, black tires. Logo: gold "BUREAU/OF/FIRE/AMBULANCE", "P.B.F." and number 3, black frames. No header. DG6-DG8 base, door lines.
1. As above.

06-PHB-DG PHILADELPHIA FIRE RESCUE 006-020 1984
Red body and chassis (shades vary), black roof, gold grille and windshield, 12-spoke gold wheels, black tires. Logo: gold "RESCUE/COMPANY/PHILADELPHIA/BUREAU OF FIRE" and number 1, black frames. No header. DG6-DG8 base, door lines.
1. As above.

06-RAF-DG ROYAL AIR FORCE 006-061? 1987
Pale gray body, dark blue chassis and roof, gold grille and windshield, 12-spoke gold wheels, black tires. Logo: blue-gold-white "ROYAL AIR FORCE" emblem, gold "216 SQUADRON/GROUND ELECTRICS". Header: white "C" FLIGHT". DG6-8 base, no door lines. In boxed set of three RAF models with certificate.
1. As above.

06-REA-DG RAILWAY EXPRESS AGENCY 006-019 1984
Dark green body, black roof and chassis, gold grille and windshield, 12-spoke gold wheels, black tires. Logo: brown-black-white design with black " RAILWAY EXPRESS/for speedy/service", white "RAILWAY EXPRESS AGENCY" on black stripe, white emblem. No header. DG6-DG8 base, door lines.
1. As above.

06-RED-LP REDDICAP HEATH FIRST SCHOOL 1987
Blue body, yellow chassis, dark yellow roof, gold grille and windshield, 12-spoke gold wheels. Logo: gold emblem, "Reddicap Heath First School", "Founded/1908" and frames. Header: blue "RHFS". Door lines. LP base.

06-REE-DG REESE'S PIECES 006-049 1986
Orange body, dark brown roof, slightly lighter brown chassis, gold grille and windshield, 12-spoke gold wheels, white tires. Logo: brown-outlined yellow "Reese's pieces" and brown-yellow-orange-white design in white frame, white "HERSHEY'S" on brown background. Header: white "HERSHEY'S" and frame. DG6-8 base, door lines.
1. Gold grille and windshield.
2. Silver grille (and windshield?)

06-ROS-DG ROSE AND CROWN 006-060? 1987
Green body and chassis, white roof, gold grille and windshield, 12-spoke gold wheels, black tires. Logo: white "Rose & Crown" and "Fine Ales/& Stouts", red-white-black-gold emblem, gold frame. Header: red "Rose & Crown". GD6-8 base.
1. Door lines.
2. No door lines.

06-ROU-LP ROUND TABLE DIAMOND JUBILEE 1987
Cream body, red roof and chassis, gold grille and windshield, 12-spoke gold wheels, black tires. Logo: black-gold-cream diamond emblem with gold "ROUND TABLE/DIAMOND JUBILEE", brown "1927-1987" and "adopt, adapt, improve", and brown and gold gem. No header. LP base, no door lines.
1. As above.

06-ROY-DG ROYAL MAIL 350 YEARS 006-041 1985
Red body, black roof and chassis, gold grille and windshield, 12-spoke gold metal wheels, black tires. Logo: circular "ROYAL MAIL/350 YEARS/SERVICE TO THE PUBLIC" and frames. No header. DG6-8 base, with or without door lines. Special box.
1. Door lines.
2. No door lines.

06-SAL-LP SALVATION ARMY 1985
Black body, roof and chassis, gold grille and windshield, 12-spoke gold wheels, white tires. Logo: white "THE/SALVATION/ARMY" on white-bordered red shield, white "MEN'S SOCIAL SERVICES", "NO. 1", "FOUNDED/1890", "12 MPH" and frames, plus white "S. A." on rear doors. Header: white "THE/SALVATION ARMY". LP base, door lines.

06-SCA-VV SCARBOROUGH 1987
Dark green body, green roof, black chassis, gold grille and windshield, 12-spoke gold wheels, black tires. Logo: picture of town, harbor and shore, gold camera and frames. Header: gold "SCARBOROUGH". View Vans box. LP base, no door lines.
1. As above.

06-SCH-LP SCHWEPPES 1987
Dark yellow body, black roof and chassis, gold grille and windshield, 12-spoke gold wheels, black tires. Logo: black "Schweppes", emblem and frames, on adhesive label. No header. LP base, door lines.
1. As above.

06-SCO-LP SCOTCH CORNER THE SWAPMEET 1985
Silver body, black roof and chassis, gold grille and windshield, 20-spoke gray wheels, black tires. Logo: black "SCOTCH CORNER/THE SWAPMEET/A1", black and maroon lines, on adhesive label. No header. LP base, door lines.
1. As above.

06-SER-LP SERVICE OFFSET 1986
No data.

06-SHP-LP SHIPSTONES 1986
Red body, black roof and chassis, gold grille and windshield, 20-spoke red wheels, black tires. Logo: white "SHIPSTONES", "Traditional Fine Ales", "Brewers/since/1852" and frame, red-white-black emblem, on adhesive label. Header: none, or white "Brit Tyres Sales". LP base, door lines.
1. No header lettering.
2. Header lettering.

06-SHR-LP SHREDDED WHEAT 1986
Yellow body, red roof and chassis, gold or silver grille and windshield, 12-spoke gold or 20-spoke red wheels, black tires. Logo: red "Nabisco/Shredded/Wheat", brown "THE ORIGINAL BRANFIBRE CEREAL", oval emblem and frames. Header: yellow "Nabisco/Shredded Wheat". LP base, with or without door lines.
1. Door lines, gold metal wheels.
2. Door lines, red plastic wheels.
3. Silver grille (which casting?)
4. No door lines, gold metal wheels.
5. No door lines, red plastic wheels.

06-SJP-LP GREAT ST. JOHN PARTY 1987
White body and chassis, black roof, gold grille and windshield, 20-spoke white wheels, black tires. Logo: black and white emblem, black "Great St. John Party/20th June 1987". Header: white "AMBULANCE". LP base, no door lines.
1. As above.

06-SPG-LP SPRING GARDEN SHOW 1987
Ivory body, orange roof and chassis, gold grille and windshield, 20-spoke orange wheels, black tires. Logo: gold "The Spring/Garden/Show/County Showrooms", figure of man plasting bush, "MAY /2-4th/1987" and frames. No header. LP base, no door lines.
1. As above.

06-STD-LP STRAND 1987
White body and roof, black chassis, gold grille and windshield, 12-spoke gold wheels, black tires. Logo: blue and gray "STRAND" envelope design, yellow lettering, blue and yellow frames. Header: blue and gray "STRAND" and underline. Adhesive labels. LP base.
1. As above.

06-STF-LP STAFFORDSHIRE COUNTY SHOW 1987
Blue body, orange roof and chassis, gold grille and windshield, 20-spoke orange wheels, black tires. Logo: gold "STAFFORDSHIRE/COUNTY SHOW", knotted rope design, "Staffordshire/Agricultural Society", "May/27-28th /1987" and frames. No header. LP base, no door lines.
1. As above.

06-STP-LP STAFFORDSHIRE POLICE DANCE ORCHESTRA 1987

Dark green body, light blue roof and slightly darker blue chassis, gold grille and windshield, 12-spoke gold wheels, black tires. Logo: silver oval, "STAFFORDSHIRE POLICE/DANCE ORCHESTRA", musical notes and frames. No header. LP base, no door lines.
1. As above.

06-STR-DG STRETTON SPRING WATER 006-011 1984
White body, green or black roof, green or blue chassis, gold grille and windshield, 12-spoke gold or gold metal wheels, black or white tires. Logo: white 'Stretton Spring Water" on blue ribbon, blue-green-black design with blue "Circa 1890", blue "Wells/Drinks/Ltd.", "12 MPH" and black-circled number 6, green frames. No header. DG6-DG8 base, door lines.
1. Black roof, blue chassis, black wheels, white tires.
2. Green roof and chassis, gold wheels, black tires.

06-SUS-LP SUSSEX EXPRESS 1987
Red body, black chassis and roof, 12-spoke gold wheels. black tires. No other data.
1. As above.

06-SWT-C3 SOUTHWESTERN TELEPHONE 1986
Black body, roof and chassis, gold grille and windshield, silver window frames, 12-spoke gold wheels, black tires. Logo: blue and white emblem with blue "SOUTHWESTERN/TELEPHONE". Header: blue "BELL SYSTEM CO." on white background. Casting B: DG6-DG8, with "C3" scratched on base. Privately made.
1. As above.

06-TAL-LP TALYLLYN RAILWAY 1986
Very dark green body, red roof, black chassis, gold grille and windshield, 12-spoke gold wheels, black tires. Logo: "THE FIRST PRESERVED RAILWAY", railroad engine design, "TALYLLYN RAILWAY/WHARF STATION/TYWYN, GWYNEDD", emblem and frame. Header: gold "TALYLLYN RAILWAY/COMPANY". DG6-8 or LP base, door lines. Special label on box.
1. DG6-8 base.
2. LP base.

06-TAY-LP TAYLORS OF GLOUCESTER 1986
White body, blue roof and chassis, gold grille and windshield, 20-spoke blue wheels, white tires. Logo: blue "Taylor's/of Gloucester/1925 1985", telephone number and frame, blue and white Ford emblem. Header: white "Taylors". Logo and header on adhesive labels. LP base, door lines.
1. As above.

06-TEL-LP TELEMEDIA CELEBRITY GOLF 1987
Black body, roof and chassis, gold grille and windshield, 12-spoke gold wheels, black tires. Logo: gold design, "TELEMEDIA CELEBRITY/GOLF TOURNAMENT/SEPTEMBER 1987" and maple leaf emblem with "Ontario/Special Olympics" circling it. Header: gold "HORSESHOE VALLEY". LP base, door lines.

06-TEN-LP TENNENT'S LAGER 1987
Green body and chassis, black roof, gold grille and windshield, 12-spoke gold wheels, black tires. Logo: red-outlined gold "TENNENT'S/LAGER", gold "Brewers of Ales & Stouts Since 1556", red-black-gold design and emblems, gold frames. Header: gold "TENNENT'S". Gold "TENNENT'S/LAGER" on rear doors. LP base, no door lines.

06-TER-LP TERRY PRINTING GROUP 1986
Black body, no other data.
1. As above.

06-THC-C3 THREE COCKS WORKING RALLY 1983
Jade green body, black roof, cream chassis, gold grille and windshield, 12-spoke gold wheels, black tires. Logo: red "Three Cocks/1983/Working Rally" around yellow-black-red emblem. No header. DG6-DG8 base, door lines.
1. As above.

06-THR-LP THRUWAY AUTOROUTE 1986
White body, black roof and chassis, gold grille and windshield, 12-spoke gold wheels,

146

black tires. Logo: white "thruway . muffler centre" on rose panel ith black frame, rose and black stripes of left side of model; similar pattern with white "centre du silencieux/autoroute" on right side. No header. LP base, no door lines.

  1. As above.

06-TIZ-DG TIZER   006-047 1986

Yellow-orange body, black roof and chassis, gold grille and windshield, 12-spoke gold wheels, black tires. Logo: white "TIZER /THE APPETIZER" and red "Registered Trade Mark" on black and white panel, black "TIZER LIMITED/440 HOLLINWOOD AVE./MOSTON/MANCHESTER", red frames. No header. DG6-8 base, with or without door lines.

  1. Door lines.
  2. No door lines.

06-TRU-LP TRUE VALUE HARDWARE   1986

Black body, roof and chassis, gold grille and windshield, 12-spoke gold wheels, black tires. Logo: light green "true value" and frames, white "hardware", white-outlined red "Our name says it all." Header: white "Our name says it all." LP base, no door lines.

  1. As above.

06-UNW-LP UNWIN'S WINE MERCHANTS   1986

Dark green body, brown or black roof, black chassis, gold grille and windshield, 12-spoke gold wheels, black tires. Logo: red-outlined pale green "UNWINS/WINE MERCHANTS", pale green "Head Office/DARTFORD 72711", "EST. 1843" and frames, two-tone green emblem, plus pale green "UNWINS/WINE MERCHANTS/EST. 1843" on rear doors. Header: pale green "UNWINS". (Pale green color might also be called cream.) LP base, no door lines. Certificate.

  1. Brown roof.
  2. Black roof.

06-VAR-LP VARITYPER   1985

No data.

  1. As above.

06-WEH-LP WESTERN EVENING HERALD/MORNING NEWS   1987

Red body and roof, black chassis, gold grille and windshield, 12-spoke gold wheels, black tires. Logo: black-outlined gold "The/Western/Morning News" on left side of model, "Western/Evening Herald" on right side. Header: black "PLYMOUTH/266626". LP base, no door lines.

06-WEL-DG WELLS DRINKS   006-036 1985

Yellow body, brown roof and chassis, gold grille and windshield, 12-spoke gold wheels, black tires. Logo: orange-green-black-yellow fruit design with black-outlined yellow "Wells" and orange "WONDERFUL WORLD", black "Wells/drinks", orange and green frames. Logo: orange "Taste the/goodness". DG6-DG8 or DG6-8 base, door lines.

  1. DG6-DG8 base.
  2. DG6-8 base.

06-WER-LP THE WERRINGTON PATISSERIE LTD.   1987

Tan body, brown roof and chassis, gold grille and windshield, 12-spoke gold wheels, black tires. Logo: brown and tan emblem with "THE WERRINGTON/PATISSERIE LTD", brown lettering and frames. No header. LP base, no door lines.

  1. As above.

06-WES-LP WESTERN AUTO SUPPLY CO.   1987

Red body, black roof and chassis, gold grille and windshield, 12-spoke gold wheels, black tires. Logo: red-white-black emblem with white "WESTERN/AUTO/SUPPLY/CO.", black "SERVES THE NATION" on black-bordered white ribbon, white "Founded/1909", "No. 1/12 MPH" and frames. No header. LP base, no door lines.

  1. As above.

06-WEV-DG WELLS BLACK VELVIT   006-058 1987

Light rose body, black roof and chassis, gold grille and windshield, 12-spoke gold wheels, white tires. Logo: gold panel with black "Wells", black and gold branch design and black "WONDERFUL WORLD" on black-bordered wite ribbon, white panel with black "BLACKCURRANT/Black Velvit", black "Wells/Drinks/Ltd." Header:

---

white "VITAMIN C". DG6-8 or LP base, no door lines.

  1. DG6-8 base (regular issue).
  2. LP base (samples).

06-WHB-LP WHITBREAD   1986

Brown body and chassis, darker brown roof, gold grille and windshield, 12-spoke gold wheels, black tires. Logo: gold FIGURE, "ESTD 1742/WHITBREAD/BLACKBURN". No header. LP base, door lines.

  1. As above.

06-WIN-VV WINDSOR   1987

Maroon body, dark red roof, black chassis, gold grille and windshield, 12-spoke gold metal wheels, black tires. Logo: picture of Round Tower, gold camera emblem and frames. Header: gold "WINDSOR". View Vans box. LP base, no door lines.

  1. As above.

06-WON-DG WONDER BREAD   006-018 1984

White body, light blue roof, blue chassis, gold grille and windshield, 12-spoke gold wheels, black tires. Logo: red-yellow-bluwe bread loaf design with red "WONDER", blue "BREAD" and "IT'S SLO-BAKED", red "It's Slo-baked". Header: white "WONDER BREAD". Varying shades of red logo color. DG6-DG8 base, door lines.

  1. As above.

06-WOO-DG WOODWARD'S   006-040 1985

Blue body, roof and chassis, gold grille and windshield, 12-spoke gold wheels, black tires. Logo: white design and "GET IT AT", blue-outlined white "WOODWARD'S", and white "WE SELL EVERYTHING". Header: blue-outlined white "WOODWARD'S". DG6-8 base, door lines.

  1. As above.

06-WOR-LP WORFIELD GARAGE   1977

Red or black body and chassis, black roof, gold grille and windshield, 12-spoke gold wheels, black tires. Logo: white "Worfield" with line, "WORFIELD GARAGE" and red-blue-yellow-white-black emblem. Header: white telephone number. Logo and header on adhesive labels. LP base, door lines.

  1. Red body and chassis.
  2. Black body and chassis.

06-YCM-LP YORK CASTLE MUSEUM   1987

Dark green body, black roof, cream chassis, gold grille and windshield, 12-spoke gold wheels, black tires. Logo: cream castle design, "York Castle/Museum" and frame. No header. LP base, no door lines. Certificate.

  1. As above.

06-YOB-DG YORKSHIRE BISCUITS   006-017 1984

Dark brown body, black roof and chassis, gold grille and windshield, 12-spoke gold wheels, black tires. Logo: white or cream "YORKSHIRE/BISCUITS/limited/HAWORTH KEIGHLEY", red lines and diamond, yellow emblem, design and frames. Header: white "YORKSHIRE/BISCUITS Ltd." DG6-DG8 base, door lines.

  1. White logo lettering.
  2. Cream logo lettering.

06-YOE-DG YORKSHIRE EVENING POST   006-012 1984

Yellow body, black roof and chassis, gold grille and windshield, 12-spoke gold wheels, black tires. Logo: black "YORKSHIRE/EVENING POST/THE ORIGINAL BUFF", lines and "12 MPH". No header. DG6-DG8 base, door lines.

  1. As above.

06-YOP-DG YORKSHIRE POST   006-002 1983

Blue body, black roof and chassis, gold grille and windshield, 12-spoke gold wheels, black tires. Logo: yellow "Yorkshire/Post/Twixt Trent & Tweed", lines and "12 MPH". No header. DG6-DG8 base, door lines.

  1. As above.

007 FORD WOODY WAGON   74mm 1984

Metal body and chassis, plastic seats, grille, base, later roof blade and spare wheel. 12-spoke metal, 20-spoke plastic or plastic disc wheels. Roof of body has either small hatch or raised support for front of roof blade. Rear of body casting has either exposed slot for chassis tab or area covered by spare wheel. Castings:

  A. Recessed body panel just under oval sign.

  B. Panel not recessed.
  C. Panel not recessed, rear spare, roof blade. Base types:
  A. DG7-DG9.
  B. DG7-DG9 plus DG13 and DG14 on axle covers.
  C. DG7-9-13-14.
  D. Lledo Promotional Model
  E. "Made in England/by Lledo"

07-CHO-DG CHOCOLATES BY DELLA   007-007 1986

Cream body, chassis, blade, seats and spare, brown trim, silver grille, 20-spoke cream wheels, black tires. Logo: brown "Chocolates by" and brown-outlined cream "Della" on pink (shades vary) oval. Header: brown "Belgian/Chocolates". Flush panel, roof blade, spare wheel. DG7-9-13-14 base.

  1. As above.

07-COC-DG COCA-COLA   007-002 1984

Light orange body (shades vary), brown trim, black chassis, silver grille, cream interior, 12-spoke gunmetal wheels, white tires. Logo: red "Drink/Coca-Cola/in bottles". Recessed or flush panel, no spare wheel or roof blade.

  1. DG7-DG9 base, recessed body panel.
  2. DG13 and DG14 on axle covers, flush panel.
  3. DG7-9-13-14 base, flush panel.

07-COM-DG COMMONWEALTH GAMES   007-008 1986

White body and blade, blue chassis, cream interior and spare, silver grille, red disc wheels, white tires. Logo: red disc with black border and "COMMONWEALTH GAMES 1986", white and black dog figure and white "Mac" and underline. Blade: black dog figures. Flush panel, roof blade, spare wheel. DG7-9-13-14 base. Special box.

  1. As above.

07-FER-LP FERGUSON'S FORD   1986

No data.

  1. As above.

07-FOR-DG FORD SALES & SERVICE   007-003 1984

White body, black trim and chassis, cream interior, silver grille, 12-spoke gunmetal wheels, white tires. Logo: white "Ford" on blue oval with white border, blue "SALES & SERVICE" under oval. Flush panel, no blade or spare.

  1. DG7-DG9 base.
  2. DG13 and DG14 on axle covers.
  3. DG7-9-13-14 base.

07-FTS-FS FORD TRI-STATE DEALER   1985

White body, blue trim and chassis, off-white blade, cream interior and spare, silver grille, 20-spoke yellow wheels, black tires. Logo: white "Ford" on blue oval with white border, blue "SALES & SERVICE" below oval. Blade: blue "Tri-State Dealer." Flush panel, roof blade, spare wheel. "Made in England/by Lledo" base. Fantastic Set of Wheels.

  1. As above.

07-GDF-DG GODFREY DAVIS FORD   007-005 1985

White body, blue trim and chassis, off-white blade, cream or white interior, cream or black spare, silver grille, 12-spoke or 20-spoke blackish wheels, white tires. Logo: white "Ford" on blue oval with white border, blue "SALES & SERVICE" below oval. Blade: white "Godfrey Davis" on blue background with white border. Flush panel, roof blade, spare wheel. DG7-9-13-14 base.

  1. 12-spoke gunmetal wheels, cream interior and spare wheel.
  2. 20 spoke blue-black wheels, cream interior and spare wheel.
  3. 20-spoke blue-black wheels, cream interior, black spare wheel.
  4. White interior, other details not known.

07-GRY-SP GRAY   1986?

Light gray body and chassis, cream blade and interior, silver grille, 20-spoke cream wheels, black tires. No logo. Flush panel, no blade or spare. DG7-9-13-14 base. Factory specimen.

  1. As above.

07-HAM-DG HAMLEYS   007-005 1984

Cream body, tan trim, red chassis, cream interior, silver or gold grille, 12-spoke gold wheels, white tires. Logo: tan "HAMLEYS" and underline on red oval with cream border, tan "TOYS & GAMES". Flush panel, no blade or spare. In special box or gift set.

1. Silver grille, DG13 and DG14 on axle covers.
2. Silver grille, DG7-9-13-14 base?
3. Gold grille, DG7-9-13-14 base.

07-KLM-LP KLM ANIMAL TRANSPORT   1987
Light blue body, white trim, interior, spare and blade, blue chassis, silver grille, 20-spoke blue wheels, white tires. Logo: white emblem and "KLM". Blade: light blue "All Animal Transport". In special 3-model box. Flush panel, roof blade, spare wheel. LP base.

1. As above.

07-PAT-DG PAT'S POODLE PARLOUR   007-001 1984
Yellow body, brown trim, red chassis, cream interior, silver grille, 12-spoke gunmetal wheels, white tires. Logo: white "POODLE/Pat's/PARLOUR" and designs on green oval. Recessed or flush panel, no blade or spare.

1. DG7-DG9 base, recessed panel.
2. DG7-DG9 base, flush panel.
3. DG13 and DG14 on axle covers, flush panel.
4. DG7-9-13-14 base, flush panel.

07-WPT-DG WEST POINT TOY SHOW   007-004 1984
Yellow body (shades vary), green trim and chassis, cream interior, silver grille, 12-spoke gunmetal wheels, white tires. Logo: blue "TOY SHOW/WEST POINT/3rd. 4th. JUNE 1984". Recessed or flush panel, no blade or spare.

1. DG7-DG9 base, recessed panel.
2. DG13 and DG14 on axle covers, flush panel.

008 MODEL T FORD TANKER   80mm 1984
Metal body and chassis, tank, roof, pipes, grille and windshield, 12-spoke metal or 20-spoke plastic wheels. Exists only with door lines. Base types:

A. DG6-DG8 base.
B. DG6-8 base.
C. Lledo Promotional base.
D. Only "Made in England/by Lledo".

08-BMF-DG BLUE MOUNTAIN BUSH FIRE BRIGADES 008-007 1986
Red body, roof, tank and chassis, gold grille, windshield and pipes, 12-spoke gold wheels, black tires. Logo: yellow "BLUE MOUNTAINS/BUSH FIRE/BRIGADES", diagonal lines and "BLAXLAND COUNTY COUNCIL", red-white-green emblem, plus yellow "FIRE/TANKER" on rear of tank. Header: yellow "FIRE TANKER". DG6-8 base.

1. As above.

08-BON-LP BONDY OIL INC.   1986
Light blue body and chassis, white roof, silver tank, grille, windshield and pipes, 20-spoke blue wheels, white tires. Logo: blue-silver-black "Bondy/Oil Inc." emblem on tank, white "NEWFIELD, N.J." on body, plus blue "FUEL OIL/AND/KEROSENE" on rear of tank. Header: blue "Bondy". All lettering on adhesive labels. LP base.

1. As above.

08-BPC-LP BP CHEMICALS   1987
White body and tank, blue chassis and roof, gold grille and windshield, 20-spoke cream wheels, black tires. Logo: blue "BP chemicals" on tank, green and yellow BP emblems on door and rear of tank. No header. LP base.

1. As above.

08-BPE-LP BRITISH PETROLEUM   1985
Dark green body, white roof, red tank, blue chassis, gold grille, windshield and pipes, 20-spoke red wheels, black tires. Logo: black-outlined gold "BP" on tank, white "2603" and "BRITISH PETROLEUM/COMPANY LTD." on body. Header: black "MOTOR BP" SPIRIT". All lettering on adhesive labels. LP base.

1. As above.

08-CAS-DG WAKEFIELD CASTROL   008-005 1985

Dark green body and tank, white roof, black chassis, gold grille, windshield and pipes, 12-spoke gold wheels, black tires. Logo: white-outlined red "Castrol", gold "WAKEFIELD" and "MOTOR OIL" on tank, gold number 27, "27, CANNON STRET, LONDON", telephone number, "ESTd 1899" and circled letter R on body. No header. DG6-8 base.

1. As above.

08-COC-DG COCA-COLA   008-002 1984
Light orange body, dark yellow or light orange tank, black roof and chassis, gold grille, windshield and pipes, 12-spoke gold wheels, black tires. Logo: black "SERVE" and "AT HOME" and red "Coca-Cola" on tank, red "The/Coca-Cola/BOTTLING Co." on body. No header. DG6-DG8 base.

1. Dark yellow tank, lighter than body.
2. Light orange tank, same color as body.

08-COL-LP COLE'S   1987
Red body, roof and tank, gold and tank, gold grille, windshield and pipes, 20-spoke red wheels, black tires. Logo: gold "COLE'S/FACTORS/MOTOR SPIRIT—PARAFFIN", other lettering, trim and frames. Header: none. LP base.

08-CRO-DG CROW CARRYING CO.   008-009 1986-87?
Yellow body, black roof, tank and chassis, gold grille, windshield and pipes, 12-spoke gold wheels, black tires. Logo: red and white design with red "as the crow flies", red and white bird figure and red-outlined white "CROW CARRYING COMPANY LTD." on tank, red "HARTS LANE, NORTH ST./BARKING, ESSEX", telephone number and "FOUNDED 1920" on body. Header: white "CROW CARRYING/CO." DG6-8 base.

1. As above.

08-CWR-LP CASTROL WORLD RALLY   1987
No data.

1. As above.

08-ESS-DG ESSO   008-001 1984
Light blue body, blue tank, darker blue chassis, white roof, gold grille, windshield and pipes, 12-spoke gold or 20-spoke white wheels, black tires. Logo: red "Esso" and stripes in blue oval on white background on tank, white "No./7/12 MPH", blue "blue" and red-white-blue Esso emblem on white background, and red "INFLAMABLE/DANGER" or "INFLAMMABLE/DANGER" on white panel on body. No header. DG6-DG8 or DG6-8 base.

1. A few factory specimens exist with red chassis.
2. DG6-DG8 base, gold wheels, "INFLAMABLE" misspelling.
3. DG6-DG8 base, gold wheels, correct "INFLAMMABLE" spelling.
4. DG6-8 base, gold wheels, correct spelling.
5. Edocar base, gold wheels, correct spelling.
6. DG6-8 base, white wheels, correct spelling.

08-GRY-SP GRAY   1986?
Light gray body and chassis, white roof, dark green tank, gold grille, windshield and pipes, 20-spoke cream wheels, white tires. No logo. DG6-8 base. Factory specimen.

1. As above.

08-HER-DG HERSHEY'S CHOCOLATE MILK   008-008 1986
White body, brown roof, tank and chassis, gold grille, windshield and pipes, 12-spoke gold wheels, white tires. Logo: white "HERSHEY'S" and brown "CHOCOLATE MILK" on white stripe on tank, brown "Real/Chocolate" and white "HERSHEY'S" and "CHOCOLATE MILK" on brown stripes on body. Header: white "HERSHEY'S" and frame. DG6-8 base. Special box.

1. As above.
2. Darker brown chassis, lighter brown logo color.

08-HOF-DG HOFMEISTER   008-004 1985
Yellow body and tank (shades vary), brown chassis and roof, gold grille, windshield and pipes, 20-spoke gold wheels, white tires. Logo: black "Hofmeister" on white ribbon with black border on tank, black bear figure, "LAGER/12 MPH" and circled number 6 on body, plus black bear figure and "For great lager/follow the bear" on rear of tank. No header. DG6-DG8 or DG6-8 base.

---

1. DG6-DG8 base, tank lighter than body, red wheels.
2. DG6-DG8 base, tank same shade as body, red wheels.
3. DG6-8 base, tank lighter than body, red wheels.
4. DG6-8 base, tank same shade as body, red wheels.
5. DG6-8 base, purplish-brown chassis, red wheels.
6. DG6-8 base, purplish-brown hassis, gold wheels.
7. DG6-8 base, muddy yellow tank: Tesco issue.
8. DG6-8 base, tank lighter than body, gold wheels.

08-LIQ-FS LIQUID BUBBLE   1985
Light blue body, white roof and tank, pink chassis, gold grille, windshield and pipes, 20-spoke red wheels, white tires. Logo: 2-tone blue and pink bubble design with light blue "LIQUID BUBBLE" on tank, pink and white bubbles, blue-outlined light blue "fill up", pink "2c" on blue disc and pink "world's/best bubbles" on blue-outlined white cloud on body. No header. Fantastic Set o' Wheels.

1. As above.

08-MAR-LP MARSHALL TRUCKING   1986
Green body, white roof and chassis, silver tank, gold grille, windshield and pipes, 20-spoke green wheels, black tires. Logo: black "MARSHALL" on black-outlined white star on green background on tank, similar star plus black "TRUCKING INC./NEWFIELD N.J." on body. Header: black "MARSHALL". All on adhesive labels. LP base.

1. As above.

08-MIL-LP MILK   1987
Blue body and chassis, white roof and tank, gold grille, windshield and pipes, 12-spoke gold wheels, black tires. Logo: white "Milk" on two-tone blue background on tank, white "Fresh From/The Farm" on body. Header: blue "Fresh From The Farm". LP base.

1. As above.

08-MMB-LP MIDWEST MINIATURE BOTTLE   1986
Black body and tank, red roof and chassis, silver grille, windshield and pipes, 20-spoke red wheels, black tires. Logo: white "MIDWEST/MINIATURE/bottle collector's club" on tank, white man-wheelbarrow-bottles design and "FOUNDED/4/14/79" on body. Header: black 'WORLD WIDE'. LP base.

08-NAM-C3 NATIONAL MILK   1985?
Lime gren body, white tank, black roof and chassis, gold grille, windshield and pipes, 12-spoke gold wheels, white tires. Logo: black "National Milk" on sides and rear of tank. No header. DG6-8 base.

1. As above.

08-PEN-DG PENNZOIL   008-006 1985
Red body, white tank, black roof and chassis, gold grille, windshield and pipes, 12-spoke gold or 20-spoke cream wheels, black tires. Logo: black "PENNZOIL" across red Liberty Bell on tank, black "PENNZOIL PLACE/HOUSTON, TEXAS", yellow-black-red can with black "PENNZOIL/MOTOR OIL", and black "Safe Lubrication" on body, plus black "Supreme Quality/PENNZOIL/Safe Lubrication", Liberty Bell and oval on rear of tank. No header. DG6-8 base.

1. 12-spoke gold wheels.
2. 20-spoke cream wheels.

08-PHI-DG/C3 PHILADELPHIA BUREAU OF FIRE 008-003 1984
Red body (shades vary), tank and chassis, black or white roof, gold grille, windshield and pipes, 12-spoke gold wheels, black tires. Logo: gold "BUREAU of FIRE/SERVICE TRUCK" in black frame on tank, gold "P. B. F." in black frame on body. No header or black "P. B. F." and frame. DG6-DG8 base.

1. Black roof, no header logo.
2. White roof, no header logo.
3. White roof, header logo. Code 3.

08-RED-EC RED   1986
Red body, black roof and chassis, yellow-orange tank, gold grille and 12-spoke wheels, black tires. No logo or header. Edocar box and A-1 base.

1. As above.

Lledo™ Models

08-SHE-LP SHELL-MEX   **1986**
Red body and tank, white roof, black chassis, gold grille, windshield and pipes, 12-spoke gold wheels, black tires. Logo: black-outlined yellow "SHELL", yellow "FUEL OIL" on tank, yellow "SHELL-MEX/LTD/FUEL OIL" and number 7002 on body. Header: red "SHELL-MEX". All on adhesive labels. LP base.
1. As above.

08-SMW-LP SMALL WHEELS   **1986**
Black body, roof, tank and chassis, gold grille, windshield and pipes, 12-spoke gold wheels, white tires. Logo: gold "SMALL WHEELS", ribbon outline and "Waterloo, Ontario" on tank, gold telephone number and frame, red and white Canadian flag on body, plus gold horsedrawn fire engine design on rear of tank. Header: gold "RARE TOYS". LP base.
1. As above.

08-WAT-DG WATER WORKS   **008-010 1987**
Dark blue body and chassis, black roof and tank, gold grille, windshield and pipes, 12-spoke gold wheels, black tires. Logo: white "WATER WORKS" on blue background, silver and white faucet on tank, silver "RUTLAND DISTRICT/ EMERGENCY SERVICE" on body, plus white "EMERGENCY/WATER SUPPLY" on rear of tank. No header. DG6-8 base.
1. As above.

08-ZER-? ZEROLENE   **1987?**
No data.
1. As above.

MODELS CHOPPED FROM 008 ORIGINALS:

X8-HOF-C3 HOFMEISTER   **1984?**
Yellow body with usual black logo, brown roof and chassis, 20-spoke red wheels, white tires, red rear bed with two brown (lighter than roof) plastic barrels.

X8-PBF-Ce PHILADELPHIA BUREAU OF FIRE   **1984?**
Red body and chassis with usual gold and black logo, black roof, two red chemical tanks, gold hose reel with red mechanism atop tanks, gold trim.

009 MODEL A FORD CAR (TOP DOWN)   **77mm 1984**
Metal body and chassis, plastic seats, grille, windshield and base, later spare wheel, 12-spoke or 20-spoke wheels. Casting change: rear body adapted to allow mounting of spare wheel. Base types:
A. DG7-DG9.
B. DG7-DG9, plus DG13 on front and DG14 on rear axle cover.
C. DG7-9-13-14, rim around lettering.
D. Lledo Promotional Model.

09-FMF-DG THE FIFTEEN MILLIONTH FORD   **009-004 1985**
Black body, chassis, black or cream interior, black spare, silver grille, silver or gold windshield, 12-spoke gunmetal or 20-spoke black wheels, white tires. Logo: white "The Fifteen Millionth/Ford". DG7-9-13-14 base.
1. Metal wheels, cream interior, no spare, silver windshield.
2. Metal wheels, black interior and spare, silver windshield.
3. Metal wheels, black interior and spare, gold windshield.
4. Plastic wheels, black interior and spare, silver windshield.
5. Metal wheels, black interior and spare, silver windshield with roof pegs.
6. Metal wheels, cream interior and spare, silver windshield with roof pegs. Note: cream interiors may not be genuine.

09-NYR-DG NEW YORK-RIO   **009-002 1984**
Silver body, red chassis, black or cream interior, silver grille and windshield, 12-spoke gunmetal wheels, white tires. Logo: blue "NEW YORK-RIO" on sides and hood, blue circled number 3, red-white-blue Union Jack.
1. Black interior.
2. Black interior, DG7-DG9 plus DG13 and DG14 on axle covers.
3. Cream interior. (may not be genuine)

09-PHI-DG PHILADELPHIA BUREAU OF FIRE   **009-003 1984**
Red body and chassis (shades vary), cream or black interior, silver grille and windshield, 12-spoke gold wheels, black tires. Logo: gold disc with black "BATTALION CHIEF/9/D.P.S./BUREAU OF FIRE".

1. Cream interior, DG7-DG9 base (may not be genuine).
2. Black interior, DG7-DG9 base.
3. Black interior, DG 13 and DG 14 on axle covers.

09-POL-DG POLICE   **009-001 1984**
Light or dark blue body, dark blue chassis, cream or black interior, cream spare or none, silver grille and windshield, 12-spoke gunmetal or 20-spoke black plastic wheels, white tires. Logo: white "POLICE" on hood and sides, white door area with black and gold 6-pointed star, white number 055.
1. Light blue body, DG7-DG9 base, cream interior, no spare, metal wheels.
2. Dark blue body, DG7-DG9 base, cream interior, no spare, metal wheels.
3. Dark blue body, DG7-DG9 base, black interior, no spare, metal wheels.
4. Dark blue body, DG13 and DG14 on axle covers, black interior, no spare, metal wheels.
5. Dark blue body, DG7-9-13-14 base, black interior, no spare, metal wheels.
6. Medium blue body (lighter than chassis), DG7-9-13-14 base, cream interior and spare, black plastic wheels.
7. Dark blue body, mushroom tan spare, 20-spoke wheels, other details unknown.
Note: black interiors may not be genuine.

010 ALBION SINGLE DECKER COACH   **83mm 1984**
Metal body and chassis, plastic roof/upper body, interior, grille and base, solid plastic (dual rear) wheels. Castings:
A. Original front end of chassis.
B. Thickened front end to stabilize grille.
C. Thick front end with two round holes under grille.
D. Wide base tab slot, otherwise as type C.
There is one other casting difference: the rear edges of the front fenders may be either thin, with a lip at the outer edge, or uniformly thick all the way across. The fender units were cast in pairs, and one of the two was modified to have the thick edges. Thus every 010, 012, 016 and 020 model can be found with either thick or thin fender edges, and these will not be listed as variations.
Base types:
A. DG10-DG12 without ridge.
B. DG10-DG12 with ridge around lettering.
C. Lledo Promotional Model, with ridge.
D. "Made in England/by Lledo" on base.

10-AMS-LP AMSTERDAM 1992   **1986**
Dark yellow body, light gray chassis, cream roof, red interior, silver or gold grille, gray 6-bolt wheels, black tires. Logo: 3 red crosses and "Amsterdam 1992" on roof, black "Amsterdam wants the world to win" in one of four languages on each side of the lower body. Header: black "AMSTERDAM" and frame. Ridged LP base. Original front end.
1. English and Dutch logo, silver grille.
2. Spanish and French logo, silver grille.
3. English and Dutch logo, gold grille.
4. Spanish and French logo, gold grille.

10-BAR-DG BARTON   **010-007 1985**
Red body, magenta chassis, cream roof and interior, gold grille, dark red 6-bolt wheels, black tires. Logo: black-outlined gold "BARTON", underline and "175", gold "T. H. Barton, Director/Beeston" and frame, black and cream or white stripes. Header: black "NOTTINGHAM" and frame. DG10-DG12 base without ridge. Original front end.
1. Cream stripe.
2. White stripe.

10-BRI-DG BRIGHTON BELLE   **010-001 1984**
Maroon body with green and yellow trim, green chassis, cream or tan roof, dark cream interior, silver or gold grille, green 6-bolt wheels, white tires. Logo: yellow "Brighton Belle" and white "HASTINGS-EASTBOURNE-WORTHING-BOGNOR". Header: black "BRIGHTON". DG10-DG12 base without, later with ridge. Original or thick front end.
1. Tan roof, silver radiator.
2. Tan roof, gold radiator.

3. Cream roof, gold radiator.
4. Cream roof, gold radiator, ridged base.
5. Ivory roof and interior, darker green 6-bolt wheels, gold radiator, ridged base, thick front end with holes and wide slot.
6. Darker green disc wheels, otherwise as type 5.

10-CEN-LP CENTRAAL NEDERLAND   **1986**
Dark yellow body and roof, light gray chassis, red interior, silver grille, gray 6-bolt wheels, black tires. Logo: blue "centraal nederland" and "CN" monogram. Header: black "ZEIST" and frame. LP base with ridge. Original front end.
1. As above.

10-COM-DG COMMONWEALTH GAMES   **010-014 1986**
White body, red chassis, blue roof, cream interior, gold grille, red 6-bolt wheels, white tires. Logo: blue-white-red " XIII". black "XIII COMMONWEALTH GAMES/ SCOTLAND 1986" AND "COURTESY COACH", RED-WHITE-BLACK "MAC" emblem. No header. DG10-DG12 base with ridge. Thick front end. Special box.
1. As above.

10-DUN-LP DUNDEE CORPORATION TRANSPORT   **1987**
Dark yellow body and chassis, light blue roof and interior, silver grille, dark blue 8-bolt wheels, black tires. Logo: black "CORPORATION TRANSPORT" on white stripe, black and gold emblem, white "No. 10". Header: white "DUNDEE" on black background. LP base, thick front end with holes and wide slot. In set of three models. Certificate.
1. As above.

10-GLA-LP GLASGOW CORPORATION   **1987**
Orange body, black chassis, green roof and interior, silver grille, black 6-bolt wheels, black tires. Logo: black-edged white stripe with black "GLASGOW CORPORATION", black emblem. Header: white "JOHNSTONE" on black background. LP base with ridge. Certificate.
1. As above.

10-GRY-SP GRAY   **date?**
Gray body and chassis, red or yellow roof, cream interior, gold grille, black 6-bolt wheels, white tires. No logo or header. DG base with ridge. Original front end. Specimen.
1. Red roof.
2. Yellow roof.

10-GWM-LP G. W. R. MUSEUM   **1987**
Brown body and chassis, cream roof and seats, gold grille, brown wheels, white tires. Logo: white "G.W.R. Museum, Swindon/Silver Jubilee/1962-1987". No header. Thick front end. LP base.
1. As above.

10-GWR-DG G. W. R.   **010-009 1985**
Dark brown body, black or purplish-brown chassis, cream or off-white roof, red seats, gold grille, gold frames. Logo: red-outlined gold "G.W.R.", gold frames. Header: black "STATION" and frame. Either front end. Special box; some models mounted on plinth.
1. Black chassis, cream roof, DG10-DG12 base without ridge, original front end.
2. Purplish-brown chassis, off-white roof, DG10-DG12 base with ridge, thick front end.

10-HAM-DG HAMLEYS   **010-006 1984**
Dark brown body, cream chassis, roof and interior, gold grille, cream 6-bolt wheels, black tires. Logo: white "HAMLEYS" and underline, yellow "THE FINEST TOYSHOP IN THE WORLD" and "REGENT STREET, LONDON". Header: black "REGENT STREET" and frame. DG10-DG12 base without ridge. Original front end. Special box.

10-HAP-LP HAPPY DAYS   **1986**
Red body, cream chassis, roof and interior, silver grille, red 6-bolt wheels, black tires. Logo: gold design and "Happy Days", red "Austin's". No header. LP base with ridge. Original front end.

149

1. As above.

10-HER-DG   HERSHEY'S MILK CHOCOLATE   010-013 1986
Brown body, cream or brown chassis, cream roof, cream or white interior, gold grille, cream 6-bolt or disc wheels, black tires. DG10-DG12 base with ridge. Thick front end. Special box.
  1. Cream chassis, cream interior, 6-bolt wheels.
  2. Cream chassis with two holes, cream interior, 6-bolt wheels.
  3. Brown chassis with two holes, cream interior, 6-bolt wheels.
  4. Purplish-brown body, ? chassis, cream interior, disc wheels.
  5. Purplish-brown body, ? chassis, white interior, 6-bolt wheels.

10-IMP-DG   IMPERIAL AIRWAYS   010-011 1986
Cream body, light blue chassis, dark blue or red roof, cream interior, gold grille, cream wheels, black tires. Logo: blue "LONDON-AFRICA-INDIA-FAR EAST", red "IMPERIAL AIRWAYS" and "Courtesy/Coach", red and blue emblem. Header: white "CROYDON" and frame. Either front end. DG10-DG12 base with ridge.
  1. Original front end, blue roof, 6-bolt wheels.
  2. Thick front end, blue roof, disc wheels.
  3. Thick front end, ? wheels, red roof.
  4. Lighter cream body, disc wheels, other details not known.

10-IRO-LP   IRONBRIDGE MUSEUMS   1986
Blue-black body, cream chassis, roof and interior, gold grille, 6-bolt blue-black wheels, black tires. Logo: blue-black "Visit the Museums at" on gold stripe, gold "Ironbridge" and underline. No header. LP base with ridges. Thick front end.
  1. As above.

10-KLM-LP   KLM PASSENGER TRANSPORT   1987
Light blue body, blue chassis, white roof and interior, silver grille, 6-bolt blue wheels, white tires. Logo: white crown and "KLM/Passenger/Transport". Header: light blue "SCHIPHOL". In special 3-model box. LP base with ridge. Thick front end.

10-LAK-LP   LAKESIDE TOURS   1987
Red body, dark red chassis, cream roof, gold grille, red 6-bolt wheels, black tires. Logo: black "WINDERMEME-CONISTON-ULLSWATER" on cream stripe, gold "LAKESIDE/TOURS". Header: black "BUTTERMERE" and frame. LP base. Thick front end with holes and slot. Fuji box.

10-LNE-LP   L N E R   1985
Apple green body and chassis, cream roof and interior, silver grille, 6-bolt cream wheels, black tires. Logo: red-outlined "L N E R" and "127" on brown stripe. Header: white "DURHAM" on black stripe. Both on adhesive labels. Cream LP base with ridge. Original front end.
  1. As above.

10-LOC-DG   LONDON COUNTRY   1986
Green body, dark green chassis, cream or off-white roof and interior, gold or silver grille, dark green wheels, black tires. Logo: light yellow "LONDON/COUNTRY" and "30/M.P.H." Header: black "ONGAR" and frame. DG10-DG12 base with ridge. Thick front end.
  1. Cream roof, gold grille, 6-bolt wheels.
  2. Off-white roof, gold grille, 6-bolt wheels.
  3. Cream roof? silver grille, 6-bolt wheels.
  4. Cream roof? gold grille, disc wheels.

10-LOM-LP   LONDON MODEL CLUB   1986
No data.

10-LOT-LP   LOTHIAN   1987
Maroon body, black chassis, white roof and interior, silver grille, maroon 6-bolt wheels, black tires. Logo: gold stripe, "LOTHIAN" and coat of arms. Header: white "Broughton St." on black. LP base. Thick front end. In boxed set of three, with or without certificate.
  1. As above.

150 10-MAI-LP   MAIDSTONE & DISTRICT   1987

Dark green body and chassis, light cream roof and interior, silver grille, dark green 6-bolt wheels, black tires. Logo: gold oval, "Maidstone & District/motor transport/ltd." and frame. Header: white "TENTERDEN" on black background. LP base with ridge. Thick front end.
  1. As above.

10-OXF-LP   OXFORD   1987
Red body, black chassis, red-brown roof, cream interior, silver grille, 6-bolt black wheels, black tires. Logo: olive stripe, gold "OXFORD", underline, "103" and frame. Header: white "ABINGDON" and frame. LP base with ridge. Thick front end. Certificate.
  1. As above.

10-POT-DG   POTTERIES   010-004 1984
Red body, black chassis, cream or red roof, cream interior, black grille, red 6-bolt wheels, black tires. Logo: black-outlined gold "CHEADLE-LONGTON" on white panel on black stripe, black-outlined gold "POTTERIES", underline and "23". Header: black (on cream roof) or white (on red roof) "LONGTON" and frame. DG10-DG12 base without or with ridge. Original front end.
  1. Cream roof, black header, no base ridge.
  2. Red roof, white header, no base ridge.
  3. Red roof, white header, ridged base.

10-RED-DG   REDBURNS   010-012 1986
Red body and chassis, cream roof, cream or white interior, gold grille, 6-bolt red wheels, black tires. Logo: black-outlined gold "REDBURNS", gold "MOTOR SERVICES Ltd.", address and "SPEED/12 MPH". Header: black "SOUTH ST." and frame. LP10-LP12 base without ridge. Original front end or thick type with holes.
  1. Original front end, cream interior.
  2. Thick front end with holes, white interior.

10-SBO-FS/DG   SCHOOL BUS: OAKRIDGE SCHOOL   1985
Yellow-orange body and roof, black chassis, cream interior, gold grille, 6-bolt black wheels, white tires. Logo: red stripes, white "SCHOOL BUS" on black panel, black "OAKRIDGE SCHOOL", "DISTRICT", "15 MPH", "No. 7" and lines, black circle with yellow number 4. Header: black "SCHOOL" and frame. Original front end, "MADE IN ENGLAND/by Lledo". Fantastic Set o' Wheels. Reissued in 1987 as DG model, with new interior, chassis and base.
  1. As above; Fantastic Set o' Wheels.
  2. White interior, ridged DG base, thick front end with two holes and wide slot; 1987 DG issue.

10-SBU-DG   SCHOOL BUS: UNION FREE SCHOOL   010-002 1984
Yellow-orange body and roof, black chassis, cream interior, gold or silver grille, 6-bolt black wheels, white tires. Logo: black "DISTRICT 17. UNION FREE SCHOOL", "No. 7", "15 MPH" and lines, white "SCHOOL BUS" on black panel. Header: black "SCHOOL" and frame. DG10-DG12 base without ridge. Original front end.
  1. Silver grille.
  2. Gold grille.

10-SIL-DG   SILVER SERVICE   010-016 1987
Silver body and chassis, red roof, white interior, silver grille, 6-bolt red wheels, black tires. Logo: black "DARLEY DALE & MATLOCK" in frame and "Silver Service". Header: white or silver "MATLOCK" and frame. DG10-DG12 base with ridge. Thick front end with two holes, later with wide slot.
  1. Silver header, darker red roof.
  2. White header, lighter red roof, wide slot.

10-SOV-DG   SOUTHERN VECTIS   010-005 1984
Green body, black chassis, cream roof and interior, gold grille, green 6-bolt or disc wheels, black tires. Logo: black-outlined yellow or white "SOUTHERN VECTIS", yellow or white "NELSON ROAD/NEWPORT I.O.W." and stripe. Header: black "NEWPORT" and frame. Boxed or on plinth. DG10-DG12 base without ridge. Original or thick front end. Certificate, special label on box.
  1. Yellow logo.
  2. Yellow logo, on plinth.
  3. White logo.

4. Yellow logo, ivory roof and interior, thick front end with holes and wide slot, darker green disc wheels.
5. Darker green disc wheels, otherwise as type 4.

10-TAN-LP   TANDHAUS   1985
Cream body and roof, dark blue chassis, red interior, silver grille, 6-bolt light blue wheels, white tires. Logo: blue "MINIATURE CARS", house design, "TANDHAUS" and "1982-85 NISHINOMIYA", lighter blue stripes. No header. DG10-DG12 base without ridge. Original front end.
  1. As above.

10-TAR-DG   TARTAN TOURS   010-008 1985
Red body, black chassis, roof and interior, gold grille, 6-bolt cream wheels, black tires. Logo: white "ECCLEFECHAN & AUCHTERMUCHTY/TARTAN/TOURS", green and white plaid design. Header: black "PERTH" and frame. DG10-DG12 base without or with ridge. Original or thick front end.
  1. Dark cream roof and interior, base without ridge.
  2. Dark cream roof and interior, ridged base.
  3. Light cream roof and interior, thick front end with two holes, ridged base.

10-THS-LP   THORPE HALL SCHOOL   1985
Green body, black chassis, light orange roof, cream seats, gold grille, 6-bolt green wheels, black tires. Logo: gold "THORPE HALL SCHOOL, WALTHAM FOREST/Golden Jubilee/1935-1985", stripes and "15 MPH". Header: black "HALE END" and frame. DG10-DG12 base without ridge. Original front end.

10-TIL-DG   TILLINGBOURNE VALLEY   010-003 1984
Maroon body and roof, black chassis, cream seats, gold grille, 6-bolt maroon wheels, black tires. Logo: yellow "Tillingbourne/Valley". Header: yellow "PEASLAKE" and frame. DG10-DG12 base without ridge. Original front end.

10-TRA-DG   TRAILWAYS   010-010 1985
White body, red chassis, off-white roof, red seats, gold grille, 6-bolt red wheels, white tires. Logo: white "Trailways" and red-white-blue American flag on red stripe. Header: black "DALLAS" and frame. DG10-DG12 base without or with ridge. Original front end.
  1. Base without ridge.
  2. Ridged base.

10-USA-DG   U. S. ARMY   1987
No data.
  1. As above.

011   HORSE DRAWN LARGE VAN   110mm 1984
Metal body, chassis, hitch, 12-spoked front and 16-spoked rear wheels, plastic roof and two tan, light or dark brown or black horses. No separate base; lettering on chassis; types:
  A. "DAYS GONE/by Lledo" on rear panel, "MADE IN/ENGLAND" and "DG 11" at front.
  B. "DAYS GONE/DG 11/by Lledo" in frame on rear panel, "MADE IN/ENGLAND" at front.
  C. "LLEDO/PROMOTIONAL MODEL" on rear panel, "MADE IN/ENGLAND" at front.
  D. "by Lledo" on rear panel, "MADE IN/ENGLAND" and "DG 11" at front.

11-ABE-DG   ABELS OF EAST ANGLIA   011-003 1985
Light beige body, red chassis and blue roof, gold wheels, tan or dark brown horses. Logo: dark blue "ABELS of EAST/ANGLIA", light blue "WORLD WIDE REMOVALS." on dark blue ribbon, red "WATTON, NORFOLK/HUNTINGDON, CAMBS.", red, white and dark blue trim. Base A.
  1. Tan horses.
  2. Dark brown horses.

11-BIG-DG   BIG TOP   011-002 1985
Light cream body, red chassis and hitch, dark blue roof, gold wheels, dark brown or black horses. Logo: black "BIG TOP" on red-outlined yellow ribbon, blue trim, multicolored circus scenes. Base A or B.

1. Dark brown horses, base A.
2. Black horses, base B.

11-BRC-LP   BRANCH-CHEMIE   1987
Yellow body, red chassis and hitch, blue roof, gold wheels, dark brown horses. Left logo: red-yellow-blue-black paint cans, black lettering. Right logo: black "BRANCH-CHEMIE" and address, blue and yellow company emblem, red-yellow-blue-black paint can. Base C. Figures included.
1. As above.

11-CLO-LP   CITY OF LONDON POLICE   1985
Blue-black body, black chassis, hitch and roof, gold wheels, dark brown horses. Logo: gold "City of London Police" and red-white-gold coat of arms on dark blue background, plus gold "POLICE" on dark blue background at front of wagon, both on adhesive labels. Base D. Special box, certificate.
1. As above.

11-CLP-LP   CITY OF LONDON POLICE (PRISON VAN)   1985
Mustard body, chassis and hitch, dark brown roof, gold wheels, dark brown horses. Logo: gold "City of London Police" on dark brown background adhesive label. Base C. Special box, certificate.
1. As above.

11-COC-LP   COCA-COLA   1986
White body, red chassis, hitch and roof, gold wheels, light or dark brown or black horses. Logo: red-tan-black cases, red "Coca-Cola" and frame, black "IN BOTTLES" and "5c". Base B. Special box.
1. Light brown horses, lighter red roof.
2. Dark brown horses, darker red roof.
3. Black horses, darker red roof.

11-EXC-LP   EXCHANGE AND MART   1986
Light tan body, dark green chassis and hitch, green roof, gold wheels, dark brown horses. Logo: brown "EXCHANGE AND MART", other lettering, oval pictures of gentleman and lady, green and brown frames. Base C. Special box.
1. As above.

11-GRY-SP   GRAY   date?
Gray body, chassis and hitch, blue roof, gold wheels, tan horses. No logo. DG base Specimen.
1. As above.

11-MAC-DG   MacCOSHAM   011-007 1986
Dark yellow body, chassis, hitch and roof, gunmetal wheels, dark brown horses. Logo: yellow "MacCOSHAM" on dark green ribbon, dark green "WE/ESTIMATES FREE/PHONE 71559", at left, banner with "MOVE/CRATE/SHIP/STORE" in center, "PIANOS/&/FURNITURE" at right. Base B.
1. As above.

11-ROY-DG   ROYAL MAIL   011-006 1985
Red body, black chassis, hitch and roof, gold wheels, black horses. Logo: black-outlined "Royal Mail" and "GviR" monogram, black and gold crown. Base A. Special box.
1. As above.

11-STA-DG   STAFFORDSHIRE COUNTY SHOW   011-004 1985
Tan body, dark brown chassis, hitch and roof, gold wheels, dark brown horses. Logo: brown "Staffordshire/Agricultural Society/COUNTY SHOW/MAY 22nd & 23rd/1985" and knotted rope-cow's head design. Base A.
1. As above.

11-TEX-LP   TEXAS SESQUICENTENNIAL   1986
White body, blue chassis and hitch, red roof, gunmetal wheels, black horses. Logo: blue "TEXAS SESQUICENTENNIAL" and map of texas with white star and "LONGVIEW", red "1836" and "1986", red-white-blue Texas and American flags. Base C. Certificate.
1. As above.

11-TUR-DG   TURNBULL & CO.   011-001 1984
White body, red chassis and hitch, green roof, gold wheels, tan horses. Logo: green "FURNITURE REMOVERS", red lines and stripe with gold "TURNBULL & CO",

green "CHURCH LANE/PRITTLEWELL, ESSEX" and number 11. Base A.
1. As above.

11-WIL-DG   WILLIAMS GRIFFIN   011-005 1985
Dark green body, red chassis and hitch, tan roof, gold wheels, black horses. Logo: gold griffin, gold-outlined "WILLIAMS GRIFFIN", yellow "DEPARTMENT STORE/HIGH STREET COLCHESTER/FAMILY BUSINESS/ESTABLISHED 1884" and telephone number. Base A.
1. As above.

012   FIRE ENGINE   82mm/100mm 1984
Metal body and chassis, plastic grille, windshield, ladders, floor, base and solid plastic wheels. Some models have one-piece plastic ladder; others have wheeled escape ladder. Casting variations include the usual thick or thin front fenders as well as. Front suspension: original or thickened at base of grille. Ladder rack atop windshield: with or without tongue. Seats: with or without mounting pins and holes for figures. Base types:
A. DG10-DG12 without ridge.
B. DG10-DG12 with ridge.
C. Lledo Promotional Model.
D. "MADE IN ENGLAND/by Lledo" only.

12-AUX-DG   AUXILIARY FIRE SERVICE   012-006? 1987
Dark green body and chassis, black floor, gold grille and windshield, cream escape ladder with gunmetal wheels, 6-bolt green wheels, light gray tires. Logo: white shield, "AUXILIARY FIRE SERVICE" and frame. Thick front end, no ladder tab, no pins or holes. DG10-DG12 base with ridge.
1. As above.

12-BER-DG   BERMUDA FIRE DEPT.   012-003 1985
Dark blue body, cream chassis, cream or white floor, cream ladder, gold grille and windshield, 6-bolt red wheels, black tires. Logo: gold "BERMUDA FIRE/DEPT" and frame on sides, "B.F.D." on hood. DG10-12 base with or without ridge, no ladder tab.
1. Cream floor, no ridge on base, original front end.
2. Cream floor, ridged base, original front end.
3. White floor, ridged base, thick front end, no holes or pegs for figures.

12-BGD-LP   BOROUGH GREEN & DISTRICT   1986
Red body, white chassis, black floor, light brown ladder, gold grille and windshield, , 6-bolt red wheels, black tires. Logo: gold "BOROUGH GREEN & DISTRICT/FIRE BRIGADE" and frame. Original front end, holes and pegs for figures, no ladder tab. LP base with ridge.
1. As above.

12-BOS-FS   BOSTON FIRE DEPT.   1985
Red body and chassis, cream floor and ladder, gold grille and windshield, 6-bolt red wheels, white tires. Logo: gold "BOSTON FIRE/DEPT" and frame on sides, "B.F.D." on hood. "MADE IN ENGLAND/by Lledo" base: Fantastic Set o' Wheels. Holes and pegs for figures, no ladder tab.
1. As above.

12-CAR-DG   CARDIFF CITY FIRE SERVICE   012-002 1985
Red body, white chassis, black floor, light brown ladder, gold grille and windshield, 6-bolt red wheels, black tires. Logo: yellow "CARDIFF CITY/FIRE SERVICE 6" on sides, "C.C.F.S." on hood. Holes and pegs for figures, no ladder tab. DG10-DG12 base without ridge.
1. As above.

12-CHE-DG/LP   CHELMSFORD TOWN FIRE BRIGADE 012-005 1986
Red body, black or red chassis, black floor, light brown escape ladder with gold wheels, gold or silver grille and windshield, green 6-bolt or black disc wheels, black tires. Logo: gold "CHELMSFORD TOWN/FIRE BRIGADE" and frame, red-white-blue shield. Thick front end, no holes or pegs for figures, no ladder tab. DG10-DG12 or LP base with ridge.
1. Red fenders, black disc wheels, gold grille and windshield, LP base.
2. Black fenders, green 6-bolt wheels, gold grille and windshield, DG base.
3. Black fenders, green 6-bolt wheels, silver grille and windshield, DG base.
4. Black fenders, green 6-bolt wheels, silver grille and windshield, DG base.

5. Black fenders, green 6-bolt wheels, gold grille, silver windshield, DG base.
6. Black fenders, green? disc wheels, other details?
7. LP base on DG issue?

12-ESS-DG   ESSEX COUNTY FIRE BRIGADE   012-007 1987
Red body, white chassis, off-white floor, dark cream escape ladder with gold wheels, gold grille and windshield, 6-bolt red wheels, black tires. Logo: gold "ESSEX COUNTY/FIRE BRIGADE" and shield. Thick front end with two holes and wide slot, no ladder tab or pegs for figures, white DG10-DG12 base with ridge.
1. As above.

12-GRY-SP   GRAY   date?
Gray body and chassis, white floor, brown ladder, gold grille and windshield, 6-bolt wheels, white tires. No logo. Ridged DG base. Original front end. Specimen.
1. As above.

12-GUI-LP   GUILDFORD FIRE BRIGADE   1986
Dark green body, chassis, floor, ladder and 6-bolt wheels, gold grille and windshield, black tires. Logo: gold "No. 7", "GUILDFORD/FIRE BRIGADE", shield and frames. Original front end, holes and pegs for figures, no ladder tab. Green LP base with ridge.
1. As above.

12-GWR-LP   G.W.R. FIRE BRIGADE   1985
Dark brown body, cream chassis, floor and ladder, gold grille and windshield, 6-bolt brown wheels, black tires. Logo: gold "No. 6", "G.W.R./FIRE BRIGADE", emblem and frames. Original front end, holes and pegs for figures, no ladder tab. Cream LP base with ridge. Special box.
1. As above.

12-LON-DG/LP   LONDON FIRE BRIGADE   012-004 1986
Red body, black chasasis and floor, cream escape ladder with light brown, black, gunmetal or gold wheels, gold or silver grille and windshield, red or green wheels, black tires. Logo number 52, "L.C.C. "LONDON FIRE BRIGADE" and frames, red-white-blue shield. Thick front end, no holes or pegs for figures, no ladder tab. DG10-DG12 or LP base with ridge.
1. Cream ladder, gold ladder wheels, silver grille, LP base.
2. Cream ladder, light brown ladder wheels, DG base.
3. Gloss black ladder wheels, DG base.
4. Gunmetal ladder wheels, DG base.
5. 6-bolt green wheels, DG base.
6. Red (or green?) disc wheels, DG base.
7. Brown ladder, DG base.
8. Gold grille and windshield, DG base.
9. Gold grille, silver windshield, DG base.
10. LP base on DG issue?
Individual features are listed above because nobody knows exactly how many of the possible combinations of them exist.

12-LUC-DG   LUCKHURST COUNTY   012-001 1984
Red body, dark green chassis, black floor, cream ladder, gold grille and windshield, 6-bolt red or green wheels, black tires. Logo: yellow or white "LUCKHURST/COUNTY" and frame on sides, "L.C.F.B." on hood. DG10-DG12 base.
1. Ladder tab, no ridge on base, original front end, holes and pegs for figures, red wheels.
2. No ladder tab, no ridge on base, original front end, holes and pegs for figures, red wheels.
3. No ladder tab, ridged base, original front end, holes and pegs for figures, red wheels.
4. No ladder tab, ridged base, original front end, no figure holes or pegs, red wheels.
5. No ladder tab, ridged base, thick front end, no figure holes or pegs, green wheels: Tesco issue.
6. White logo, other details unknown?

12-MIL-LP   MILTON VOLUNTEER BRIGADE   1986
Red body, white chassis, black floor, light brown ladder, gold grille and windshield, 6-bolt red wheels, black tires. Logo: gold "MILTON VOLUNTEER BRIGADE/

BRISBANE" and frame. Original front end, holes and pegs for figures, no ladder tab. LP base with ridge.
1. As above.

12-NAT-LP   NATIONAL FIRE SERVICE   1986
Light gray body, floor and ladder, white chassis, gold grille and windshield, 6-bolt light gray wheels, black tires. Logo: white NFS emblems, "NATIONAL/FIRE SERVICE" and frames. Original front end, holes and pegs for figures, no ladder tab. Light gray LP base with ridge.
1. As above.

12-RED-EC   RED   1986
Red body and chassis, white floor, gold grille and windshield,, cream ladder, red 6-bolt wheels, black tires. No logo. Thick front end with holes, no holes or pegs for figures, no ladder tab. Edocar base.
1. As above.

12-SUR-LP   SURREY FIRE BRIGADE   1985
Red body, black chassis and floor, white ladder, gold grille and windshield, 6-bolt red wheels, black tires. Logo: gold "SURREY/FIRE BRIGADE", number 1 and frame. Original front end, holes and pegs for figures, no ladder tab. LP or DG base with ridge. Certificate.
1. LP base.
2. DG base.

12-WAL-LP   JAMES WALKER & CO.   1986
Plum body, black chassis and floor, light brown ladder, gold grille and windshield, 6-bolt black wheels, black tires. Logo: gold emblem and "JAMES WALKER & CO./WOKING SURREY". Original front end, holes and pegs for figures, no ladder tab. LP base with ridge.
1. As above.

12-WAR-LP   WARRINGTON   1987
Red body and chassis, black floor, gold grille and windshield with no tab, dark cream ladder with gold wheels, 6-bolt red wheels, black tires. Logo: gold "WARRINGTON FIRE BRIGADE" and frame. Thick front end with two holes and wide slot. No figure pegs or holes. White LP base. Special Persil box; one of four Persil models.
1. As above.

12-WIN-DG   WINDSOR FIRE BRIGADE   012-   1987
Red body and chassis, black floor, gold grille and windshield with no tab, dark cream ladder with gold wheels, 6-bolt black wheels, black tires. Logo: gold "WINDSOR FIRE BRIGADE" and lines. Thick front end with two holes and wide slot. No figure pegs or holes. DG base. Special box, part of Ruby Wedding set.
1. As above.

013   MODEL A FORD VAN   77mm   1984
Metal body and chassis; plastic roof, roof blade if any, grille and base; 12-spoke metal or 20-spoke plastic wheels. Roofs with blades have transverse ridges, those without have longitudinal ridges. This is the only casting change, and the type of roof can be inferred from the presence or absence of a roof blade. Base types:
A. DG7-DG9. No model with this base has a roof blade.
B. DG7-DG9, plus DG13 on front and DG14 on rear axle cover.
C. DG7-9-13-14.
D. Lledo Promotional.
E. Made in England/by Lledo: Fantastic Set o' Wheels.

13-AIM-LP   A.I.M./HAROLD'S PLACE   1985
Dark red body, black chassis, tan roof and blade, gold grille, 12-spoke gunmetal wheels, white tires. Logo: gold AIM club emblem and "1970-1985". Blade: black "HAROLD'S PLACE, INC." LP base. Certificate.
1. As above.

13-ANL-LP   ADVERTISER NORTH LONDON GROUP   1987
White body, jade green chassis, roof and blade, gold grille, 12-spoke gold wheels, black tires. Logo: jade green emblem and "NORTH LONDON GROUP", black "First for/News", "Best for/Ads and telephone number. Blade: black "Delhome", green "Distribution" on black stripe. LP base. Special box.
1. As above.

13-BAG-LP   BAGEL WORLD   1986
Salmon body, brown chassis and roof, gold grille, 12-spoke gold wheels, white tires. Logo: brown "BAGEL WORLD", emblem, phone numbers, address and "F.D.M." LP base.
1. As above.

13-BAS-DG   BASILDON BOND   013-007   1985
White body, dark blue chassis, blue roof and blade, gold grille, 12-spoke gold wheels, black tires. Logo: gold "Basildon Bond" on gold-rimmed blue panel, blue and black "DRG/STATIONERY" and lines on door, black frames. Blade: gold "BRITAIN'S MOST POPULAR/WRITING PAPER". Base B: DG13 and DG14 on axle covers.
1. Pale matt finish, gold grille.
2. Darker gloss finish, gold grille
3. Silver grille..

13-BBC-LP   BBC 1936-1986/RADIO TIMES   1986
Dark green body, black chassis, roof and blade, gold grille, 20-spoke green wheels, black tires. Logo: gold "BBC" in circle, "1936 1986/FIFTY YEARS OF TELEVISION". Blade: white "RADIO TIMES 2d/EVERY FRIDAY". LP base. Special box, certificate.
1. As above.

13-BEA-LP   BEAVER LUMBER   1986
Dark yellow body, chassis, roof and blade, gold grille, 12-spoke gold wheels, black tires. Logo: green and yellow "Beaver Lumber" on green panel. Blade: black "Your Lumber One Store". LP base.
1. As above.

13-BIL-LP   BILL SWITCHGEAR   1986
Cream body, black chassis and roof, gold grille, 12-spoke gold wheels, black tires. Logo: white "BILL" and red circle on black shield held by two dark red and black figures, black-rimmed dark red ribbon with black "YOU CANNOT BUY BETTER GEAR", black "1906-1986". LP base.
1. As above.

13-BEP-LP   BRISTOL EVENING POST   1987
Dark yellow body, black chassis, roof and blade, gold grille, 12-spoke gold wheels, black tires. Logo: black "BRISTOL/EVENING/POST", other lettering and frame, plus "BRISTOL/EVENING/POST" on rear doors. Blade: yellow "LATEST NEWS". LP base.
1. As above.

13-BUC-LP   BUCKTROUT & COMPANY   1985
Dark blue body, black chassis, roof and blade, gold grille, 12-spoke gold wheels, black tires. Logo: black-outlined gold "BUCKTROUT & COMPANY LIMITED", gold lettering, yellow and black town design in oval, black-white-gold coat of arms and gold number 4. LP base. Certificate.
1. As above.

13-CAB-LP   CADBURY'S CHOCOLATE—BOURNVILLE   1986?
Purple body and roof, brown chassis, gold grille, 20-spoke cream wheels, black tires. Logo: brown-outlined tan "Cadbury's" and brown " Chocolate" on red panel, red "BOURNVILLE", tan "Cadbury's". LP base.
1. As above.

13-CAD-LP   CADBURY'S HERITAGE   1986
No data.
1. As above.

13-CAM-DG   CAMP COFFEE   013-016   1986
Dark cream body, black chassis, brown roof, gold grille, 20-spoke cream wheels, black tires. Logo: blue "CAMP" and "ESTd. 1885", brown "COFFEE" and trim, red-blue-brown-cream emblem with brown "R. Paterson & Sons Ltd." and cream "Glasgow". DG7-9-13-14 base.
1. As above.

13-CAR-LP   CARR'S PET STORES   1986
Cream body, bright green chassis, dull green roof, silver grille, 20-spoke cream wheels, black tires. Logo: black-outlined green "CARR'S/PET STORES", black "Broadway Market/LONDON E.8/EST. 1947" in green frame on adhesive label. LP base.
1. As above.

Certificate.
1. As above.

13-CHA-LP   CHARCOAL STEAK HOUSE   1986
Cream body, brown chassis and roof, gold grille, 12-spoke gold wheels, white tires. Logo: maroon "Charcoal/STEAK HOUSE", address, telephone number and steer figure. LP base. Certificate.
1. As above.

13-CHE-LP   CHERRY CIGARETTES   1986
Dark cream body, blue chassis, red roof, gold grille, 20-spoke red wheels, white tires. Logo: black and white "CHERRY", black "CIGARETTES" and Japanese lettering in oval, black-white-cream flower design. LP base.
1. As above.

13-CHI-LP   CHICHESTER OBSERVER CENTENARY   1987
Powder blue body, chassis, roof and blade, silver grille, 20-spoke powder blue wheels, white tires. Logo: red and yellow emblem with yellow "Chichester Observer/ Centenary". Blade: yellow "1887-1987" and frame. Adhesive labels. LP base.
1. As above.

13-CHM-LP   ETS. COMM. HOLL. MAROCAIN   1987
Cream body, blue chassis, dark yellow roof, gold grille, 20-spoke cream wheels, black tires. Logo: red "ETS. COMM. HOLL. MAROCAIN", address, telephone number and red and gold Moroccan flag on left side, red Arabic lettering and red and gold Moroccan flag on right. LP base.
1. As above.

13-CHS-VV   CHESTER   1987
Dark brown body, roof and blade, black chassis, gold grille, 12-spoke gold wheels, black tires. Logo: picture of buildings, archway and clock, gold camera and frames. Blade: gold "CHESTER". View Vans box. LP base.
1. As above.

13-CHU-LP   CHUBB LIFE AMERICA   1986
White body, blue chassis, roof and blade, gold grille, 12-spoke gold wheels, white tires. Logo: blue emblem and "CHUBB/LIFE AMERICA/Frederic K. Clausen/Reginal Group Sales Manager", address, telephone number and frame. Blade: white "GROUP INSURANCE". LP base.
1. As above.

13-CLO-LP   CLOWNS CONVENTION   1986
Light tan body, black chassis, roof and blade, gold grille, 20-spoke cream wheels, black tires. Logo: black-outlined red "Clowns", black "CONVENTION", red-black-cream design. Blade: yellow "2nd International Clowns Convention/Bognor Regis, April 11th-to-13th 1986". LP base.
1. As above.

13-COA-DG   COCA-COLA   013-006   1984
Yellow-orange body, black chassis and roof, silver grille, 12-spoke gold wheels, black tires. Logo: red "Coca-Cola/"AT SODA FOUNTAINS". DG7-DG9 base with DG13 and DG14 on axle covers.
1. As above.

13-COB-DG   COCA-COLA   013-010   1985
Yellow-orange body, chassis, roof and blade, gold or silver grille, 20-spoke red wheels, white tires. Logo: red "DRINK/Coca-Cola/IN BOTTLES", red-white brown bottle, brown frame and red "The/Coca-Cola/Bottling Co." Blade: black "EVERY BOTTLE STERILIZED".
1. DG7-DG9 base with DG13 and DG14 on axle covers, gold grille.
2. Same base as type 1, silver grille.
3. DG7-9-13-14 base, gold grille.

13-COC-DG   COCA-COLA   013-020   1986
Yellow-orange body, roof and blade, black or yellow-orange chassis, silver grille, 20-spoke yellow wheels, white tires. Logo: white "DRINK/Coca-Cola/IN BOTTLES" and brown and white hand holding bottle on red panel with white border, brown "ADVERTISING/CAR, red "Coca-Cola" and brown "BOTTLING CO." Blade: brown "Join the seven million". DG7-9-13-14 base. Special box.
1. Black chassis.
2. Yellow chassis.

13-COD-LP   COCA-COLA   1987
Red body, black chassis and roof, silver grille, 20-spoke cream wheels, black tires.
Logo: white "DRINK/Coca-Cola/registered trade mark" and stripe on red adhesive label. LP base.
1. As above.

13-CPG-LP   TIMEX CPGA CHAMPIONSHIP   1986
White body, blue chassis and roof, gold grille, 12-spoke gold wheels, white tires. Logo: red design and black "TIMEX/CPGA/CHAMPIONSHIP/Sept. 10-14, 1986". LP base.
1. As above.

13-DUN-VV   DUNSTER   1987
Cream body, black chassis, brown roof and blade, gold grille, cream 20-spoke wheels, black tires. Logo: picture of Dunster Yarn Market, gold camera and frames. Blade: gold "DUNSTER". View Vans box. LP base.
1. As above.

13-EDI-VV   EDINBURGH   1987
Cream body, black chassis, brown roof and blade, gold grille, 20-spoke cream plastic wheels, black tires. Logo: picture of Edinburgh Castle, gold camera and frames. Blade: gold "EDINBURGH". View Vans box. LP base.
1. As above.

13-ELP-LP   EL PASO, TEXAS/SUN BOWL   1985
Light blue body, black chassis and roof, silver grille, 12-spoke gold wheels, black tires. Logo: blue "December 28/1985/EL PASO/TEXAS", gold and blue "SUN/BOWL" emblem, blue "52nd/Annual", gold frames. LP base. Certificate.
1. As above.

13-EVA-LP   EVENING ARGUS   1987
Green body, black chassis, roof and blade, gold grille, green 20-spoke wheels, black tires. Logo: gold "Evening/Argus" on black panel, black and white newspaper design. Blade: white "INCORPORATING/SUSSEX DAILY NEWS". LP base.
1. As above.

13-EVG-LP   EVENING GAZETTE   1986
Yellow body, black chassis and roof, silver grille, 20-spoke yellow wheels, black tires. Logo: black "EVENING/GAZETTE/VICTORIA St. BLACKPOOL", telephone number, frame and "EST./1873" on yellow adhesive labels. LP base.
1. As above.

13-EVN-DG   EVENING NEWS   013-001 1984
Yellow-orange body, black chassis, roof and blade, silver grille, 12-spoke gold wheels, black tires. Logo: red "EVENING NEWS", red shield with white "6:30", black and white newspaper rack design and black telephone number. Blade: "FIRST WITH/THE NEWS".
1. DG7-DG9 base.
2. DG7-DG9 plus DG13 and DG14 on axle covers.

13-EVS-DG/LP   EVENING SENTINEL   013-013 1985-1986
Navy blue body, black chassis, roof and (on LP) blade, silver grille, 20-spoke cream wheels, black tires. Logo: gold "EVENING/SENTINEL", blue and white newspaper rack design. Blade of LP issue: gold "FESTIVAL YEAR".
1. DG7-9-13-14 base: 1985 DG issue.
2. LP base, roof blade: 1986 LP issue.

13-EWC-LP   ERNIE WHITT CHARITY CLASSIC   1986
White body, blue chassis and roof, gold grille, 12-spoke gold wheels, white tires. Logo: blue design, "Ernie Whitt/Charity Classic/August/18th/1986", autograph and frame. LP base.
1. As above.

13-EXC-LP   EXCHANGE & MART   1986
White body, black chassis, roof and blade, silver grille, 20-spoke red wheels, black tires. Logo: white-outlined "The/EXCHANGE/& MART" on red panel, black and red lettering, black frame. Blade: white circles with "4d", "Every Thursday". LP base. Special box.
1. As above.

13-EXS-LP   EXPRESS & STAR   1986
Red body, black chassis, white roof, silver grille, 20-spoke black wheels, black tires. Logo: gold "EXPRESS & STAR". LP base. Certificate.
1. As above.

13-FAH-LP   FARNHAM MALTINGS   1985
No data.
1. As above.

13-FAM-LP   FARNHAM MALTINGS   1986
Dark green body, red chassis, roof and blade, gold grille, 12-spoke gold wheels, white tires. Logo: gold "FARNHAM/MALTINGS" and emblem, light green "SWAPMEET" and background, dark green "F/M" on light green panels, plus light green "21st SEPTEMBER 1986" across rear doors. Blade: green lines and "THE BEST IN THE SOUTH". LP base.
1. As above.

13-FAR-LP   FARNHAM MALTINGS   1987
Red body, black chassis and roof. No other data.
1. As above.

13-FDB-DG   F. D. B.   013-021 1986
Gray body, black chassis and roof, gold or silver grille, 12-spoke black wheels, black tires. Logo: blue dragon and "F.D.B." DG7-9-13-14 base.
1. Light bluish gray body, gold grille.
2. Light bluish gray body, silver grille.
3. Darker greenish gray body, gold grille.

13-FES-DG   FESTIVAL GARDENS   1985
Cream body, brown chassis and roof, gold grille, 20-spoke cream wheels, black tires. Logo: green-outlined cream "FESTIVAL", green "GARDENS/LIVERPOOL", black "MAY 23rd—SEPTEMBER 8th 1985". DG7-9-13-14 base.
1. As above.

13-FIN-LP   FINDLATER MACKIE TODD   1986
Dark green body, black chassis and roof, silver grille, 20-spoke cream wheels, black tires. Logo: gold coat of arms and "FINDLATER/MACKIE TODD/& CO. LTD." on green adhesive label. LP base.

13-FOT-LP   FOTORAMA   1985
White or silver body, red chassis, roof and (on silver version) blade, gold grille, 12-spoke gold or 20-spoke red wheels, black tires. Logo: red-blue or red-yellow-blue "FOTORAMA", blue "A World of Colour" and frames, and (on silver version) red F monogram. Blade (of silver version): blue "COLOUR PRINT FILM". DG or LP base.
1. White body, red and blue logo, no blade, gold wheels, LP base.
2. DG base, otherwise as type 1.
3. Silver body, three-color logo, roof blade, monogram, red wheels, LP base.

13-GER-LP   MICHAEL GERSON 25 YEARS   1986.
Silver body, dark green or black chassis and roof, silver grille, 20-spoke green or black disc wheels, black tires. Logo: green or black "MICHAEL GERSON/25/YEARS", wreath, "OVERSEAS REMOVALS" and "OCTOBER/1961/OCTOBER/1986". LP base. Special box, certificate.
1. Green chassis, roof, wheels and logo.
2. Black chassis, roof, wheels and logo.

13-GET-VV   GETTYSBURG/P.M.C.C.   1987
Cream body, brown chassis, roof and blade, 20-spoke cream wheels. Blade: "P.M.C.C. 1987". LP base. View Vans box. No other data.
1. As above.

13-GRY-SP   GRAY   1986?
Light gray body and chassis, white or other color roof, silver grille, 20-spoke cream wheels, black tires. No logo. DG7-9-13-14 base. Factory specimen.
1. White roof.
2. ? roof.

13-GUE-VV   GUERNSEY   1987
Brown body and roof, black chassis, gold grille, 12-spoke gold wheels, black tires. Logo: Picture of harbor, gold camera and frames. LP base. View Vans box.

13-HAM-DG   HAMLEYS   1984
Yellow-orange body, chassis and roof, silver grille, 12-spoke gold wheels, black tires. Logo: white "HAMLEYS" and underline, "of/Regent Street, London" on red panel, black frames. In special box or gift set.
1. DG7-DG9, plus DG13 and DG14 on axle covers; sold singly.
2. DG7-9-13-14 base; in gift set.

13-HAP-LP   HAROLD'S PLACE, INC.   1985
Green body, red chassis, roof and blade, silver grille, 20-spoke yellow wheels, black tires. Logo: white-outlined red "HAROLD'S/PLACE, INC.", yellow address and "FEATURING LLEDO MODELS", red-white-yellow Christmas design. Blade: white "MERRY", snowman figure and "CHRISTMAS". LP base.
1. As above.

13-HAR-LP   HARROW 18 PLUS   1985
Cream body, green chassis, roof and blade, gold grille, 20-spoke cream wheels, black tires. Logo: green "HARROW/18 PLUS", design and frame on dark cream adhesive label. No logo on blade. LP base.

13-HER-DG   HERSHEY'S KISSES   013-018 1986
Brown body, dark cream chassis and roof, gold grille, 20-spoke brown wheels, white tires. Logo: White "HERSHEY'S/Kisses", candy design, line and "MILK/CHOCOLATE/COCOA". DG7-9-13-14 base. Special box.

13-HES-DG   HERSHEY'S MILK CHOCOLATE   013-019 1986
Light cream body, brown chassis, roof and blade, gold grille, 12-spoke gold wheels, white tires. Logo: cream "HERSHEY'S" on brown background, brown "MILK CHOCOLATE" on cream panel, brown designs, red frames. Blade: white "SWEETS AND TREATS". DG7-9-13-14 base. Special box.
1. Chocolate brown chassis, gold grille.
2. Purplish brown chassis, gold grille, lighter brown logo background.
3. Silver grille, otherwise as type 2.

13-HEW-LP   HEWITT FORD   1987
White body, blue chassis and roof, no other data.
1. Hewitt of Chippenham.
2. Hewitt of Weymouth.

13-HGR-LP   H & G RESTAURANT   1987
Black body, chassis, roof and blade, gold grille, 12-spoke gold wheels, white tires. Logo: red-outlined gold "H & G", white "Restaurant/RT. 50/Easton/MD" and "Pies/&/Rolls", red-white-black chef figure, gold frames. Blade: white "40th ANNIVERSARY". LP base.
1. As above.

13-HOL-LP   HOLME VALLEY EXPRESS   1987
Blue body, black chassis, yellow roof and blade, gold grille, 12-spoke gold wheels, black tires. Logo: white-outlined gold "Holme Valley Express", gold address and "Estab./1886", gold and white trim and frames. Blade: black "The Voice of the Valley". LP base. Certificate.
1. As above.

13-HOR-LP   HORNBY'S DAIRIES   1986
Red body, black chassis, white roof, silver grille, 20-spoke red wheels, black tires. Logo: black-outlined white "HORNBY'S DAIRIES/BRISTOL'S SAFEST MILK", two red-white-black triangle emblems, black frames. LP base.
1. As above.

13-HPS-DG   H. P. SAUCE   013-023 1987
Magenta body and chassis, white roof and blade, gold grille, 20-spoke dark blue wheels, gold grille. Logo: white "THE ONE & ONLY/H.P./SAUCE" and stripes, dark blue panel. Blade: white "H.P." on blue background. DG7-9-13-14 base.

13-HRA-LP   HARRY RAMSDEN'S FISH & CHIPS   1987
Cream body, blue chassis and roof, gold grille, 20-spoke gold wheels, black tires. Logo: red and black fish, red "Harry Ramsden's" and stripe, black "the most famous Fish &

Lledo™ Models

Chip Store in the world" and "12 MPH". LP base.
1. As above.

13-ILL-LP 5th ILLINOIS PLASTIC KIT & TOY SHOW   1985
Black body, chassis and roof, gold grille, 12-spoke gold wheels, white tires. Logo: gold car design, "5th Illinois Plastic Kit & Toy Show Sept. 22,/1985", "Die Cast/Toys" and frame. LP base.
1. As above.

13-IOM-LP ISLE OF MAN TT   1986
Light blue body, black chassis, gray roof, gold grille, 12-spoke gold wheels, black tires. Logo: blue and silver "ISLE OF MAN/TT 86", emblem and blue "26 MAY—6 JUNE" on light blue adhesive label. LP base. Certificate.
1. As above.

13-IOW-VV ISLE OF WIGHT   1987
Brown body, roof and blade, black chassis, gold grille, 12-spoke gold wheels, black tires. Logo: picture, gold camera and frames. Blade: gold "ISLE OF WIGHT". LP base. View Vans box.
1. Picture of houses with tower behind them.
2. Picture of street scene with pedestrians.

13-JEL-LP JELLY BEANS TV SHOW   1986
White body, red chassis and roof, gold grille, 12-spoke gold wheels, white tires. Logo: red music with "JELLY BEANS TV SHOW", man, guitar, girl and boy design, "JELLY BEANS/TV SHOW/with your host/DANNY COUGHLAN" and autograph. LP base.
1. As above.

13-JEP-DG JERSEY EVENING POST   013-005 1985
White body, black chassis, pink roof and blade, gold grille, 12-spoke gold wheels, black tires. Logo: black "Jersey/Evening Post" and address, pink stripe. Blade: black "REPORTING ISLAND LIFE". DG7-9 plus DG13 and DG14 on axle covers.
1. As above.

13-JER-VV JERSEY   1987
Brown body, roof and blade, black chassis, gold grille, 12-spoke gold wheels, black tires. Logo: picture and gold camera and frames. Blade: gold "JERSEY". View Vans box. LP base.
1. Picture of castle, town and harbor.
2. Picture of rocky seacoast.

13-JOL-FS JOLLY TIME ICE CREAM   1985
Cream body, pink chassis, roof and blade, silver grille, 20-spoke red wheels, white tires. Logo: red-outlined orange "JOLLY TIME", brown "ICE CREAM", list and "42 VARIETIES", brown and cream popsicle on orange disc in cream and red circles, red music. Blade: red music and "TREAT/TIME". "MADE IN ENGLAND/by Lledo" base: Fantastic Set o' Wheels.

13-KAL-LP KALAMAZOO LOOSE LEAF BOOKS   1986
Black body, chassis and roof, gold grille, 12-spoke gold wheels, black tires. Logo: gold "Loose Leaf/Kalamazoo/Books" and address. LP base.
1. As above.

13-KEL-LP KELLOGG'S CORN FLAKES   1987
White body, red chassis and roof, silver grille, 12-spoke gold wheels, black tires. Logo: Red-yellow-black-white cereal box design, black "KELLOGG TOASTED CORN FLAKE CO." and other lettering, red signature. LP base.
1. As above.

13-KEM-LP THE KENTISH MERCURY   1987
Yellow body, black chassis, roof and blade, silver grille, 20-spoke black wheels, black tires. Logo: black "The Kentish Mercury" and "Est./1833", red frame and lines.
1. As above.

13-KIT-LP KITCHENER COIN MACHINE CO.   1986
Blue body, red chassis, roof and blade, gold grille, 12-spoke gold wheels, white tires. Logo: white-outlined "kitchener/coin/machine/co. ltd.". white address. Blade: white "service" and telephone number. LP base.
1. As above.

13-KLM-LP KLM PARTY AND CATERING SERVICE   1987
Light blue body, blue chassis, white roof, silver grille, 20-spoke blue wheels, white tires. Logo: white "Party/and/Catering/Service". In special 3-model box. LP base.
1. As above.

13-KUN-LP KUNTZ ELECTROPLATING   1986
Dark blue body, black chassis and roof, silver grille, 20-spoke blue wheels, white tires. Logo: silver "Kuntz/ELECTROPLATING INC.", address and Telex number. LP base. Certificate.
1. As above.

13-LEI-LP LEICESTER MERCURY   1985
Dark blue body, black chassis, white roof, silver grille, 12-spoke gold wheels, black tires. Logo: white "Leicester/Mercury/Largest Circulation". LP base.
1. As above.

13-LIE-LP LINCOLNSHIRE ECHO   1985
No data.
1. As above.

13-LIN-VV LINCOLN   1987
Brown body, roof and blade, black chassis, gold grille, 12-spoke gold wheels, black tires. Logo: picture of Lincoln Cathedral, gold camera and frames. Blade: gold "LINCOLN". View Vans box. LP base.

13-LIO-LP LIONEL LINES   1986
Orange body, blue chassis, roof and blade, gold grille, 12-spoke gold wheels, white tires. Logo: blue "LIONEL/LINES", emblem, "SERVICE TRUCK", other lettering and frames, plus "WE/BUY TOY/TRAINS" across rear doors. Logo: gold "Nicholas Smith est./1909." LP base.

13-LIS-LP LINCOLNSHIRE STANDARD   1987
White body, red chassis, 20-spoke red wheels, black tires. No other data.
1. As above.

13-LLA-VV LLANGOLLEN   1987
Brown body and roof, black chassis, gold grille, 12-spoke gold wheels, black tires. Logo: picture of bridge over River Dee, gold camera and frames. Blade: gold "LLANGOLLEN". View Vans box. LP base.

13-LON-VV LONDON   1987
Cream body, black chassis, brown roof, gold grille, 20-spoke cream wheels, black tires. Logo: picture, gold camera and frames. Blade: gold "LONDON". View Vans box. LP base.
1. Picture of Tower Bridge.
2. Picture of Westminster Abbey.

13-MAB-DG MARY ANN BREWERY   013-003 1984
Dark blue body and roof, white chassis, gold grille, 12-spoke gold wheels, black tires. Logo: white "ANN STREET BREWERY CO. LTD. and address, blue and white arms and map of Jersey with black MARY ANN/The beers that make Jersey/famous". DG7-DG8 plus DG13 and DG14 on axle covers.
1. As above.

13-MAN-LP MANCHESTER EVENING NEWS   1985
Yellow body, chassis, roof and blade, silver grille, 20-spoke yellow wheels, black tires. Logo: black "Manchester/Evening News", telephone number and address, on yellow adhesive label. Blade: black "A FRIEND/DROPPING IN!" Certificate.
1. As above.

13-MAR-VV MARGATE   1987
Brown body, roof and blade, black chassis, gold grille, 12-spoke gold wheels, black tires. Logo: picture of beach, gold camera design and frames. Blade: gold "MARGATE". Adhesive labels. LP base. In View Vans box.

13-MER-LP MERCANTILE CREDIT   1986
Dark blue body, chassis and roof, 20-spoke cream wheels, black tires. No other data.
1. As above.

13-MIC-DG MICHELIN   013-008 1985
Yellow body, blue chassis and roof, gold or silver grille, 12-spoke gold or 20-spoke white wheels, black tires. Logo: blue "Michelin" and stripe, black and white tire and man, black frames.
1. Gold grille and wheels, DG7-DG9 plus DG13 and DG14 on axle covers.
2. Gold grille and wheels, DG7-9-13-14 base.
3. Silver grille, gold wheels, DG7-9-13-14 base.
4. White plastic wheels, ? grille, DG7-9-13-14 base.

13-MIT-DG/LP MITRE 10   013-017 1986
Light brown body, chassis and roof, gold grille, 20-spoke white wheels, black tires. Logo: red-white-black figure, black-white-yellow "MITRE 10" emblems, and black "AUSTRALIA'S BIGGEST HARDWARE SPECIALISTS" (DG), or red and yellow stripes and black-white-yellow "MITRE 10" emblems (LP). DG7-9-13-14 or LP base.
1. Logo with figure, DG7-9-13-14 base.
2. Logo without figure, LP base.

13-NEA-LP JAMES NEALE & SONS   1986
Yellow body, blue chassis, white roof, gold grille, 20-spoke yellow wheels, black tires. Logo: black-outlined gold "JAMES NEALE & SONS", black-outlined yellow "LIMITED", black other lettering and frame. LP base.
1. As above.

13-NED-LP NEDERLANDSE LLEDO   1985
Cream body, blue chassis, red roof and blade, 20-spoke white wheels, black tires. Logo: gold and red oval emblem with blue "NEDERLANDSE/Lledo/VERZAMELAARS VERENIGING", blue "Opgericht/13 September/1984". Blade: white "NEDERLANDSE LLEDO/VERZAMELAARS VERENIGING". LP base.
1. As above.

13-NEP-LP NEWS PLUS NEWSAGENT   1986
White body, blue chassis, roof and blade, silver grille, 20-spoke cream wheels, black tires. Logo: blue "NEWS PLUS" and red "NEWSAGENT" on white panel in yellow-red-blue stripes. Blade: "We're More than just newsagents." LP base.
1. As above.

13-NEY-LP NEWEY & EYRE LTD.   1986
Blue body, chassis and roof, gold grille, 20-spoke black wheels, black tires. Logo: white "NEWEY & EYRE LTD.", design and lettering. LP base.
1. As above.

13-NIA-LP NIAGARA FALLS, CANADA   1986
Red or light blue body, black chassis and roof, silver grille, 20-spoke red or black wheels, black or white tires. Logo: black-outlined gold "NIAGARA/FALLS/CANADA", design and "1986", black frames. LP base.
1. Red body and wheels, black tires.
2. Blue body, black wheels, white tires.

13-NOF-LP NORFRAN PRODUCTS   1986
Blue body, chassis and roof, gold grille, 20-spoke black wheels, black tires. Logo: white "Norfran/Products/Ltd" and Viking ship emblem. LP base.
1. As above.

13-NTC-C3 NORTHLAND TOY CLUB   1987
White body, blue chassis and roof, gold grille, 12-spoke gold wheels, white tires. Logo: black emblem, "NORTHLAND/TOY CLUB", frame and "EST/1974". LP base.
1. As above.

13-OHA-LP O'HARA BAR   1986
Dark brown body, gray chassis, roof and blade, gold grille, 12-spoke gold wheels, black tires. Logo: gold "BAR BODEGA COFFEE SHOP/THAI AND DUTCH FOOD", white-outlined red "O'HARA", red and white telephone, white phone number and "PATTAYA/THAILAND", on blue adhesive label. Blade: blue "DE KOFFIE IS KLAAR" on silver adhesive label. LP base.

13-OLT-LP OLD TOYLAND SHOWS   1986
Dark orange body, black chassis, dark brown roof and blade, silver grille, 12-spoke

154

Lledo™ Models

gold wheels, white tires. Logo: black fire truck, show sites, "U.S.A. 1986" and circled number 2. Blade: gold "OLD TOYLAND SHOWS". LP base.
1. As above.

13-ONB-LP ONTARIO BEAVER PELTS 1986
Cream body, brown chassis and roof, gold grille, 12-spoke gold wheels, white tires. Logo: brown beaver, "Ontario/Beaver Pelts" and "F.D.M." LP base.
1. As above.

13-PEA-VV THE PEAKS 1987
Brown body, roof and blade, black chassis, gold grille, 12-spoke gold wheels, black tires. Logo: picture of Peak District scene, gold camera and frames. Blade: gold "THE PEAKS". View Vans box. LP base.
1. As above.

13-PEP-LP PETERBOROUGH PARACHUTE CENTRE 1986
Maroon body, cream chassis, roof and blade, silver grille, 20-spoke dark red wheels, white tires. Logo: white and gold emblem, gold "PETERBOROUGH PARACHUTE CENTRE", white phone number and "Sibson Airfield", on adhesive label. Blade: maroon "LEARN TO SKYDIVE". LP base. Certificate.
1. As above.

13-PLY-VV PLYMOUTH/ROYAL MARINES 1987
Cream body, black chassis, brown roof and blade, gold grille, 20-spoke cream wheels, black tires. Logo: picture of marine officers on left, of Marine Band on right; gold camera and frames. Blade: gold "FLAG OFFICER, PLYMOUTH" on left, "THE BAND OF HER/MAJESTY'S ROYAL MARINES" on right. View Vans box. LP base.
1. As above.

13-POL-LP POLK'S MODEL CRAFT HOBBIES 1985
cream body, black chassis, roof and blade, silver grille, 20-spoke cream wheels, black tires. Logo: blue-white-black design, black "POLK'S Model/Craft HOBBIES Inc.", address and design, blue frame. Blade: white "50 YEARS OF SERVICE/1935-1985". LP base.
1. As above.

13-POT-LP (C3?) POTTER'S WAREHOUSE 1986
Cream body, brown chassis and roof, gold grille, 20-spoke cream wheels, black tires. Logo: brown-outlined "POTTERS", brown "Warehouse/FACTORY SHOPS/STOKE-ON-TRENT". DG7-9-13-14 base.
1. As above.

13-QUA-LP ALFRED QUAIFE & CO. 1987
Black body, chassis and roof, 20-spoke black wheels, black tires. No other data.
1. As above.

13-ROB-DG ROBINSONS SQUASHES 013-015 1986
Cream body and chassis, green roof, gold grille, 20-spoke cream wheels, black tires. Logo: "ROBINSONS/ORIGINAL/HIGH JUICE/SQUASHES and green and black design on cream emblem, white lettering on black ribbon, green and black vertical stripes, black emblem with "ROBINSONS". DG7-9-13-14 base. Also sold as a Tesco model.
1. As above.

13-ROM-DG ROYAL MAIL 013-002 1984
Red body, black chassis and roof, silver grille, 12-spoke gold wheels, black tires. Logo: black "ROYAL MAIL" and round "POST OFFICE" emblem, gold crown, gold "GR" monogram. DG7-DG9 plus DG13 and DG14 on axle covers, or DG7-9-13-14 base. Special box.
1. DG13 and DG14 on axle covers, Royal Mail box.
2. DG7-9-13-14 base, special box, part of Ruby Wedding set: 1987.

13-ROY-DG ROYAL MAIL 350 YEARS 013-014 1985
Red body, black chassis and roof, silver grille, 20-spoke red wheels, black tires. Logo: black "ROYAL MAIL" and gold crown, black-outlined gold "GR" monogram, black frame and round gold "350 YEARS" emblem. DG7-9-13-14 base. Special box.
1. As above.

13-RYD-DG RYDER TRUCK RENTAL 013-022 1986
Yellow-orange body and roof, black chassis, silver grille, 20-spoke cream wheels,

black tires. Logo: black "RYDER" and "TRUCK RENTAL", red-white-black stripes and "RYDER" emblem. DG7-9-13-14 base.
1. As above.

13-STI-VV STIRLING 1987
Cream body, black chassis, brown roof and blade, gold grille, 20-spoke cream wheels, black tires. Logo: picture of Stirling Castle, gold camera and frames. Blade: gold "STIRLING". View Vans box. LP base.
1. As above.

13-STR-DG STROH'S BEER 013-009 1985
Red body, black chassis and roof, silver or gold grille, 12-spoke gold wheels, white tires. Logo: gold and black emblem, "Stroh's" and "Beer", white lettering, line and "EST. 1850", black "NO. 9", gold frames.
1. Silver grille, DG7-DG9 plus DG13 and DG14 on axle covers.
2. Silver grille, DG7-9-13-14 base.
3. Gold grille, DG7-9-13-14 base.

13-SUA-VV STRATFORD-UPON-AVON 1987
Brown or cream body, black chassis, brown roof and blade, gold grille, 12-spoke gold or 20-spoke cream wheels, black tires. Logo: picture, gold camera and frames. Blade: gold "STRATFORD-UPON-AVON". View Vans box. LP base.
1. Brown body, gold wheels, picture of Anne Hathaway's cottage.
2. Cream body and wheels, picture of Shakespeare's birthplace and street.

13-SWA-LP SWAN PENS 1986
Black body, chassis and roof, gold grille, 20-spoke black wheels, black tires. Logo: silver "SWAN PENS" and design. LP base.
1. As above.

13-SWI-LP SWISS CENTRE 1986
Maroon body, black chassis, white roof, silver grille, 20-spoke red wheels, black tires. Logo: white-outlined yellow "SWISS", white "CENTRE", emblem and other lettering, black "RESTAURANTS/& SHOPS" on black-outlined white ribbon, plus similar logo, including telephone number, across rear doors. LP base.
1. As above.

13-TAY-LP TAYLORS OF WOODFORD 1987
White body, black chassis, blue roof, gold grille, 12-spoke gold wheels, black tires. Logo: blue "Taylors of Woodford Ltd./Retail Dealer", address and telephone number, blue and white "Ford" emblem, on adhesive labels. LP base.
1. As above.

13-TEL-LP TELEGRAPH CENTENARY 1986
Red body, black chassis and roof, gold grille, 20-spoke black wheels, black tires. Logo: gold and black emblems with black "Telegraph/1886/Centenary/1986", white and black newspaper designs, black "We have stood the test of time" on black-bordered gold ribbon. LP base.
1. As above.

13-TIM-LP THE TIMES 1986
Yellow body, chassis, roof and blade, silver grille, 20-spoke cream wheels, black tires. Logo: black "First with the News." Blade: black "THE TIMES". LP base.
1. As above.

13-TOC-LP TOWN CRIER 1987
No data.
1. As above.

13-TUC-DG TUCHER BRAU 013-012 1985
Turquoise body, blue chassis, black roof, gold grille, 20-spoke yellow-orange wheels, black tires. Logo: black and gold emblems, gold-outlined black "Tucher", black "BRAU-TRADITION/SEIT 1672", gold and blue frames. DG7-9-13-14 base.
1. As above.

13-TUR-LP TURANO BREAD 1986
Cream body, brown or black chassis and roof, gold grille, 20-spoke brown wheels, white tires. Logo: cream "TURANO", yellow "OLD FASHIONED/FRENCH 7 ITALIAN BREAD" and red-white-black-yellow emblem on brown panel, brown "Classic" and other lettering, brown-outlined cream "TURANO". LP base.
1. Brown chassis and roof.
2. Black chassis and roof: 1987.

13-VEC-LP VECTIS MODELS 1986
Dark green body, red chassis, yellow roof and blade, gold grille, 12-spoke gold wheels, white tires. Logo: gold truck design, "THE ISLAND'S/PREMIER DIECAST/CENTRE", "V/M" monogram and frames, plus gold "COWES, I.O.W." and telephone number across rear doors. Blade: red "VECTIS MODELS" and lines. All are on adhesive labels. LP base.
1. As above.

13-VIM-LP DRINK VIMTO 1985
Plum body, black chassis, black or white roof and blade, silver grille, 20-spoke wheels, black tires. Logo: white "DRINK", yellow-outlined red "VIMTO", white "AND KEEP FIT", yellow "EST./1908". Blade: red or yellow "J. N. Nichols & Co. Ltd." LP base. Certificate.
1. White roof and blade with red lettering.
2. Black roof and blade with yellow lettering.

13-VIW-LP VICTORIA WINE COMPANY 1987
Dark green body, black chassis and roof, silver grille, 20-spoke green wheels, black tires. Logo: red emblem, white "THE VICTORIA/WINE COMPANY/Britain's leading wine merchant", similar emblem and lettering on door, white frames. LP base.
1. As above.

13-WEP-LP WEEKLY POST/MOTOR SHOW 1985
Light yellow body, black chassis, roof and blade, gold grille, 12-spoke gold wheels, black tires. Logo: black-outlined "'85", red "MOTOR/SHOW/St. Clare Holiday Centre/October 31—November 2", red and black lines. Blade: white "Isle of Wight/Weekly Post". Both on adhesive labels. LP base.
1. As above.

13-WIM-VV WINDERMERE 1987
Cream body, black chassis, brown roof and blade, gold grille, 20-spoke cream wheels, black tires. Logo: picture of lake and town, gold camera and frames. Blade: gold "WINDERMERE". View Vans box. LP base.
1. As above.

13-WIN-VV WINDSOR 1987
Brown body, roof and blade, black chassis, gold grille, 12-spoke gold wheels, black tires. Logo: picture of Windsor Castle, gold camera and frames. View Vans box. LP base.
1. As above.

13-WPT-LP WEST POINT TOY SHOW 1985
Cream body, green chassis, roof and blade, gold grille, 20-spoke black wheels, black tires. Logo: black "WEST POINT/TOY SHOW/June 23/1985", black-white-cream "LLEDO USA" journal design, black frame. Blade can have black "HOTEL THAYER" and frame. Both on dark cream adhesive labels. LP base.
1. Hotel Thayer logo on blade.
2. No logo on blade.

13-WYE-VV WYE COLLEGE 1987
Brown body, no other data. View Vans box.
1. As above.

13-YOH-LP YOUNGS OF HAYES 1985
Blue body, chassis, roof and blade, gold grille, 12-spoke gold wheels, black tires. Logo: white "YOUNGS/HAYES/1925-1985", blue and white emblem, black and white newspaper rack. Blade: white "FIRST WITH THE NEWS". Both on adhesive labels. LP base.
1. As above.

13-YOR-VV YORK 1987
Brown body, roof and blade, black chassis, gold grille, 12-spoke gold wheels, black tires. Logo: picture of cathedral, gold camera and frames. Blade: gold "YORK". View Vans box. LP base.
1. As above.

13-ZEA-LP ZEALLEY 1986
Blue body, black chassis and roof, gold grille, 20-spoke blue wheels, white tires. Logo: yellow "ZEALLEY/NEWTON ABBOT 67676", "EST./1836" and frames. LP base.

Lledo™ Models

1. As above.

014 MODEL A FORD CAR (TOP UP)   80mm 1985
Metal body and chassis, plastic top, interior, spare wheel, windshield, grille and base. Metal 12-spoke or plastic solid disc or 20-spoke wheels. Same basic model as 009 with addition of raised top. All issues have spare wheel and body casting modified to take it. Casting differences: Top bar of windshield with or without two pegs to hold roof in place; interior with or without figure holes in seats. Base types:
A. DG7-DG9, plus DG13 and DG14 on axle covers.
B. DG7-9-13-14.
C. Lledo Promotional.
D. "MADE IN ENGLAND/by Lledo": Fantastic Set o' Wheels.

14-ACM-DG ACME OFFICE CLEANING CO.   014-003 1985
Light cream body and chassis, cream top, interior with holes and spare, silver grille and windshield with or without pegs, cream disc wheels, white tires. Logo: black "ACME" on hood and sides, "OFFICE CLEANING CO./17" DG7-9-13-14 base.
1. No pegs on windshield.
2. Two pegs on windshield.

14-BEN-LP HAROLD L. BENNETT STATE FARM INSURANCE   1986
White body, red chassis, cream or black top, interior with or without holes, and spare, gold grille and windshield with pegs, 12-spoke gold wheels, black tires. Logo: red "STATE FARM/INSURANCE" on hood, red and white State Farm emblem and red "HAROLD L. BENNETT/INSURANCE AGENCY INC." on sides. LP base. Certificate.
1. Black top, spare, and interior with holes.
2. Cream top, spare, and interior without holes.

14-COV-LP COVE PHOTOGRAPHIC   1986
No data. (Cave?)
1. As above.

14-GRA-DG GRAND HOTEL   014-004 1986
Dark brown body, yellow or tan chassis, cream top, interior without holes, and spare, gold grille and windshield without or with pegs, red disc wheels, white tires. Logo: Gold "Grand/Hotel", "BRIGHTON/77" and "COURTESY CAR". DG7-9-13-14 base.
1. No pegs on windshield, cream roof, interior and spare, yellow chassis.
2. Two pegs on windshield, otherwise as type 1.
3. Two pegs on windshield, tan textured roof, interior and spare, dark tan chassis.

14-GRY-DG GRAY   year?
Light gray body and chassis, cream top, interior without holes and spare, silver grille and windshield with pegs, 20-spoke cream wheels, black tires. No logo. LP base. Factory specimen.
1. As above.

14-HAM-DG HAMLEYS   014-005 1986
Red body, black chassis, top, interior with or without holes, and spare, gold grille and windshield with pegs, 20-spoke red wheels, black tires. Logo: gold "HAMLEYS" and underline. DG7-9-13-14 base. Special box.
1. Holes in interior.
2. No holes in interior.

14-KLM-LP KLM TRAVEL AGENCIES   1987
Light blue body, blue chassis, white top, interior with holes and spare, silver grille and windshield with pegs, 20-spoke blue wheels, white tires. Logo: white crown and "KLM" on both hood and sides, white "TRAVEL AGENCIES" on sides. Special 3-model box. LP base.

14-MEP-LP METROPOLITAN POLICE   1986
Black body, chassis, top, interior without holes and spare, silver grille and windshield with pegs, 20-spoke black wheels, white tires. Logo: white "METROPOLITAN/POLICE". LP base.

14-POL-FS POLICE   1985
Black body, chassis, top, interior with holes, and spare, silver grille and windshield

without pegs, 12-spoke black wheels, white tires. Logo: white "POLICE" on hood and sides, white "055" on hood, gold and black star badge on sides. "MADE IN ENGLAND/by Lledo" base: Fantastic Set o' Wheels.
1. As above.

14-SDF-DG SAN DIEGO FIRE CHIEF   014-001 1985
Red body, yellow chassis, tan top, interior with or without holes, and spare, gold grille and windshield without or with pegs, 20-spoke red wheels, white tires. Logo: black-outlined gold "SAN DIEGO" on gold-bordered white panel, gold or red "FIRE CHIEF" on white panel, gold and black helmet, black "No. 1/COMPANY" and black and white checkered stripes, plus white "FIRE DEPT."/1" on hood.
1. DG7-DG9 base with DG13 and DG14 on axle covers, gold "FIRE CHIEF", windshield without pegs, interior with holes.
2. Red "FIRE CHIEF", otherwise as type 1.
3. Red "FIRE CHIEF", windshield with pegs, otherwise as type 1.
4. DG7-9-13-14 base, red "FIRE CHIEF", windshield without pegs, interior with holes.
5. Windshield with pegs, otherwise as type 4.
6. Windshield wth pegs, interior presumably without holes, Tesco box, otherwise as type 4.

14-SFS-FS SAN DIEGO FIRE CHIEF   1985
Red body and chassis, black top, interior with holes, and spare, gold grille and windshield without pegs, 12-spoke black wheels, white tires. Logo: black-outlined gold "SAN DIEGO" on white panel, red "FIRE CHIEF" on white panel, black "No. 1/COMPANY" and black-white checkered stripes on sides, plus white "FIRE DEPT./1" on hood. "MADE IN ENGLAND/by Lledo" base. Fantastic Set o' Wheels.
1. As above.

14-STP-DG STATE PENITENTIARY   014-006 1987
Ivory body and chassis, black textured roof, interior without holes, and spare, silver grille and windshield with pegs, 20-spoke black wheels, white tires. Logo: black and red stripes, black "STATE/PENITENTIARY" and red-outlined shield and "R S B". DG7-9-13-14 base.
1. As above.

14-TAX-DG TAXI   014-002 1985
Yellow body and chassis, black top, interior with or without holes, and spare, gold grille and windshield without or with pegs, 20-spoke yellow wheels, black tires. Logo: black "TAXI" on hood and sides, black "57" and "5c/PER MILE", black-white checkered stripe. DG7-9-13-14 base.
1. No windshield pegs.
2. Two windshield pegs.
3. 12-spoke metal wheels?
4. Edocar issue, presumably without interior holes.

14-TXE-EC TAXI   1986
Yellow body and chassis, black top, interior with holes, and spare, silver grille and windshield with pegs, 20-spoke yellow wheels, black tires. Logo: black "TAXI". Edocar box and A3 base.
1. As above.

14-TXI-LP TAXI   1986
Black body, chassis, top, interior without holes, and spare, silver grille and windshield with pegs, 20-spoke black wheels, black tires. Logo: white "TAXI".
1. LP base.
2. DG7-9-13-14 base?

14-WES-LP WESTERN STUDIOS   1987
Cream body, red chassis, white top and interior, gold grille and windshield, 20-spoke red wheels, white tires. Logo: red "Western Studios/film/crew", black camera design and "on/location". LP base. Fuji box.
1. As above.

015 AEC DOUBLE DECKER BUS   86mm 1985
Metal body, chassis, roof and stairs, plastic windows/upper seats, grille and solid 8-bolt single front and dual rear wheels. Casting change: the very first models had roofs

with smooth undersides; all subsequent castings have been ridged. Base lettering on chassis: DG 15, at first on smooth base, since then on a recessed area, or LP, always recessed. This and subsequent models were never sold with figures and have no figure attachment pins or slots. Stair castings have to date always been attached to bodies before painting and are thus the same color as that stated for the body.

15-ADC-LP ADMIRALS' CUP   1985
No data.
1. As above.

15-ADM-LP ADMIRALS' CUP   1987
Green body, chassis and roof, white windows, silver grille, light gray wheels, black tires. Upper logo: black "1987 ADMIRALS' CUP" and lines, blue and white trim. Lower: white "Southern Vectis" and black-white-green emblem. Both on adhesive labels. LP base.

15-ALT-LP ALTON TOWERS   1987
Magenta body, chassis and windows, silver roof, silver grille, magenta wheels, black tires. Upper logo: black-outlined gold "Alton Towers" and black "Europe's Premier/Leisure Park" on white background. Lower logo: gold emblem. LP base.

15-AUB-LP AUSTRALIAN BICENTENARY   1987
Green body, black chassis, cream roof and windows, silver grille, green wheels, black tires. Upper logo: red-white-blue British and Australian flags, blue "AUSTRALIAN BICENTENARY/CELEBRATIONS 1787-1987" on white adhesive label. Lower logo: gold stripe and "SOUTHERN VECTIS". Front and rear: white "RYDE" on black. LP base.
1. As above.

15-AUT-LP AUTOCAR   1987
Dark purple body and chassis, cream roof and windows, silver grille, black 5-star front/6-spoke rear wheels including tires. Logo: cream stripes, gold "Autocar". LP base.
1. As above.

15-AVD-LP AVON DIECAST CLUB   1986
Dark green body and roof, black chassis, cream windows, silver grille, green wheels, black tires. Upper logo: gold "1st AVON DIECAST CLUB SWAPMEET 27-2-86". Lower logo: gold "Bristol". Both on adhesive labels. Front and back white "YATE" on black. LP base.

15-BAE-LP BARCLAYS EALING   1986
Red body and roof, cream chassis and windows, silver grille, light blue wheels, black tires. Upper logo: white "BARCLAYS EALING" and eagle on blue background. Lower logo: white "LONDON TRANSPORT" and underline. LP base.

15-BAL-LP BARCLAYS (LONDON)   1986
Dusty blue body and roof, cream chassis and windows, gold grille, light blue wheels, white tires. Upper logo: blue "BARCLAYS", black eagle and "FOUNDED/1986" on white background. Lower logo: white "WELLINGTON ROAD/ST. JOHN'S WOOD/LONDON". LP base.
1. Eagle faces right.
2. Eagle faces left.

15-BAM-LP BARCLAYS IN MILTON KEYNES   1985
Dark blue body and chassis, dark yellow roof and windows, silver grille, yellow wheels, black tires. Upper logo: white "BARCLAYS in Milton/Keynes". Lower logo: red "Ask Barclays/FIRST!" on yellow background. LP base. Certificate.
1. As above.

15-BAN-LP BANBURY STEAM SOCIETY RALLY   1987
Dark green body and windows, black chassis and roof, dark green wheels, black tires. Upper logo: "21st Anniversary Rally 1987/Bloxham". Lower logo: "Banbury/Steam Society".
1. As above.

15-BAS-LP BARCLAYS SUPER SAVERS   1986

Dusty blue body and roof, cream chassis and windows, gold grille, light blue wheels, black tires. Upper logo: blue "BARCLAYS", black eagle and "FOUNDED/1896" on white background. Lower logo: red "Super Savers", black "CLUB" on white parallelogram. LP base.
1. As above.

15-BEA-LP   BEAMISH   1987
Red body, black chassis, light cream roof, dark cream windows, silver grille, black 5-star front and 6-bolt rear wheels including tires. Upper logo: white-outlined blue "BEAMISH", red trim, gold-white-blue mine cars, blue background. Lower logo: gold "NORTHERN" and underline. LP base. Special box.
1. As above.

15-BIR-LP   BIRD'S   1987
Red body and roof, black chassis, cream windows, gold grille, red wheels, black tires. Upper logo: white-outlined blue bird figures and "BIRD'S" on tan background. Lower logo: yellow "London TRANSPORT" and underline. LP base.
1. As above.

15-BIS-LP   85 B.I.S.-SPLIT   1985
Dark green body and chassis, brown roof, cream windows, silver grille, green wheels, black tires. Upper logo: blue and white emblem, blue "85 B.I.S.-SPLIT" on white background. Lower logo: gold "LONDON TRANSPORT" and underline. Both on adhesive labels. LP base.
1. As above.

15-BMO-LP   BANVIL MILTON ONTARIO   1987
Red body, black chassis, silver roof, cream windows, silver grille, black 5-star front/6-spoke rear wheels including tires. Upper logo: gold "BANVIL MILTON ONTARIO" on black background. Lower logo: gold "GENERAL" and underline. LP base.
1. As above.

15-BRG-LP   BRIGADE AID   1987
Light blue body and roof, blue chassis, orange windows, silver grille, blue wheels, black tires. Upper logo: black "BRIGADE AID", yellow-black-red emblems. Lower logo: red "WATER/MEANS LIFE". LP base. Special box.
1. As above.

15-BRK-LP   BROOKLANDS MOTORCOURSE   1985
Red body, black chassis, cream windows, silver grille, red wheels, black tires. Upper logo: black track maps and "VISIT/BROOKLANDS MOTOR-COURSE" on yellow adhesive label. Lower logo: black-outlined gold "GENERAL". Recessed DG15 base. Certificate.
1. As above.

15-BTM-LP   BOURNEMOUTH TRANSPORT MUSEUM   1986
Dark yellow body, black chassis, brown or cream roof, dark yellow or cream windows, silver grille, maroon wheels. Upper logo: black "Visit" and "Transport Museum", yellow "BOURNEMOUTH" on red or green background with brown stripe. Front and rear white "SQUARE" on black. LP base.
1. Red upper logo background, cream roof and windows.
2. Green upper logo background, brown roof and yellow windows.

15-BTR-LP   BOURNEMOUTH TRANSPORT MUSEUM   1987
Dark blue body and roof, black chassis, light blue windows, silver grille, black wheels and tires. Upper logo: black "Visit" and "Transport Museum", red "BOURNEMOUTH" on cream background with orange stripe. Lower logo: orange stripe and "VERWOOD TRANSPORT". Both on adhesive labels. Front and rear white "VERWOOD" on black. LP base.
1. As above.

15-BTV-LP   VISIT THE TRANSIT MUSEUM IN BOURNEMOUTH   1987
Dark green body, black chassis, cream roof, tan? windows, black wheels and tires. Upper logo: "VISIT THE TRANSPORT MUSEUM IN/BOURNEMOUTH". Lower logo: "HANTS & DORSET".
1. As above.

15-CAS-DG   CASTLEMAINE   015 006   1985
Red body, cream chassis, roof and windows, silver grille, black tires. Upper

logo: red "CASTLEMAINE", black-outlined "XXXX" on yellow background. Lower logo: red "CORPORATION TRANSPORT" on yellow stripe. Smooth or recessed DG15 base.
1. Smooth base.
2. Recessed base.

15-CCC-LP   CATHERINE COOKSON COUNTRY   1987
Dark blue body and chassis, cream roof and windows, silver grille, black wheels and tires. Upper logo: red "Catherine Cookson", cream "COUNTRY" on blue panel, cream background with red frame. Lower logo: white "SOUTH SHIELDS/CORPORATION" and lines. LP base. Special box.

15-CHA-LP   CHASEWATER LIGHT RAILWAY   1985
Navy blue body, black chassis, cream roof and windows, silver grille, red wheels, black tires. Upper logo: cream "CHASEWATER LIGHT RAILWAY/Transport Rally 1985" and vehicles on blue ribbon on cream background. No lower logo. LP base.
1. As above.

15-CHO-LP   CHORLEY GUARDIAN   1986
Red body, black chassis and roof, cream windows, silver grille, red wheels, black tires. Upper logo: gold "Chorley Guardian" and shield on blue background. Lower logo: yellow "RIBBLE" and underline. LP base.
1. As above.

15-CIC-LP   CITY OF COVENTRY   1985
Magenta body and chassis, cream roof and windows, silver grille, magenta wheels, black tires. Upper logo: gold "100 YEARS/OF PUBLIC TRANSPORT IN COVENTRY", trim and frame. Lower logo: gold "CITY OF COVENTRY". Both on adhesive labels. LP base.

15-CIN-DG   CINZANO VERMOUTH   013-005   1985
Red body and roof, black chassis, cream or white windows, silver grille, black wheels, black tires. Upper logo: white "VERMOUTH CINZANO VERMOUTH" on red and blue background. Lower logo: white "LONDON TRANSPORT" and underline. DG15 base, either smooth or recessed.
1. Cream windows, smooth base.
2. White windows, recessed base.

15-CLB-LP   COUNTRY LIFE ENGLISH BUTTER   1987
Red body, black chassis, cream roof and windows, silver grille, red wheels, black tires. Upper logo: green "COUNTRY LIFE ENGLISH BUTTER" on yellow background. Lower logo: yellow "You'll never put a better bit of butter on your knife". LP base.
1. As above.

15-COC-DG   COCA-COLA/CHICAGO TRANSIT   015-002   1985
Red body and roof, black chassis, cream windows, silver grille, red wheels, black tires. Upper logo: brown and white bottles, white "IN BOTTLES" and "DRINK", red "Coca-Cola" on tan background. Lower logo: yellow "CHICAGO TRANSIT" and underline. Smooth DG15 base.

15-COM-DG   COMMONWEALTH GAMES   015-009   1986
Red body and roof, black chassis, cream windows, silver grille, red wheels, black tires. Upper logo: white "British Caledonian Airways" and gold shield on blue background. Lower logo: red-white-blue XIII Commonwealth Games emblem and white lettering. Recessed DG15 base. Special box.

15-COW-LP   COWES TOY & MODEL MUSEUM   1987
Green body, black chassis, cream roof and windows, silver grille, green wheels, black tires. Upper logo: "COWES TOY & MODEL MUSEUM/OPENED WHITSUN 1987" on dark cream adhesive label. Lower logo: gold "SOUTHERN VECTIS" and stripe. LP base.
1. As above.

15-COY-LP   COWES TOY & MODEL MUSEUM   1987
Dark brown body, tan chassis and roof, white windows, silver grille, dark tan wheels, black tires. Upper logo: gold "COWES TOY & MODEL MUSEUM", red frame. Lower logo: gold "HIGH STREET/WEST COWES" and red frame. Both on

adhesive labels. LP base.
1. As above.

15-DEL-LP   THE DELAINE   1987
Dull blue body, black chassis and roof, cream windows, silver grille, black 5-star front/6-spoke rear wheels including tires. Logo: silver "The Delaine" and underline, red and cream stripes. White "BOURNE" on black frot board. LP base. Certificate.
1. As above

15-DNA-LP   DONINGTON AUTOJUMBLE   1987
Blue body and roof, cream chassis and windows, silver grille, black 5-star front/6-spoke rear wheels including tires. Upper logo: black "DONINGTON INTERNATIONAL/1ST AUTOJUMBLE 87" on clear adhesive label. Lower logo: white "DONINGTON" and emblem on clear adhesive label. LP base.

15-DUN-LP   DUNDEE CORPORATION TRANSPORT   1987
Dark blue body and chassis, light blue roof and windows, silver grille, dark blue wheels, black tires. Upper logo: white "MODEL MOTORING" and trim on black, black lettering on white. Lower logo: black "CORPORATION TRANSPORT" on white stripe, gold and blue emblem, white "No. 15". LP base. In set of three. Certificate.

15-EDM-LP   CITY OF EDMONTON   1987
Light blue or red body, black chassis, light blue or silver roof, cream windows, silver grille, light blue or red wheels, black tires. Upper logo: gold or silver "CITY OF EDMONTON" on black background. Lower logo: gold or silver "GENERAL" and underline. LP base.
1. Light blue body, roof and wheels, gold logo.
2. Red body and wheels, silver roof and logo.

15-ETF-LP   ESSEX TOY FAIR   1987
White body, black chassis, green roof, dark green windows, silver grille, green wheels, black tires. Upper logo: black "Essex Toy Fair" and frame, red and gold shield, red car, Lower logo: black "For Collectors Of Tinplate,/Die Cast & Model Railways". Both on adhesive labels. LP base. Certificate.

15-EVA-DG   EVENING ARGUS   015-007   1986
Red body, black chassis, cream roof and windows, silver grille, black wheels and tires. Upper logo: black "Evening Argus" on cream background. Lower logo: cream stripe, gold "BRIGHTON HOVE & DISTRICT/TRANSPORT" and underline. Recessed DG base.

15-EVT-LP   EVENING TELEGRAPH   1987
Dark green body and roof, black chassis, cream windows, silver grille, dark green 8-bolt wheels, black tires. Upper logo: gold "Evening Telegraph" on red background. Lower logo: black-outlined gold "LINCOLNSHIRE", gold "ROAD CAR CO. LTD." LP base.
1. As above.

15-EXC-LP   EXCHANGE & MART   1987
Red body, black chassis, silver roof, cream windows, silver grille, red wheels, black tires. Upper logo: gold-white-black "EXCHANGE & MART", gold "Every Thursday", red "Just the Ticket", black "4d" in gold-rimmed white circle, white background. Lower logo: black-outlined gold "GENERAL" and underline. LP base. Special box.
1. As above.

15-EXE-LP   EXPRESS & ECHO   1987
Red body and roof, black chassis, cream windows, silver grille, red wheels, black tires. Upper logo: red "Express & Echo/YOUR LOCAL/EVENING NEWSPAPER" on white background. Lower logo: gold "EXETER CORPORATION", coat of arms and frame. LP base.
1. As above.

15-EXS-LP   EXPRESS & STAR   1987
Green body and roof, black chassis, yellow windows, silver grille, black 8-bolt wheels

and tires. Upper logo: black "FIRST WITH/THE NEWS/Express and Star Est. 1874" on white background. Lower logo: "WOLVERHAMPTON CORPORATION/TRANSPORT". LP base.
1. As above.

15-FAR-LP   FARNHAM MALTINGS   1985
Red body, chassis and roof, tan windows, red wheels. No other data.
1. As above.

15-FLE-LP   FLEETWOOD 150 CELEBRATIONS   1986
Cream body, brown chassis, roof and windows, cream wheels, black tires. Upper logo: "Fleetwood 150/Celebrations 1836-1986". Lower logo: "Fleetwood". DG or LP base.
1. LP base.
2. DG15 base.

15-FOA-LP   FOTORAMA—A WORLD OF COLOUR   1985
Red body and roof, black chassis, cream windows, silver grille, red wheels, black tires. Upper logo: red "F", blue "OTORAMA A World of Colour" on white adhesive label. Lower logo: white "LONDON TRANSPORT" and underline. LP base.
1. As above.

15-FOF-LP   FOTORAMA FILM   1985
Red body and roof, black chassis, cream windows, silver grille, red wheels, black tires. Upper logo: red "F", blue "OTORAMA FILM" on white adhesive label. Lower logo: white "LONDON TRANSPORT" and underline. LP base.
1. As above.

15-GEM-LP   GEMINI DIECAST   1985
Pink body and roof, black chassis, cream windows, silver grille, cream wheels, black tires. Upper logo: black "GEMINI DIECAST" and frame. Lower logo: gold "SHROPSHIRE" and frame. Both on adhesive labels. LP base.
1. As above.

15-GLA-LP   GLASGOW CORPORATION   1987
Orange body, black chassis, green roof and windows, silver grille, black wheels and axles. Upper logo: white "MODEL MOTORING" and trim on black panel, black lettering on white panels". Lower logo: black "GLASGOW CORPORATION" and lines on white stripe, black coat of arms. LP base. In set of 3. Certificate.
1. As above.

15-GUA-LP   GUARDIAN—POST   1986
Dark green body, chassis and roof, cream windows, silver grille, dark green wheels, black tires. Upper logo: yellow "GUARDIAN . POST/MORNING . EVENING" on blue background. Lower logo: white "NOTTINGHAM CORPORATION PASSENGER/TRANSPORT DEPARTMENT/B. ENGLAND/General Manager" and gold-red-green coat of arms. LP base.
1. As above.

15-GUE-LP   GUELPH, THE ROYAL CITY   1986-1987
Yellow or red body, black chassis, cream or silver roof, cream windows, silver grille, red wheels, black tires. Upper logo: gold or silver "GUELPH—THE ROYAL CITY" on black background. Lower logo: silver or gold "GENERAL" and underline. LP base.
1. Red body, cream roof, gold logo.
2. Yellow body, cream roof, gold logo.
3. Red body, silver roof and logo: 1987.

15-GWS-LP   GREAT WESTERN SOCIETY   1986
Brown body, black chassis, cream roof and windows, silver grille, brown wheels, black tires. Upper logo: "GWS" emblems and "25th ANNIVERSARY/1961-1986". Lower logo: "GREAT WESTERN SOCIETY" and "814". LP base. Certificate.

15-HAG-DG   HALL'S WINE/GENERAL   013-001   1985
Bright or brick red body, black or red chassis, silver or pale blue-gray roof, dark or light cream windows, silver or gold grille, dark or light red wheels, black or white tires. Upper logo: black "Take", black-outlined red "HALL'S WINE" and black "and defy Influenza" on yellow background. Lower logo: black-outlined gold "GENERAL" and underline. Smooth or recessed DG15 base. Earliest issues had smooth underside of roof.

1. Smooth silver roof, red body, black chassis, silver grille, dark cream windows, dark red wheels, black tires, smooth base.
2. Ridged silver roof, otherwise as type 1.
3. Ridged silver roof, gold grille, otherwise as type 1.
4. Brick red body, ridged blue-gray roof, red chassis, dark cream windows, light red wheels, white tires, silver grille, recessed base.
5. Ridged silver roof, red body, black chassis, silver grille, light cream windows, dark red wheels, black tires, recessed base. Sold in Days Gone or Tesco box.

15-HAH-LP   HALL'S WINE/HASTINGS   1985
Maroon body and chassis, silver roof, cream windows, silver grille, dark red wheels, black tires. Upper logo: black "Take", black-outlined maroon "HALL'S WINE" and black "and defy/ Influenza" on yellow background. Lower logo: gold "HASTINGS & DISTRICT". LP base. Certificate.
1. As above.

15-HAM-DG   HAMLEYS   015-004   1985
Red body and roof, black chassis, cream windows, silver grille, red wheels, black tires. Upper logo: yellow "REGENT/STREET. HAMLEYS LONDON/W.1" and underline on blue background. Lower logo: gold "LONDON TRANSPORT". Smooth or recessed DG15 base. Special box.
1. Smooth base.
2. Recessed base.

15-HAN-LP   HANNINGTONS DEPT. STORE   1986
Red body, chassis and roof, cream windows, silver grille, red wheels, black tires. Upper logo: gold "HANNINGTONS Dept./Store" on blue background. Lower logo: gold "BRIGHTON CORPORATION TRANSPORT" and coat of arms. LP base. Certificate.
1. As above.

15-HAP-LP   HAPPY EATER   1986
Red body, black chassis, silver roof, cream windows, silver grille, red wheels, black tires. Upper logo: red-yellow-black faces and red "HAPPY EATER/FAMILY RESTAURANTS" on yellow background. Lower logo: red-yellow-black emblem and yellow "LOOK OUT FOR/OUR SIGNS". LP base.
1. As above.

15-HEI-DG   HEINZ/THOMAS TILLING   015-...   1987
Red body and roof, black chassis, cream windows, silver grille, red wheels, black tires. Upper logo: white "57 HEINZ/TOMATO KETCHUP 57" on light blue background. Lower logo: white stripe and panel, gold "THOMAS TILLING/LIMITED" and underlines. Recessed DG base.
1. As above.

15-HMQ-LP   VISIT OF H. M. THE QUEEN   1987
Green body, black chassis, cream roof and windows, silver grille, green wheels, black tires. Upper logo: red-white-blue Union Jack, blue "VISIT OF H. M. THE QUEEN", red "RYDE I.O.W. MAY 13th 1987" on white adhesive label. Lower logo: gold "SOUTHERN VECTIS" and stripe. LP base.
1. As above.

15-IWR-LP   ISLE OF WIGHT STEAM RALLY   1985
Green body and chassis, cream roof and windows, silver grille, green wheels, black tires. Upper logo: green "Isle of Wight Steam Rally AUGUST/1985" on yellow background. Lower logo: gold "WESTRIDGE" and underline on green background. Both on adhesive labels. LP base.
1. As above.

15-IWS-LP   ISLE OF WIGHT STEAM RAILWAY   1987
Green body and chassis, cream roof and windows, silver grille, green wheels, black tires. Upper logo: red "ISLE OF WIGHT STEAM RAILWAY" and frame on white adhesive label. Lower logo: gold "SOUTHERN VECTIS" and stripe. LP base. Certificate.
1. As above.

15-IWW-LP   ISLE OF WIGHT WEEKLY POST   1985
Green body and chassis, cream roof and windows, silver grille, green wheels, black tires. Upper logo: white map, stroe, "Isle of Wight/Weekly Post" and panel with red "1975-1985" on red background. Lower logo: gold "SOUTHERN VECTIS" and

underline. Both on adhesive labels. LP base.
1. As above.

15-KIT-LP   CITY OF KITCHENER   1986-1987
Red or yellow body, black chassis, cream or silver roof, cream windows, red wheels, black tires. Upper logo: gold or silver "CITY OF KITCHENER" on black background. Lower logo: gold or silver "GENERAL" and underline. LP base.
1. Red body, cream roof, gold logo.
2. Yellow body, cream roof, gold logo.
3. Red body, silver roof and logo: 1987.

15-KLM-LP   KLM   1987
Light blue body, blue chassis, cream roof and windows, silver grille, blue wheels, white tires. Upper logo: white "FLY WITH KLM THE NO. 1", crown and frame. Lower logo: "The Reliable Airline KLM" and crown. LP base. In 3-model box.
1. As above.

15-KOY-LP   KOYANAGI   1987
Red or white body and roof, black or green chassis, cream or green windows, silver grille, red or green 6-bolt wheels, black tires. Upper logo: green square "MG" emblems and Japanese lettering on cream background. Lower logo: gold Japanese lettering and telephone number. LP base.
1. Red body, roof and wheels, black chassis, cream windows.
2. White body and roof, green chassis, windows and wheels.

15-LBS-LP   LAMBETH BUILDING SOCIETY   1987
Red body and roof, black chassis, white windows, silver grille, red 8-bolt wheels, black tires. Upper logo: blue "Lambeth Building Society/A safe home for investors since 1852" and emblem on white adhesive label. Lower logo: gold "LONDON TRANSPORT" and underline on red adhesive label. White "LAMBETH" on black front and rear boards. LP base. Certificate.

15-LIN-LP   LINCOLNSHIRE ECHO   1986
Olive body, chassis and roof, cream windows, silver grille, black wheels and tires. Upper logo: gold "Lincolnshire Echo" on brown background. Lower logo: red-white-gold coat of arms and gold "CITY OF LINCOLN TRANSPORT". LP base.

15-LIV-DG   LIVERPOOL FESTIVAL GARDENS 015-003   1985
Cream body and roof, brown chassis and windows, silver grille, cream wheels, black tires. Upper logo: green-outlined "FESTIVAL", green "GARDENS" and black "LIVERPOOL/MAY 23rd—SEPT. 8th, 1985". Lower logo: green "FESTIVAL TRANSPORT" and underline. Smooth or recessed DG15 base.
1. Smooth base
2. Recessed base..

15-LMC-LP   LONDON MODEL CLUB   1986
Dark yellow body and windows, black chassis and roof, silver grille, yellow wheels, black tires. Upper logo: black design and "LONDON MODEL CLUB—1986" on yellow adhesive label. No lower logo.

15-LOT-LP   LOTHIAN   1987
Maroon body, black chassis, white roof and windows, silver grille, maroon 8-bolt wheels, black tires. Upper logo: white "MODEL MOTORING" on black, black lettering on white. Lower logo: gold stripe, "LOTHIAN" and coat of arms. LP base. In boxed set of three, with or without certificate.
1. As above.

15-MAI-LP   MAIDSTONE & DISTRICT   1986
Dark green body, chassis and roof, cream windows, silver grille, green wheels, gray tires. Upper logo: green "See the Countryside by M & D Bus" on dark cream background. Lower logo: gold "Maidstone & District/Motor Services/Co." and oval. Green "75 years/behind us" on dark cream panel on stairs. All on adhesive labels. LP base.
1. As above.

15-MAT-DG   MADAME TUSSAUDS   015-011   1987
Red body and roof, black chassis, cream windows, silver grille, red wheels, black tires. Upper logo: blue "MADAME TUSSAUDS" on dark cream background. Lower

logo: yellow "LONDON TRANSPORT" and underline. Recessed DG15 base.
1. As above.

15-MBF-LP   MODEL BUS FEDERATION   1987
No data.
1. As above.

15-MON-LP   VILLE DE MONTREAL   1987
Red or light blue body, black chassis, silver or light blue roof, cream windows, silver grille, red or light blue wheels, black tires. Upper logo: silver or gold "VILLE DE MONTREAL" on black background. Lower logo: silver or gold "GENERAL" and underline. LP base.
1. Light blue body, roof and wheels, gold logo.
2. Red body and wheels, silver roof and logo.

15-MSM-LP   MSMC WINDSOR SWAPMEET   1986
Dark blue body, black chassis, silver roof, cream windows, silver grille, lightblue wheels, white tires. Upper logo: black "WINDSOR SWAPMEET January 25th 1986" and frame on blue background. Lower logo: gold "MSMC". Both on adhesive labels. LP base.
1. As above.

15-NAG-LP   NATIONAL GARDEN FESTIVAL   1986
Red body and roof, green chassis, cream windows, silver grille, red wheels, black tires. Upper logo: white "NATIONAL GARDEN FESTIVAL 1986". Lower logo: red-white-two-tone green emblem and white "STOKE-ON-/-TRENT". LP base.
1. As above.

15-NAP-LP   NATIONAL & PROVINCIAL   1986
Red body, chassis, roof, windows and wheels, black tires. No other data.
1. As above.

15-NDM-LP   NORTHERN DAILY MAIL   1987
Maroon body, black chassis, light gray roof, cream windows, silver grille, maroon wheels, black tires. Upper logo: cream "Don't-Miss/The Northern Daily Mail" on green background. Lower logo: maroon-cream-green emblem. LP base.
1. As above.

15-NEW-LP   NEWS OF THE WORLD   1986
Red body, chassis and roof, cream windows, silver grille, red wheels, black tires. Upper Logo: blue "BEST/SUNDAY/PAPER NEWS OF/THE WORLD/WORLD'S/RECORD/SALE" on white background. Lower logo: white "LONDON TRANSPORT" and underline. LP base.
1. As above.

15-NIA-LP   NIAGARA FALLS—CANADA   1986
Red body and roof, black chassis, silver roof, silver grille, red wheels, black tires. Upper logo: gold "NIAGARA FALLS—CANADA" on black background. Lower logo: black-outlined gold "GENERAL" and underline. LP base.
1. As above.

15-NOR-LP   6th NORFOLK SWAPMEET   1986
Black body, chassis and roof, maroon windows, silver grille, black wheels and tires. Upper logo: gold "SUNDAY 30th/NOVEMBER 1986/6th NORFOLK SWAPMEET" and frame. Lower logo: gold "THE EAST ANGLIAN/DIECAST MODEL CLUB" and frame. Gold "NORFOLK SWAPMEET/ST. ANDREWS HALL—NORWICH", date and frame on stairs. Front and rear white "6/NORWICH" on black. All on adhesive labels. LP base.
1. As above.

15-NOT-LP   NOTTINGHAM EVENING POST   1986
Dark green body, chassis and roof, cream windows, silver grille, green wheels, black tires. Upper logo: yellow "NOTTINGHAM/EVENING POST" on blue background. Lower logo: white "NOTTINGHAM CORPORATION PASSENGER/TRANSPORT DEPARTMENT/B. ENGLAND/General Manager" and red-green-gold coat of arms. LP base.
1. As above.

15-OXF-LP   OXFORD MAIL   1986
Red body, black chassis, maroon roof and windows, silver grille, black wheels and tires. Upper logo: gold "READ/THE" and "DAILY", red "OXFORD MAIL" on black background and light gray-green or blue stripe. Lower logo: black-outlined gold

"OXFORD" and underline, light gray-green or blue stripe. Front and rear "1/STATIONS" on black. Black "VISIT THE/OXFORD/BUS MUSEUM" on dark cream adhesive label on stairs. LP base.
1. Light gray-green stripes.
2. Blue stripes.

15-PER-LP   PERSIL   1987
Red body and roof, black chassis, white windows, silver grille, red wheels, black tires. Upper logo: green-outlined white "Persil", green " washes whiter" on white background. Lower logo: white "LONDON TRANSPORT" and underline. LP base. Special box. One of four Persil models.
1. As above.

15-PLA-LP   PLYMOUTH ARGYLE FOOTBALL CLUB   1987
Dull green body, roof and windows, black chassis, silver grille, green wheels, black tires. Upper logo: green "PLYMOUTH ARGYLE FOOTBALL/CLUB" on white background. Lower logo: white "WESTERN NATIONAL". LP base.
1. As above.

15-QUE-LP   QUEBEC CITY   1987
Light blue or red body, black chassis, light blue or silver roof, cream windows, silver grille, light blue or red wheels, black tires. Upper logo: silver or gold "QUEBEC CITY" on black background. Lower logo: silver or gold "GENERAL" and underline. LP base.
1. Blue body, roof and wheels, gold logo.
2. Red body and wheels, silver roof and logo.

15-RAD-LP   RADIO TIMES   1986
Red body, chassis and roof, cream windows, silver grille, red wheels, black tires. Upper logo: black "RADIO TIMES EVERY FRIDAY 2d" and lines on tan background. Lower logo: yellow "LONDON TRANSPORT" and underline. LP base.

15-RAE-DG   RADIO TIMES/STRATFORD BLUE   015- 1987
Light blue body, darker blue chassis, silver gray roof, cream windows, silver grille, black 5-star front/6-spoke rear wheels including tires. Upper logo: red "RADIO TIMES" and "2d", black design and "Special Wedding Edition" on white background. Lower logo: red-outlined gold "STRATFORD/BLUE" and underline, white "SHOTTERY—HATHAWAY COTTAGE—STRATFORD" in gold frame. Recessed DG base. Special box, part of Ruby Wedding set.
1. As above.

15-RDB-LP   REDBRIDGE VICTIMS SUPPORT SCHEME   1986
Red body and roof, black chassis, cream windows, silver grille, red wheels, black tires. Upper logo: red "REDBRIDGE VICTIMS SUPPORT SCHEME" on white adhesive label. Lower logo: gold "LONDON TRANSPORT" and underline. LP base.
1. As above.

15-RFG-LP   RED FUNNEL GROUP   1986
Black body, light blue chassis, white roof, red windows, silver grille, red wheels, black tires. Upper logo: "1986 SOUTHAMPTON ISLE OF WIGHT AND SOUTH OF ENGLAND/ROYAL MAIL STEAM PACKET COMPANY LIMITED" on white adhesive label on left side; right label has same lettering but ends with "1861". Label ends with dates fold onto front of bus. Lower logo: gold "RED FUNNEL GROUP/125th Anniversary" and frame. LP base.
1. As above.

15-ROY-DG/C3?   THE ROYAL WEDDING   015-008 1986
Blue body and roof, black chassis and roof, gold grille, red wheels, black tires. Upper logo: gold "THE ROYAL WEDDING JULY 23rd 1986" and frame. Lower logo: gold "H.R.H. PRINCE ANDREW/MISS SARAH FERGUSON", line and frame. With or without gold "WESTMINSTER ABBEY/LONDON" and frame on blue adhesive label on stairs. Recessed DG15 base.
1. No rear label, gold grille: DG.
2. No rear label, silver grille: DG.
3. With rear label, silver grille: C3?

15-RYH-LP   RYDE HARRIERS   1986
Red body, white chassis, roof and windows, silver grille, black wheels, black tires. Upper logo: white map, "30th Isle of Wight Marathon/Ryde Harriers" and panel with red

"1886-1986". Lower logo: gold "SOUTHERN VECTIS" and underline. Both on adhesive labels. LP base. Certificate.
1. As above.

15-RYR-LP   RYDE RAIL FESTIVAL   1986
Dark blue body, light gray chassis and roof, cream windows, silver grille, black wheels, black tires. Upper logo: white "RYDE RAIL FESTIVAL" and map, gold lines. Lower logo: gold "I.W.R. 1864" and frame. Dark blue "RYDE RAIL 1986/Saturday 21st June" and lines on dark cream panel on stairs. All on adhesive labels. LP base.
1. As above.

15-SHW-LP   SHOWGARD MOUNTS   1985
Red body, black chassis, cream roof and windows, silver grille, red wheels, black tires. Upper logo: red and black "SHOWGARD MOUNTS", black "For stamps of all nations". Lower logo: black square and number 8, black-outlined gold "GENERAL" and underline. LP base.
1. As above.

15-SPG-LP   THE SPRING GARDEN SHOW   1986
Cream body and windows, light blue chassis and roof, silver grille, light blue wheels, black tires. Upper logo: blue "The Spring/Garden Show 1986" and figure. Lower logo: blue "COUNTY SHOWGROUND". LP base.
1. As above.

15-STE-LP   STEVENSON'S BUS SERVICES   1987
Yellow-orange body and windows, black chassis and roof, silver grille, yellow-orange wheels, black tires. Upper logo: black "Stevenson's BUS SERVICES". Lower logo: black stripe, "STEVENSONS" and emblem. LP base.
1. As above.

15-STF-LP   STAFFORDSHIRE COUNTY SHOW   1986
Cream body and windows, green chassis and roof, silver grille, green wheels, black tires. Upper logo: green rope design and "STAFFORDSHIRE COUNTY SHOW/MAY 28-29 1986". Lower logo: green "Staffordshire/Agricultural Society". LP base.
1. As above.

15-STO-LP   STOCKTON CORPORATION   1986
Dark green body, chassis and roof, cream windows, silver grille, green wheels, black tires. Upper logo: gold "STOCKTON CORPORATION", red and gold coat of arms. No lower logo. LP base.
1. As above.

15-STR-LP   STRETTON MODELS   1985
Dark blue body and roof, black chassis, cream windows, cream wheels, black tires. Upper logo: gold "STRETTON MODELS", address, phone number and frame. Lower logo: gold "SHROPSHIRE" and frame. LP base.
1. As above.

15-SWV-DG   SWAN VESTAS—SOUTHDOWN   015-010 1986
Light green body, dark green chassis and roof, cream or white windows, silver grille, dark green wheels, black tires. Upper logo: black "SWAN VESTAS/BRITISH MADE BY BRYANT & MAY", "THE/SMOKER'S/MATCH" and matchbox design. Lower logo: black-outlined gold "SOUTHDOWN". Recessed DG15 base.
1. Cream windows.
2. White windows.

15-TOC-LP   TOWN CRIER   1987
Red body and chassis, black roof, white? windows, white wheels, black tires. Upper logo: "TOWN CRIER". Lower logo: "ORTONA" and underline.
1. As above.

15-TOH-LP   TORONTO HARBOUR FRONT   1986-1987
Red or yellow body, black chassis, cream or silver roof, cream windows, silver grille, red or maroon wheels, black tires. Upper logo: silver or gold "TORONTO HARBOUR FRONT" on black background. Lower logo: silver or gold "GENERAL" and underline. LP base.
1. Red body, cream roof, gold logo.
2. Yellow body, cream roof, gold logo.
3. Red body, silver roof and logo: 1987.

Lledo™ Models

15-TOR-LP   CITY OF TORONTO   1987
Light blue or red body, black chassis, light blue or silver roof, cream windows, silver grille, light blue or red wheels, black tires. Upper logo: silver or gold "CITY OF TORONTO" on black background. Lower logo: silver or gold "GENERAL" and underline. LP base.
1. Light blue body, roof and wheels, gold logo.
2. Red body and wheels, silver roof and logo.

15-TVT-DG   TV TIMES   015- 1987
Red body, black chassis, cream windows, silver grille, red 8-bolt wheels, black tires. Upper logo: black-outlined "TV Times" and similar emblem. Lower logo: white "LONDON TRANSPORT" and underlines. Recessed DG base.
1. As above.

15-TYF-LP   THE TOYFAIR AT THE CENTRE HALLS   1986
Tan body and chassis, silver roof, brown windows, silver grille, dark tan wheels, black tires. Upper logo: brown "THE TOYFAIR AT THE CENTRE HALLS" and frame. Lower logo: brown car design with tan "SURREY". Front and rear white "9/WOKING" on black. All on adhesive labels. LP base.
1. As above.

15-UAS-LP   UNITED AUTOMOBILE SERVICES   1987
Red body and roof, black chassis, cream windows, silver grille, black 5-star front/6-spoke rear wheels including tires. Upper logo: red "1912" and "1987", black "Serving the North East for 75 Years" on gold background. Lower logo: black-outlined gold "UNITED" and underline, cream stripe. White "UNITED/75" on black front board. LP base. Certificate.
1. As above.
2. As above plus gold and black "The Model Bus/Federation" and emblem on clear adhesive label on rear stairs.

15-UNP-SP   UNPAINTED   1986
Unpainted body, chassis and roof, cream windows, silver grille, red wheels, black tires. No logo. Recessed DG base. Factory specimen.
1. As above.

15-VAN-LP   CITY OF VANCOUVER   1987
Light blue or red body, black chassis, light blue or silver roof, cream windows, light blue or red wheels, black tires. Upper logo: silver or gold "CITY OF VANCOUVER" on black background. Lower logo: silver or gold "GENERAL" and underline. LP base.
1. Blue body, roof and wheels, gold logo.
2. Red body and wheels, silver roof and logo.

15-VIE-LP   VIENNA BEEF/LITTLE JOE'S   1986
Yellow body, black chassis and windows, yellow or blue roof, silver grille, yellow wheels, black tires. Upper logo: blue "Vienna Beef", red and blue V emblem. Lower logo: red and blue "Little Joe"s", blue "COUNTRYSIDE, IL." LP base.
1. Yellow roof.
2. Blue roof.

15-VIG-LP   VIGIL RESCUE   1986
Dark green body and chassis, silver roof, cream windows, silver grille, dark green wheels, black tires. Upper logo: black "VIGIL RESCUE" and dog figure on dark cream background. Lower logo: gold "LONDON TRANSPORT" and underline/Both on adhesive labels. LP base.

15-VIM-LP   VIMTO KEEPS YOU FIT   1986
Red body, black chassis, cream roof, brown windows, silver grille, red wheels, black tires. Upper logo: red "VIMTO", black "KEEPS YOU FIT!" on cream background. Lower logo: yellow "GENERAL" and underline. LP base.

15-WAT-LP   CITY OF WATERLOO   1986-1987
Red or yellow body, black chassis, cream or silver roof, cream windows, silver grille, red or maroon wheels, black tires. Upper logo: silver or gold "CITY OF WATERLOO" on black background. Lower logo: silver or gold "GENERAL" and underline. LP base.

1. Red body, cream roof, gold logo, red wheels.
2. Yellow body, cream roof, gold logo, maroon wheels.
3. Red body, silver roof and logo, red wheels: 1987.

15-YOR-LP   YORKVILLE AND DISTRICT   1986-1987
Red or yellow body, black chassis, cream or silver roof, cream windows, silver grille, red or maroon wheels, black tires. Upper logo: silver or gold "YORKVILLE & DISTRICT" on black background. Lower logo: silver or gold "GENERAL" and underline. LP base.
1. Red body, cream roof, gold logo, red wheels.
2. Yellow body, cream roof, gold logo, maroon wheels.
3. Red body, silver roof and logo, red wheels: 1987.

016   HEAVY GOODS VAN   82mm 1985
Metal body and chassis, plastic roof, grille, base and six-bolt plastic or plain disc single front and dual rear wheels. Casting variations: the first few bodies had a small groove on each side near the bottom; this groove is only found on the first few Mayflower and Croft vans. There are three chassis castings:
A. Original front end with thin bar forward of bottom of grille.
B. Thickened bar, as already noted on 10-12 chassis.
C. Thickened bar plus two small holes.
D. Thickened bar, two holes, and wide slot.
In addition, all chassis castings exist with thick or thin rear edges of the front fenders; this will not be listed.
Base variations:
A. DG16 without ridge around lettering.
B. DG16 with ridge around lettering.
C. Lledo Promotional Model with ridge around lettering.

16-AIR-EC   AIRFIX/HUMBROL   1986
Green body, white chassis and roof, silver or gold grille, white disc wheels, black tires. Logo: white "HUMBROL" on red panel with white border, white "The Image of/Perfection", red and white disc with black "AIRFIX" and trim. Thick front end with holes. "Edocar No. A4" base; Edocar box.
1. Gold grille.
2. Silver grille.

16-ALT-LP   ALTON TOWERS   1987
Cream body, black chassis, brown roof, gold grille, cream 6-bolt wheels, black tires. Logo: gold emblem with black-outlined white "Alton Towers", gold "Europe's Premier Leisure Park". Thick front end with holes? LP base. Special box.
1. As above.

16-ALV-LP   ALLIED VAN LINES   1987
Dull orange body and chassis, white roof, silver grille, cream 6-bolt wheels, black tires. Logo: white "ALLIED/The Careful Movers", black-white-yellow-orange road design with white maple leaf and number 1. Thick front end with holes. LP base.
1. As above.

16-AMR-LP   ASSOCIATION OF MODEL RAILWAY CLUBS   1986
Light yellow body, blue chassis and roof, gold grille, yellow-orange 6-bolt wheels, black tires. Logo: blue map emblem, "ASSOCIATION/OF MODEL/RAILWAY CLUBS/Wales & West of England Ltd./2nd-5th MAY 1986". Thick front end. LP base.
1. As above.

16-APU-LP   APURA   1986
White body and roof, black chassis, gold grille, cream 6-bolt wheels, black tires. Logo: black "APURA" and "efficient en betrouwbar -ook in service", green emblem with white "A", green "handdoek/en zeepautomaten". One or two green and white "A" emblems on rear doors. Original front end. LP base.
1. One A emblem on rear doors.
2. Two A emblems on rear doors.

**16-AVO-LP   AVON DIECAST AND MODEL
                COLLECTOR SOCIETY   1985**
Black body, chassis, roof, 6-bolt wheels and tires, gold grille. Logo: silver "Avon Diecast And/Model/Collectors/Society". gold bridge design and frame, plus gold

"1985" on front, all on adhesive labels. Original front end. LP base.

16-BPQ-LP   BRITISH POLICE SPONSORED QUEST   1987
Navy blue body, black chassis and roof, silver grille, bright blue 6-bolt wheels, black tires. Logo: silver "BRITISH POLICE/ENGLAND 1987 TURKEY/SPONSORED QUEST" and circle, plus emblems on doors and "POLICE" on front, all on adhesive labels. Thick front end with two holes. LP base. Certificate.
1. As above.

16-BRD-LP   J. J. BRODSKY & SONS,   INC. 1985
Cream body, blue chassis and roof, gold grille, cream 6-bolt wheels, black tires. Logo: black-outlined white "J. J. BRODSKY & SONS, INC.", black "WHOLESALE DESTRIBUTORS/CANDIES/HOBBIES/TOBACCO'S/SUNDRIES" and emblem with "1935-1985/50 YEARS/OF/SERVICE", plus black "7300 S. KIMBARK/CHICAGO, ILLINOIS" on tan background on front, all on adhesive labels. Original front end. LP base.
1. As above.

16-BUS-DG   BUSHELLS TEA   016-004 1986
Navy blue body, black chassis and roof, gold grille, cream or white 6-bolt wheels, black tires. Logo: white-outlined tan "Bushells", maroon-white-black teacup design, tan "The Tea of Flavor", plus orange "Bushells" on front. Original front end or thick type with holes. DG base with ridge.
1. Cream wheels, original front chassis, light yellow front logo.
2. Cream wheels, thick front end with holes, light yellow front logo.
3. White wheels, thick front end with holes, light yellow front logo.
4. Cream wheels, thick front end with holes, light orange front logo.

16-CAD-DG   CADBURY'S DAIRY MILK CHOCOLATE   016-013 1987
Dark purple body and chassis, white roof, gold grille, white 6-bolt wheels, black tires. Logo: white pouring glasses design, gold "Cadbury's", white "DAIRY MILK CHOCOLATE", white and gold stripes. Thick front end with two holes and wide slot. LP base.
1. As above.

16-CAV-LP   CAVALIER—H.G.V. REMOULDS   1986
Black body, chassis, roof, 6-bolt wheels and tires, silver grille. Logo: gold and whitecavalier figure, gold "Cavalier/H.G.V. Remoulds", green stripe. Original front end. LP base.
1. As above.

16-CHA-LP   P. H. CHANDLERS   1986
Cream body, no other data.
1. As above.

16-COC-DG   COCA-COLA   016-010 1986
Red body, black chassis and roof, gold grille, cream or black 6-bolt wheels, black or white tires. Logo: white stripes and "DRINK/Coca-Cola, plus same lettering in red on white circle on rear doors. Thick front end without or with two holes. Ridged DG base. Special box.
1. Black wheels, white tires, front end without holes.
2. Cream wheels, black tires, front end without holes.
3. Black wheels, white tires, front end with two holes.
4. Cream wheels, black tires, front end with two holes.

16-COL-LP   COLD CHOICE—PELHAM MEATS   1986
Cream body, black chassis and roof, gold grille, 6-bolt black wheels, black tires. Logo: cream "COLD CHOICE" on black arc, black and cream figure, black "PELHAM MEATS LTD.", address, telephone number and list of products, on adhesive label. Original front end. LP base.
1. As above.

16-COO-LP   CO-OP ENGLISH BUTTER   1987
Dark green body, chassis and roof, 6-bolt brown wheels, white tires, gold grille. Logo: dark green "CO-OP/ENGLISH BUTTER", brown farm scene on cream background. Cream "Co-op" on front. Thick front end with two holes and wide slot. LP base.
1. As above.

16-CRO-DG   CROFT ORIGINAL SHERRY   016-002 1985

Lledo™ Models

Cream body, black chassis, brown roof, gold grille, cream 6-bolt wheels, black tires. Logo: white "Croft/ORIGINAL" on gold-brown-black emblem, black "The Sherry/of/Distinction". All three front ends. Grooved or plain body. Smooth or ridged DG base.
1. Grooved body, original front end, smooth base.
2. Plain body, original front end, smooth base.
3. Plain body, original front end, ridged base.
4. Plain body, thick front end, ridged base.
5. Plain body, thick front end with holes, ridged base, lighter cream wheels.

15-DUN-LP DUNLOP   **1987**
Red body, black chassis, white roof, gold grille, black 6-bolt wheels and tires. Logo: yellow-outlined black "DUNLOP", black-outlined yellow "THE WORLD'S/MASTER TYRE". Thick front end with holes. LP base.
1. As above.

16-EPM-LP ENFIELD PAGEANT OF MOTORING   **1986**
Black body, chassis, roof, 6-bolt wheels and tires, silver grille. No other data.
1. As above.

16-EXC-LP EXCHANGE & MART   **1986**
Black body, red chassis, white roof, gold grille, red 6-bolt wheels, black tires. Logo: black-outlined white "EXCHANGE & MART" on red and white design, white "PACKED FULL OF BARGAINS", red and white "Every Week!", white underline. Thick front end with two holes. LP base. Special box.
1. As above.

16-FER-LP FERGUSON'S CARRIERS/REMOVERS   **1986**
Light blue body and chassis, cream roof, gold grille, black 6-bolt wheels and tires. Logo: black-outlined yellow "FERGUSON'S/CARRIERS/REMOVERS/Bath Lane/BLYTH" and "BLYTH/2398", plus yellow "FERGUSON'S/Removals" on front. Original front end. LP base.
1. As above.

16-FYF-DG FYFFES   **016-012 1987**
Yellow-orange body, navy blue chassis, white roof, gold grille, yellow-orange 6-bolt wheels, black tires. Logo: light blue "BLUE LABEL/FYFFES/BRAND" and trim on dark blue oval, light and dark blue stripes. Thick front end with holes. Ridged DG base.
1. As above.

16-GER-LP OVERSEAS REMOVALS BY MICHAEL GERSON   **1985**
Dark green body, black chassis and roof, gold grille, black 6-bolt wheels and tires. Logo: yellow "OVERSEAS REMOVALS/BY", telephone number and address, black-outlined yellow "MICHAEL GERSON", plus yellow "OVERSEAS REMOVALS BY/MICHAEL GERSON" on front. Original front end. LP base.
1. As above.

16-GRE-LP ALAN GREENWOOD   **1986**
Red body, black chassis, white roof, black or gold grille, black 6-bolt wheels and tires. Logo: black-outlined white "ALAN GREENWOOD", red-wehite-blue Union Jack, white "International Removal Specialists/KINGSTON . WORCESTER . GUILDFORD" and telephone numbers, on adhesive label. Thick front end with two holes. LP base.
1. Black grille.
2. Gold grille.

16-GRM-LP GRIMLEY & SON   **1986**
Red body, no other data.
1. As above.

16-GRY-SP GRAY   **year?**
Light gray body and chassis, cream roof, gold grille, brown 6-bolt wheels, white tires. No logo. Original front end. Ridged DG base. Specimen.

16-GWS-LP GREAT WESTERN SOCIETY   **1986**
Brown body, black chassis, cream roof, gold grille, brown 6-bolt wheels, black tires. No other data.
1. As above.

16-HAM-DG HAMLEYS   **016-007 1986**
Black body, chassis, roof, 6-bolt wheels and tires, gold grille. Logo: gold "HAMLEYS/ALL THE WORLD'S/FINEST TOYS", toy design and frame. Thick front end. Ridged DG base. Special box.
1. As above.

16-HAR-LP HAROLD'S PLACE, INC.   **1986**
Bright green body and chassis, dark green roof, silver grille, dark green 6-bolt wheels, black tires. Logo: white-outlined red "MERRY CHRISTMAS/1986/to our Customers/HAROLD'S PLACE, INC." Thick front end with holes. LP base.
1. As above.

16-HEG-DG HERSHEY'S MR. GOODBAR   **016-009 1986**
Yellow body, brown chassis and roof, gold grille, brown 6-bolt wheels, white tires. Logo: white "HERSHEY'S" on brown panel, red "mr. Goodbar", yellow "PEANUTS IN MILK CHOCOLATE" on brown stripe. Thick front end, without or with holes. Ridged DG base. Special box.
1. Pale brown stripe, no front end holes.
2. Dark brown stripe, two holes.

16-HEK-DG HERSHEY'S KRACKEL   **016-008 1986**
Red body, brown chassis and roof, gold grille, red 6-bolt wheels, white tires. Logo: white "HERSHEY'S" on brown panel, white "krackel" with red line through it, yellow "CRISPED RICE IN/MILK CHOCOLATE". Thick front end without or with holes. Ridged DG base. Special box.
1. Chocolate brown, no front end holes, light brown logo panel.
2. Purplish brown chassis, two front end holes, dark brown logo panel.

16-HIV-LP HISTORIC COMMERCIAL VEHICLE RUN   **1986**
Dark green body, black chassis, cream roof, gold grille, dark green 6-bolt wheels, black tires. Logo: black-outlined silver The Historic/Conmmercial Vehicle Run/LONDON-BRIGHTON/1st Sunday in May 1986: and "HISTORIC COMMERCIAL/VEHICLE SOCIETY" emblem on left, silver "Wheels of/Yesterday/Rally/3rd 4th 5th MAY 1986/Battersea Park/LONDON SW11" on right. Thick front end. LP base.
1. As above.

16-IDE-LP THE NOTTINGHAM IDEAL HOME EXHIBITION   **1986**
Cream body, red chassis and roof, gold grille, cream 6-bolt wheels, black tires. Logo: red roof, "THE NOTTINGHAM", "EXHIBITION" and "28th March-/ 1st April 1986", red-outlined cream "IDEAL HOME", on adhesive label. Original front end. LP base.
1. As above.

16-JON-LP JONES & SON   **1987**
Light brown body, light cream chassis, cream roof, gold grille, cream 6-bolt wheels, black tires. Logo: white "JONES & SON/HORSE & PONY TRANSPORT/SERVICES/ TEL./436", black woodwork design. White "HORSES" on front. LP base. Thick front end with holes and wide slot.
1. As above.

16-KIW-DG KIWI POLISHES   **016-011 1986**
Black body, chassis, roof, 6-bolt or disc wheels and tires, gold or silver grille. Logo: black-outlined gold "KIWI/POLISHES", maroon-cream-gold-black emblem, cream or light green frame. Thick front end with holes. LP base.
1. Silver grille, 6-bolt wheels, cream logo frame.
2. Gold grille, 6-bolt wheels, cream logo frame.
3. Gold grille, disc wheels, cream logo frame.
4. Gold grille, disc wheels, light green logo frame.

16-KLE-LP THE KLEEN-E-ZE MAN   **1987**
Pale or rich blue body, light or rich blue chassis, white roof, silver grille, light or rich blue 6-bolt wheels, black tires. Logo: black figure, black-outlined gold "The/Kleen-e-ze/MAN/stands for satisfaction/SEE HIM WHEN HE CALLS/BRUSHES . MOPS . POLISHES/Hanham . Bristol." Thick front end. LP base. Certificate on plain white box.
1. Pale blue body, light blue chassis and wheels.
2. Rich blue body, chassis and wheels.

16-KLM-LP KLM CARGO   **1987**
Light blue body, blue chassis, white roof, silver grille, blue 6-bolt wheels, white tires. Logo: white crown, "KLM DOORSPEED/CARGO", plus white "AMSTERDAM" on front and crown and "KLM" on rear. Thick front end. LP base.
1. As above.

16-LMS-LP L M S EXPRESS PARCELS SERVICE   **1986**
Magenta body, black chassis and roof, silver grille, 6-bolt magenta wheels, black tires. Logo: gold "L M S/EXPRESS/PARCELS/SERVICE" and Derby telephone number. Thick front end. LP base.
1. As above.

16-LNE-DG L.N.E.R. EXPRESS PARCELS SERVICES **016-006 1986**
Navy blue body, black chassis and roof, gold or black grille, 6-bolt cream wheels, black tires. Logo: white emblem and "L.N.E.R./EXPRESS/PARCELS/SERVICES", plus "L.N.E.R" on front and "LONDON NORTH/EASTERN RAILWAY" on rear. Thick front end. LP base.
1. Gold grille.
2. Black grille.

16-LUC-LP LUCKING FURNITURE   **1986**
Blue body, no other data.
1. As above.

16-MAH-LP MANNERS & HARRISON   **1986**
Light cream body, black chassis and roof, gold grille, cream disc wheels, black tires. Logo: green "MANNERS & HARRISON" and "Auction Department", blue "CHARTERED SURVEYORS" and telephone number, green and blue stripes. Thick front end. LP base. Certificate.
1. As above.
2. Does it exist with 6-bolt wheels?

16-MAY-DG AERO MAYFLOWER TRANSIT CO.   **016-001 1985**
Dark yellow body, black chassis, green roof, gold grille, cream 6-bolt wheels, black tires. Logo: black-outlined yellow "38", black outlined red "AERO/Mayflower Transit Co.", black "LOCAL and/LONG DISTANCE/MOVING", green Mayflower and ocean design. A few early issues have grooved body. Original or thick base with holes. Smooth or ridged DG base.
1. Grooved body, smooth base, original front end, dark cream wheels.
2. Plain body, smooth base, original front end, dark cream wheels.
3. Plain body, ridged base, original front end, light cream wheels.
4. Plain body, ridged base, thick front end with holes, light? cream wheels.
5. Plain body, ridged base, lighter green roof, different shade yellow body, other details not known.

16-MIN-LP MINSTER TOY AND TRAIN FAIR   **1987**
Maroon body, black chassis, tan roof, gold grille, black wheels and tires. Logo: cream "The 1st Minster/1987/TOY & TRAIN FAIR", gold car, locomotive, stripes and emblem. Adhesive labels. LP base. Certificate.
1. As above.

16-NAS-LP NATIONAL SYSTEMS   **1986**
Yellow-orange body, green chassis and roof, gold grille, 6-bolt yellow-orange wheels, black tires. Logo: green and orange "N" emblem, green "National Systems Co./P.O. BOX 157, WATERLOO/ONTARIO N2J 3Z9", telephone number and "PATIENT/CHARTING". Thick front end with holes. LP base.
1. As above.

16-NFS-LP NFS (NATIONAL FIRE SERVICE)   **1986**
Red or light gray body, black or white chassis, white or gray roof, gold grille, black or gray 6-bolt wheels and tires. Logo: white and red "NFS" emblem, black and gray doors and windows, red and white checkered stripes. Thick front end with holes. LP base.
1. Red body, black chassis, white roof, black wheels.
2. Light gray body, white chassis, gray roof, gray wheels.

16-NMC-LP N.M.C.C. MINIATURE CAR YEAR   **1985**
Dark yellow body, black chassis and roof, gold grille, cream 6-bolt wheels, black tires.
1. As above.

Lledo™ Models

16-NOR-LP NORTHLAND LUMBER   1986
Yellow-orange body, dark green chassis and roof, gold grille, yellow-orange 6-bolt wheels, black tires. Logo: green "F.D.M.", trees and "Northland Lumber", plus "CANADA" on front. Thick front end. LP base.
1. As above.

16-OLT-LP OLD TOYLAND SHOWS   1985
Light gray body, red chassis and roof, gold grille, red 6-bolt wheels, black tires. Logo: red and black fire truck design, black circled number 1, "ON THE MOVE WITH/OLD TOYLAND/SHOWS" and list of sites. Original front end. LP base.
1. As above.

16-OVE-LP OVER'S OF CAMBERLEY   1985
Red body, black chassis, white roof, gold grille, black 6-bolt wheels and tires. Logo: white "INTERNATIONALE MOBELSPEDITION/REMOVALS/STORAGE/PACKING/SHIPPING", addresses and telephone numbers, black-outlined white "OVER'S", white "of Camberley" on black stripe, on adhesive label. Thick front end with holes. LP base.
1. As above.

16-PEA-LP J. & B. PEARCE & CO.   1986
Light blue body, dark blue base, white roof, gold grille, red 6-bolt wheels, white tires. L@No data. Announced for late 1987.
1. As above?

16-REL-LP RELIANCE WHOLESALE ELECTRICAL   1986
Cream body, no other data.
1. As above.

16-ROY-DG ROYAL MAIL   016-003 1986
Red body, blacke, on adhesive label. Thick front end with holes. LP base.
1. As above.

16-PEA-LP J. & B. PEARCE & CO.   1986
Light blue body, dark blue base, white roof, gold grille, red 6-bolt wheels, black tires. L chassis and roof, gold grille, red 6-bolt wheels, black tires. Logo: black "ROYAL MAIL" and frame, gold and black crown, black-outlined "GR" monogram. Original front end. DG base. Special box.
1. Smooth DG base.
2. Ridged DG base.

16-RRM-LP READING M.L.O.—ROYAL MAIL   1987
Red body, black chassis and roof, silver grille, red 6-bolt wheels, black tires. Logo: black circle emblem with black-Outlined yellow "READING M.L.O./ROYAL MAIL" inside outer circle, yellow "RG1 1AA and black-outlined and underlined "OPERATIONAL 1987" inside inner circle. Thick front end with holes. LP base.
1. As above.

16-SCA-LP SCALE AUTO ENTHUSIAST   1985
Light gray body, black chassis and roof, gold grile, red 6-bolt wheels, black tires. Logo: white "Scale Auto enthusiast" on red panel, white "world's leading automotive modeling magazine", plus red "DECEMBER/1985" on silver background, both on adhesive labels. Original front end. LP base.
1. As above.

16-SCF-LP STONEY CREEK FURNITURE   1987
Cream body, brown chassis and roof, gold grille, cream 6-bolt wheels, black tires. Logo: brown building design, "FURNITURE/REAL FURNITURE AT REALISTIC PRICES" and frame, green "Stoney Creek". Thick front end. LP base.
1. As above.

16-SHL-LP SHELTONS   1986
White body, black chassis, brown roof, gold grille, cream 6-bolt wheels, black tires. Logo: brown and pink stripes, brown "Sheltons", address, and "EAST ANGLIA'S LARGEST INDEPENDENT/FURNITURE CENTER", plus brown "Sheltons" and underline on front, both on adhesive labels. Thick front end with holes. Certificate.
1. As above.

16-SLU-LP SLUMBERLAND BEDS   1986

Red body and roof, black chassis, gold grille, red 6-bolt wheels, black tires. Logo: black-outlined gold "Slumberland/BEDS", gold coat of arms and lettering on doors, plus gold "Over 20 years of/POSTURE SPRINGING" across rear doors, all on adhesive labels. Thick front end. LP base.
1. As above.

16-SOE-LP SOUTH ESSEX TOY FAIR   1986
White body, black chassis, brown roof, gold grille, cream 6-bolt wheels, black tires. Logo: brown "SOUTH ESSEX DIECAST MODEL CLUB", red "Toy Fair '86/BASILDON, ESSEX" and horse bus design, white "DIECASTS-TINPLATE-RAILWAYS" on brown stripe, plus red "S.E.D.M.C." on front, both on adhesive labels. Thick front end with holes. LP base.
1. As above.

16-SUR-LP SURREY DIECAST MODEL CLUB   1985
Tan body, black chassis, brown roof, gold grille, brown 6-bolt wheels, black tires. Logo: gold car design with brown "SURREY", gold "DIECAST MODEL CLUB", plus gold "SEPTEMBER/1988" on front, both on brown adhesive labels. Original front end. LP base.

16-THR-LP THRESHOLD RECORDS & TAPES   1985
White body, black chassis, blue roof, silver grille, white 6-bolt wheels, black tires. Logo: white "THRESHOLD" on blue design, blue "RECORDS & TAPES" and address. Original front end. LP base.

16-TRE-DG TREBOR PEPPERMINTS   016-005 1986
Dark green body, black chassis, white roof, gold grille, green 6-bolt wheels, black tires. Logo: dark green "TREBOR" and "NONE SO GOOD" on white panels, white "EXTRA STRONG/PEPPERMINTS" and line, light green stripes. Original or thick front end. Ridged DG base.
1. Original front end, dark green wheels.
2. Thick front end, dark green wheels.
3. Thick front end, lighter green wheels: Tesco issue.
4. Thick front end with two holes, green disc wheels.
5. Thick front end with two holes and wide slot, brighter logo, ? wheels.

16-VAK-LP VAKUUM VULK   1986
Black body, chassis, roof, 6-bolt wheels and tires, silver grille. Logo: gold "Vakuum Vulk/THE LONG DISTANCE RETREAD", gold and white cavalier figure and globe. Original front end. LP base.
1. As above.

16-VAN-LP VAN MAGAZINE   1986
White body, red chassis and roof, gold grille, red 6-bolt wheels, black tires. Logo: white "V A N" on red panels, black "MAGAZINE" and telephone number, red "AT YOUR NEWSAGENT/Now!" Thick front end with holes. LP base.
1. As above.

16-VEN-LP VEN GROOTHANDELCENTRUM   1986
White body, green chassis and roof, silver grille, green 6-bolt wheels, black tires. Logo: green and white "VEN", green "VEN Groothandelcentrum" and red lettering, plus green and white "VEN" and green lettering across rear doors. Thick front end. LP base.
1. As above.

16-VEP-LP VERNON'S PLAICE   1987
Dark maroon body, black chassis, tan roof, gold grille, black 6-bolt wheels and tires. Logo: maroon "VERNON'S PLAICE" on silver ribbon, other silver lettering, silver-yellow-green fish design, silver telephone number on doors, both on adhesive labels. Thick front end with holes. LP base.
1. As above.

16-VER-LP VERS MARKT   1986
White body, green chassis and roof, silver grille, green 6-bolt wheels, black tires. Logo: white "VEN" on green stripe, black and white world map, red "INTERNATIONALE" and lines, green "VERS MARKT", plus green and white rear logo identical to that of the VEN model. Thick front end. LP base. Certificate.
1. As above.

16-WES-LP WESTWARD TOOLS   1986
White body, blue chassis and roof, gold grille, light red 6-bolt wheels, white tires. Logo: blue "WESTWARD . TOOLS and EQUIPMENT/Fully Guaranteed/Across Canada", wrench design and stripes. Thick front end. LP base.
1. As above.

017 HALF CAB SINGLEDECK BUS   92mm 1985
Metal body, chassis and roof, plastic windows/interior, grille, base and 8-bolt single front and dual rear wheels. Casting variations: first few Southend buses had fuel filler cap which was eliminated from all future castings; all models since 1986 Commonwealth Games have a vertical bar in the center of the rear seat. Base types (no heavy ridges):
   A. Smooth DG17.
   B. DG17 with faint line around lettering.
   C. Smooth Lledo Promotional.
   D. Lledo promotional with faint line.

17-ALD-LP ALDERSHOT & DISTRICT   1986
Lime green body, black chassis, dark green roof and windows, black wheels, gray tires. Logo: orange "ALDERSHOT & DISTRICT/Traction Co. Ltd." and oval, yellow stripe. White "ALTON" or "GUILDFORD" on black front board. Lined LP base.
   1. Destination Alton.
   2. Destination Guildford.

17-ALT-LP ALTON TOWERS   1987
Red body, black chassis, cream roof and windows, silver grille, red wheels, black tires. Logo: black-outlined red "Alton Towers", gold emblem and "Europe's/Premier/Leisure/Park". Black "ALTON" and frame on front board. Lined LP base. Special box.

17-BIG-DG BIG TOP   017-009 1986
Cream body and roof, black chassis, red windows, silver grille, red wheels, black tires. Logo: blue "BIG TOP" on orange-red-blue ribbon, multicolored circus design. Lined DG base.
   1. Red windows.
   2. Darker red windows.

17-BLA-LP BLACKBURN TRANSPORT   1987
Green body and chassis, dark green roof, cream windows, silver grille, dark green 8-bolt wheels, black tires. Logo: silver and black emblem, white "BLACKBURN/TRANSPORT". Lined LP base.
   1. As above.

17-BOA-DG B.O.A.C. CORPORATION TRANSPORT   017-002 1985
Yellow body, light gray chassis and roof, cream windows, silver grille, red wheels, white tires. Logo: red "CORPORATION TRANSPORT No. 37" on red-bordered white stripe, blue emblem and "FLY B.O.A.C" on white panel. Smooth or lined DG base.
   1. Smooth DG base.
   2. Rear vertical bar, lined DG base.
   3. No white logo background (not a regular DG issue).

17-BOU-LP BOURNEMOUTH CORPORATION   1987
Yellow body and windows, black chassis, cream roof, silver grille, black wheels and tires. Logo: gold "BOURNEMOUTH CORPORATION MOTORS" on brown stripe, brown and gold coat of arms, on adhesive label. White "MOORDOWN" on black front board. Lined LP base.
   1. As above.

17-BRI-LP BRISTOL   1987
Cream body, roof and windows, black chassis, silver grille, black wheels and tires. Logo: green trim with silver "2144", "Bristol" and greyhound emblem. Cream "YATE 87" on black front board. Lined LP base.
   1. As above.
   2. As above plus rear adhesive label: green "AVON/DIECAST/CLUB/3rd SWAPMEET".

17-BUR-DG BURNLEY CORPORATION   017-010 1987

Navy blue body, white chassis and roof, medium blue windows, silver grille, navy blue wheels, black tires. Logo: navy blue "BURNLEY CORPORATION TRAMWAYS & OMNIBUS" on white stripe, white coat of arms. Lined DG base.

1. As above.

17-COM-DG   COMMONWEALTH GAMES   017-005 1986
White body, chassis and roof, blue windows, silver grille, white wheels, black tires. Logo: blue and red "XII" design, blue "XIII COMMONWEALTH GAMES/SCOTLAND 1986", red "COMPETITORS COACH", blue and white emblem. Lined DG base. First model with vertical rear bar. Special box.

1. As above.

17-DEL-LP   THE DELAINE   1987
Dull dark blue body, black chassis and roof, cream windows, silver grille, dark blue wheels, black tires. Logo: silver "The Delaine" and underline. White "BOURNE" and frame on black front board. Lined LP base.

1. As above.

17-DEV-LP   DEVON GENERAL   1987
Red body and roof, black chassis, dark red windows, silver grille, black 5-star/6-spoke wheels including tires. Logo: gold "DEVON GENERAL" and underline on red adhesive label. White "TORQUAY" on black front board. LP base. Certificate.

1. As above.

17-DUN-LP   DUNDEE CORPORATION TRANSPORT   1987
Dark blue body and chassis, light blue roof and windows, silver grille, dark blue wheels, black tires. Logo: black "CORPORATION TRANSPORT" on white stripe, gold and blue emblem, white "No. 17". Header: white "DUNDEE" on black background. LP base. In set of three. Certificate.

1. As above.

17-EAB-LP   EASTBOURNE CORPORATION   1986
Navy blue body and chassis, cream roof and windows, silver grille, navy blue wheels, black tires. Logo: plain or red-outlined gold "EASTBOURNE CORPORATION", red and gold coat of arms, sometimes a gold stripe. White "BRIGHTON" or "OLD TOWN" on black front board. Lined LP base.

1. Gold stripe, light cream windows, destination Old Town.
2. No stripe, dark cream windows, destination Old Town.
3. No stripe, dark cream windows, destination Brighton.

17-EAK-LP   EAST KENT   1985
Maroon body and chassis, cream roof and windows, silver grille, maroon wheels, black tires. Logo: gold "EAST KENT" and underline, on adhesive label. White "ASHFORD" or "DOVER" on black front board. Lined LP base.

1. Light maroon body and chassis, destination Ashford.
2. Dark maroon body and chassis, destination Dover.
3. Other possibilities?

17-EUR-DG   EUROTOUR CRUISES   017-003 1985
Green body, cream chassis, roof and windows, silver grille, cream wheels, black tires. Logo: white "EUROTOUR/Cruises" and stripes, red-white-blue national flags. Smooth DG base.

1. As above.

17-EXC-LP   EXCHANGE AND MART   1987
Red body and roof, black chassis, white windows, silver grille, red wheels, black tires. Logo: red-white-black "EXCHANGE & MART", black "Every Thursday", black "3d" on black-rimmed gold oval, gold "LONDON TRANSPORT" and underline. LP base. Special box.

1. As above.

17-GBM-LP   G. & B. MOTOR SERVICES   1987
Light brown body, black chassis, roof and windows, silver grille, brown wheels, black tires. Logo: black and yellow stripes, black-outlined yellow "G & B/MOTOR SERVICES", black address and "30 MPH". White "DURHAM" on black front board. Lined LP base. Certificate.

1. As above.

17-GLA-LP   GLASGOW CORPORATION   1987
Orange body, black chassis, jade green roof and windows, silver grille, black wheels

and tires. Logo: black "GLASGOW CORPORATION" on black-bordered white stripe, black coat of arms. White "JOHNSTONE" on black front board. Lined LP base. Certificate.

1. As above.

17-GRY-SP   GRAY   year?
Light gray body, chassis and roof, white windows, silver grille, light bluye wheels, black tires. No logo. Lined DG base. Specimen.

1. As above.

17-HAM-DG   HAMLEYS   017-008 1986
Dark green body and roof, crea, chassis and windows, gold grille, dark green wheels, black tires. Logo: cream "HAMLEYS/WORLD OF TOYS", other lettering and underline. Lined DG base. Special box.

1. As above.

17-HAP-LP   HAPPY DAYS   1986
Red body, cream chassis, roof and windows, silver grille, red wheels, black tires. Logo: gold "Happy Days" and design with red "Austin's". Lined LP base.

1. As above.

17-HED-LP   HEDINGHAM & DISTRICT   1986
Dark blue body, black chassis, cream roof and windows, silver grille, cream wheels, black tires. Logo: gold triangle and "HEDINGHAM & DISTRICT" on blue adhesive label. white "4 GOSFIELD/HEDINGHAM" on black front board. Smooth DG base. Certificate.

1. As above.

17-HEG-LP   HEDINGHAM & DISTRICT   1987
Cream body, black chassis and roof, cream 6-bolt wheels, black tires. No other data.

1. As above.

17-IOM-LP   ISLE OF MAN TT   86 1986
Light blue body, yellow chassis, light gray roof, cream windows, silver grille, cream wheels, black tires. Logo: dark blue ansd silver "ISLE OF MAN/TT86" and design, blue "26 MAY-6 JUNE". Lined LP base. Certificate.

1. As above.

17-LON-DG/LP   LONDON TRANSPORT   017-004 1986
Red or dark green body and roof, black or dark green chassis, red, cream or dark green windows, silver or black grille, , red or green wheels, black tires. Logo: gold "LONDON TRANSPORT", underline and other lettering, on adhesive labels on LP issues. No destination on DG issue, white "COBHAM" or "213A" on black front board on LP issues. Lined DG or LP base.

1. Red body, wheels and roof, cream windows, black chassis, tampo-print logo, no destination, lined DG base: DG issue.
2. Rear seat bar, otherwise as type 1.
3. Red body, roof, windows and wheels, black chassis, adhesive labels, 213A front board, lined LP base: LP issue.
4. Dark green body, chassis, roof, windows and wheels, adhesive labels, destination Cobham, lined LP base: LP issue.

17-LOT-LP   LOTHIAN   1987
Maroon body, black chassis, white roof and windows, silver grille, maroon 8-bolt wheels, black tires. Logo: gold stripe, "Lothian" and coat of arms. White "BROUGHTON ST." on black front board. LP base. In boxed set of three models, with or without certificate.

1. As above.

17-MAD-LP   MAIDSTONE & DISTRICT   1985
Dark green body and chassis, cream roof and windows, silver grille, green wheels, black tires. Logo: gold "Maidstone & District/Motor Services/Ltd." and oval, on green adhesive label. White "RYE" or "MAIDSTON" on black front board. Lined LP base.

1. Destination Maidstone.
2. Destination Rye.

17-MAI-LP   MAIDSTONE & DISTRICT   1987
Cream body, dark green chassis, roof and windows, silver grille, dark green wheels, black tires. Logo: gold "Maidstone & District/Motor Services/Ltd." and oval, green

stripe, on adhesive label. White "LEYSDOWN" on black front board. Lined LP base.

1. As above.

17-MID-LP   MIDDLESBOROUGH CORPORATION   1986
Blue body, roof and windows, black chassis, silver grille, black wheels and tires. Logo: yellow and gold stripes and coat of arms, gold "MIDDLESBOROUGH CORPORATION". Lined LP base. Certificate.

1. As above.

17-MOX-DG   MORRELL'S/OXFORD   017-007 1986
Red body, black base, maroon roof and windows, silver grille, black wheels and tires. Logo: blue and gold emblems, blue "MORRELL'S CASTLE ALE MORRELL'S MALT STOUT" and lines on cream stripe, black-outlined gold "OXFORD" and underline. Lined DG17 base.

1. As above.

17-OXF-LP   OXFORD   1987
Cream body and windows, brown chassis and roof, silver grille, maroon wheels, black tires. Logo: gold "OXFORD", underline and "703", brown trim. White "DIDCOT" and frame on front board. LP base. Certificate.

1. As above.

17-PEN-DG   PENNINE   017-011 1987
Orange body, black chassis and roof, light gray windows, silver grille, 5-star front and 6-spoke rear black wheels including tires. Logo: gold "Pennine" on sides, "TRAVEL THE/Pennine/WAY/GARGRAVE 215" on rear. white "MALHAM" on black front board. Lined DG base.

1. As above.

17-POT-LP   POTTERIES   1986
Red body and windows, black chassis, cream roof, silver grille, black wheels and tires. Logo: gold "POTTERIES", underline and frames. Lined LP base.

1. As above.

17-RAF-DG   ROYAL AIR FORCE   017-012 1987
Pale gray body, dark blue chassis, roof and windows, silver grille, yellow 8-bolt wheels, black tires. Logo: blue "ROYAL AIR FORCE" on yellow stripe, blue and gold eagle. Header: white "216 SQUADRON". Lined DG17 base. In boxed set of three RAF models with certificate.

1. As above.

17-RDP-LP   RDP LLEDO COLLECTORS GUIDE   1986
Cream body and roof, red chassis and windows, silver grille, red wheels, black tires. Logo: red "RDP LLEDO COLLECTORS GUIDE/1986" and other lettering. White "HALESOWEN" on black front board. Lined LP base. Certificate.

1. As above.

17-RIB-LP   RIBBLE   1986
Red body, black chassis, cream roof and windows, silver grille, red wheels, black tires. Logo: gold "RIBBLE", underline, stripes and frame. White "PRESTON" on black front board. LP base.

1. As above.

17-SOD-LP   SOUTHDOWN   1985
Light green body and roof, dark green chassis, cream roof and windows, silver grille, dark green wheels, black tires. Logo: gold "SOUTHDOWN" on front adhesive label. White "BRIGHTON" or "11 WORTHING" on black front board. Lined LP base.

1. Destination Brighton.
2. Destination Worthing.

17-SOE-DG/SP   SOUTHEND CORPORATION   017-001 1985
Blue, red or orange body, cream chassis and windows, blue or red roof, silver grille, light blue or red wheels, black or white tires. Logo: black "SOUTHEND CORPORATION" on yellow or orange stripe, black-white-body color coat of arms, black lettering. Smooth or lined DG base.

1. Blue body and roof, light blue wheels, black tires, light yellow logo stripe, smooth base, fuel filler cap, no rear bar.
2. No filler cap, otherwise as type 1.
3. Filler cap, lined base, rear bar, otherwise as type 1.
4. No filler cap, otherwise as type 3.
5. Red body, roof and wheels, white tires, light orange logo stripe, lined base, no

Lledo™ Models

filler cap, rear bar, lined base: special version.
  6. Orange body, blue roof, light blue wheels, black tires, yellow-orange logo stripe, smooth base, no filler cap.
(Note: varying logo stripe colors are probably caused by the body colors under them.)

17-SOU-LP SOUTHERN VECTIS 1987
Green body, black chassis, cream roof and windows, silver grille, green wheels, black tires. Logo: gold stripe, "SOUTHERN VECTIS/NELSON ROAD/NEWPORT I.O.W.". White "COWES" or "NEWPORT" on black front board. Lined LP base.
  1. Destination Cowes.
  2. Destination Newport.

17-SOV-LP SOUTHERN VECTIS 1987
Cream body and windows, cream or green roof, green chassis, silver grille, gray wheels, black tires. Logo: green and black map emblem, green "SOUTHERN VECTIS". Black "NEWPORT" and frame on cream front board. Lined LP base.
  1. Cream roof.
  2. green roof.

17-STE-LP STEVENSON'S BUS SERVICES 1986
Dark yellow body and roof, black chassis and windows, silver grille, yellow wheels, black tires. Logo: black "Stevenson's/BUS SERVICES", emblem and trim. Lined LP base.
  1. As above.

17-STR-DG STRATFORD BLUE 017-006 1986
Light blue body, dark blue chassis, silver roof, white windows, silver or gold grille, blue wheels, gray tires. Logo: red-outlined gold "STRATFORD/BLUE" and underline, gold-bordered light blue stripe with white "SHOTTERY—HATHAWAY COTTAGE—STRATFORD", other white lettering. Lined DG base.
  1. Medium gray tires, silver grille.
  2. Light gray tires, silver grille.
  3. Light gray tires, gold grille.

17-SUT-LP SUTTON SCHOOL OF GYMNASTICS 1985
Cream body, roof and windows, black chassis, silver grille, dark red wheels, black tires. Logo: maroon "Sutton School of Gymnastics" and figure on dark cream adhesive label. Lined LP base. Certificate.
  1. As above.

17-ULS-LP ULSTER TRANSPORT 1987
Dark green body and chassis, cream roof and windows, silver grille, green 6-bolt wheels, black tires. Logo: yellow circle with "ULSTER/TRANSPORT", white and red emblem. No header. Lined LP base.
  1. As above.

17-WBC-LP WEST BROMWICH CORPORATION 1987
Navy blue body, black chassis, dark greenish-blue roof, light blue windows, silvergrille, black wheels and tires. Black "OLDBURY" and frame on roof-color front board. Lined LP base. Certificate.
  1. As above.

17-WHI-EC WHITE 1986
White body, chassis and roof, blue windows, silver grille, white 6-bolt wheels, black tires. No logo. Edocar box and A5 base.
  1. As above.

17-YCM-LP YORK CASTLE MUSEUM 1987
Blue body and roof, cream chassis and windows, gold grille, blue 8-bolt wheels, black tires. logo: yellow "York/CASTLE/Museum", rectangle and frames. Lined LP base. Certificate.
  1. As above.

018 PACKARD VAN 90mm 1985
Metal body and chassis, plastic roof, grille, base and disc wheels. The model is meant to use the Packard grille, with notched upper corners, but also exists with the Rolls-Royce (angled upper corners) and Ford (rounded upper corners) grilles. Casting types:
  A. Small rear flange, with rounded corners, on chassis.
  B. Big rear flange, with ends angling out from chassis.

Base types:

  A. DG18-19.
  B. DG18-19-22.
  C. DG18-19-22-24-25.
  D. Lledo Promotional.
  E. Edocar E6.

18-AMB-DG/EC AMBULANCE 018-001/002 1985
Cream body and roof, black chassis, silver or gold grille, green wheels, including two side spares, white tires. Logo: black "AMBULANCE" and windows, red plain or circled crosses, plus red cross on roof. Models with mixed plain and circled crosses have been reported, but are probably the result of private individuals switching roofs. Later issues probably have wide rear flange. All DG base types plus Edocar.
  1. Plain crosses, silver Packard grille, DG18-19 base.
  2. Plain crosses, silver Rolls frille, DG19-19 base.
  3. Plain crosses, silver Ford grille, DG18-19 base.
  4. Circled crosses, silver Packard grille, DG18-19 base.
  5. Circled crosses, silver Rolls grille, DG18-19 base.
  6. Circled crosses, silver Ford grille, DG18-19 base.
  7. Plain crosses, gold Packard grille, DG18-19 base.
  8. Plain crosses, gold Ford grille, DG18-19-22 base.
  9. Plain crosses, gold Packard grille, DG18-19-22-24-25 base.
  10. Plain crosses, silver Packard grille, DG18-19-22-24-25 base.
  11. Other combinations may well exist, and at least one of the listed variations is found in a Tesco box.
  12. Plain crosses, gold Packard grille, white disc wheels, Edocar box and A6 base.

18-BBC-LP BBC SERVICES 1986
White body, no other data.
  1. As above.

18-CHI-DG THE CHILDREN'S HOSPITAL 018-006 1986
Yellow-orange body, black chassis and roof, silver grille, yellow wheels, black tires. Logo: black windows and "THE CHILDREN'S HOSPITAL", red cross and "CAMPERDOWN", red and black figure, plus white figure and "THE/CHILDREN'S/HOSPITAL/CAMPERDOWN" on roof. DG or LP base. Certificate.
  1. Packard grille, DG18-19 base.
  2. Packard grille, DG18-19-22 base.
  3. Rolls grille, DG18-19-22 base.
  4. Ford grille, DG18-19-22 base.
  5. Packard grille, LP base.

18-COL-DG COLMAN'S MUSTARD 018-008 1987
Yellow body and roof, black chassis, silver grille, red wheels, black tires. Logo: black and red frame, black design, black-outlined red "Colman's Mustard", black "EST./1814". DG18-19-22-24-25 base.
  1. Packard grille.
  2. Ford grille.
  3. Rolls grille.

18-COM-DG COMMONWEALTH GAMES 018-004 1986
White body and chassis, blue roof, silver or gold Packard or Ford grille, white wheels, black tires. Logo: blue and red XIII design, black "XIII COMMONWEALTH GAMES/SCOTLAND 1986" and "SERVICES", blue-white-black emblem. DG18-19 or DG18-19-22-24-25 base. Special box.
  1. DG18-19 base, silver grille.
  2. DG18-19-22-24-25 base, gold grille.
  3. DG18-19-22-24-25 base, silver Ford grille.

18-EXC-LP EXCHANGE AND MART 1987
Dark blue body, black chassis, dark cream roof, gold grille, black disc wheels, white tires. Logo: white-outlined gold "The/Exchange/& Mart" and underline, white "OVER 6000 BARGAINS" and lines, blue "2d" on gold-rimmed white circle, blue and white "MARBLE/ARCH/MOTEX OIL" emblem. LP base. Special box.
  1. As above.

18-FIR-DG FIRESTONE 018-005 1986

White body, red chassis, roof and wheels, white tires, gold or silver grille. Logo: white "Firestone" on red panel with white border, red lines. DG base.
  1. Light red roof, silver Packard griller, DG18-19 base.
  2. Light red roof, silver Rolls grille, DG18-19 base.
  3. Darker red roof, wide rear flange, DG18-19-22-24-25 base, gold Packard grille.
  4. Silver Packard grille, otherwise as type 3.

18-GRY-SP GRAY year?
Gray body and chassis, light brown roof, silver grille, cream wheels, white tires. No logo. DG18-19 base. Large rear flange. Specimen.
  1. As above.

18-JON-LP JON ACC SERVICES 1986
Cream body and roof, black chassis, silver Packard grille, cream wheels, black tires. Logo: black windows, blue "Jon Acc Services, address and telephone number on yellow stripe with blue borders. LP base. Certificate.
  1. As above.

18-KEN-LP KENT COUNTY BRANCH 1986
Dark blue body, black chassis, white roof, black wheels, LP base. No other data.
  1. As above.

18-MIL-LP MILK MARKETING BOARD
Dark green body, no other data.
  1. As above.

18-RAF-DG ROYAL AIR FORCE 018- 1987
Pale gray body, dark blue chassis and roof, gold grille, white disc wheels, black tires. Logo: blue-white-red roundel, red cross on white disc, red "AMBULANCE"; white "AMBULANCE" on roof. DG18-19-22-24-25 base. In boxed set of three ARF models with certificate.
  1. As above.

18-RAP-DG RAPID CASH TRANSIT 018-003 1986
Green body, black chassis, cream roof, silver grille, green wheels, cream tires. Logo: black-outlined white "RAPID CASH/TRANSIT", red-white-black shield design, white "UNIT 6", plus black "UNIT 6" on roof. DG18-19 base.
  1. Packard grille.
  2. Rolls grille.
  3. Ford grille.

18-STJ-LP ST. JOHN AMBULANCE 1986
Black body and chassis, white roof, silver Packard grille, white wheels, black tires. Logo: white Maltese cross, windows, "St. John Ambulance/Association/PLYMOUTH SERVICE/Police Force & Fire Brigade Auxiliary", and frames. LP base.
  1. As above.

18-WEW-LP WESTERN WOOLLENS 1986
Pinkish cream body, black chassis and roof, silver Packard grille, red wheels, black tires. Logo: red "Western/Woollens", farm scene and "F.D.M." LP base.
  1. As above.

18-WHS-DG WHITE STAR STEAMSHIP CO. 018-007 1987
Red body and chassis, white roof, gold or silver grille, black wheels and tires. Logo: white-outlined yellow "WHITE STAR", black-outlined white star emblem, black black lines and "STEAMSHIP Co. LTD". DG18-19-22-24-25 base. Medium or wide flange, presumably with any grille type.
  1. Gold Packard grille.
  2. Silver Packard grille.
  3. Silver Rolls grille.
  4. Gold Rolls grille.
  5. Gold Ford grille.

019 ROLLS-ROYCE CAR 87mm 1985
Metal body and chassis, textured plastic roof, interior-trunk, grille and base. Metal 12-spoke or plastic 20-spoke or disc wheels, including two side-mounted spares. Casting types:
  A. Vertical flange on chassis under trunk.
  B. Small horizontal flange under trunk.

Base types, all with ridge around lettering:
- A. DG18-19.
- B. DG18-19-22.
- C. DG18-19-22-24-25.
- D. Lledo Promotional.
- E. Edocar A7.

19-BLK-LP BLACK   1987
Black body, chassis, roof, interior and trunk, silver grille, red 20-spoke wheels, black tires. Horizontal flange. LP base.
1. As above.

19-BLU-LP BLUE   1986
Dark blue body, red chassis and roof, blue interior and trunk, gold grille, red disc wheels, white tires. Horizontal flange. LP base.
1. As above.

19-BLW-LP BLACK/WHITE   1987
No data.
1. As above.

19-BUR-DG BURGUNDY   019-001 1985
Burgundy body, black chassis and roof, tan interior and trunk, silver grille, dark red disc wheels, white tires. With or without certificate. Vertical or horizontal flange. DG base.
1. DG18-19 base, vertical flange, silver Rolls grille.
2. DG18-19-22-24-25 base, horizontal flange, silver Rolls grille.
3. Silver Ford radiator, otherwise as type 2.

19-CON-LP CONGRATULATIONS   1987
Light blue body, darker blue chassis and roof, cream interior and trunk, gold grille, 20-spoke white wheels, black tires. Logo: gold "Congratulations". Horizontal flange. LP base.
1. As above.

19-CRM-DG CREAM   019-002 1985
Cream body, chassis, roof, interior and trunk, silver grille, cream disc wheels, white tires. Vertical flange. Boxed or on plinth. For factory promotional use. DG18-19 base.
1. On plinth.
2. Not on plinth.

19-GOL-DG GOLD   019-005 1987
Gold body and chassis, white roof, interior and trunk, gold grille, 12-spoke gold wheels, white tires. Horizontal flange. DG18-19-22-24-25 base.
1. As above.

19-GRY-SP GRAY   year?
Gray body and chassis, black roof, light brown interior and trunk, silver grille, tan wheels and tires. DG18-19 base. Specimen.
1. As above.

19-MAR-LP HAPPY 40th BIRTHDAY MARILYN   1987
White body and chassis, black roof, tan interior and trunk, gold grille, white disc wheels, black tires. Logo: gold "Happy/40th/Birthday/Marilyn/Oct. 3, 1987" and design. Horizontal flange. LP base.
1. As above.

19-OLI-DG OLIVE AND WICKER   019-004 1986
Light tannish olive body with red-brown wickerwork tampo-printed on sides, tannish yellow chassis, light tan or brown roof, interior and trunk, gold or silver grille, bright yellow disc wheels, gray or tan tires. Vertical or horizontal flange. DG base.
1. Brown roof, tan interior, gray tires, gold grille, DG181-9 base, vertical flange.
2. Tan roof and interior, gray tires, gold grille, DG18-19 base, vertical flange.
3. Brown roof and interior, gray tires, gold grille, DG18-19 base, horizontal flange.
4. Tan roof and interior, gray tires, gold grille, DG18-19 base, horizontal flange.
5. Tan roof and interior, gray tires, gold grille, DG18-19-22 base, horizontal flange.
6. Tan roof and interior, gray tires, silver grille, DG18-19-22 base, horizontal flange.
7. Tan roof and interior, gray tires, gold grille, DG18-19-22-24-25 base, horizontal flange.
8. Tan roof, interior and tires, gold grille, DG18-19-22-24-25 base, horizontal

flange.

19-QEP-DG QUEEN ELIZABETH/PRINCE PHILIP   019- 1987
Magenta body, black chassis, dark cream roof, interior and trunk, gold grille, reddish-purple disc wheels, white tires. Logo: gold "H.M./Queen Elizabeth II/H.R.H./Prince Philip". Small rear flange. DG18-19-22-24-25 base. Special box, part of Ruby Wedding set.
1. As above.

19-ROY-LP ROYAL WEDDING   1986
White body, chassis and roof, black interior and trunk, gold grille, white disc wheels, black tires. Logo: gold "The Royal Wedding 23 July 1986" and coat of arms on each side, "H.R.H. Prince Andrew" on left side, "Miss Sarah Ferguson" on right. Horizontal flange. LP base. Special box.
1. As above.

19-SIL-EC SILVER   1986
Silver body, black chassis, roof, interior and trunk, black disc wheels, white or black tires. Horizontal flange. Edocar box and A7 base.
1. White tires.
2. Black tires.

19-WHI-LP WHITE   1986
White body, chassis and roof, black or ivory interior and trunk, silver grille, white disc wheels, black tires. Vertical flange. LP base.
1. Black interior.
2. Ivory interior, in special Persil box; one of four Persil models.

19-YEL-DG YELLOW   019-003 1985
Yellow body and chassis, dark tan roof, interior and trunk, silver or gold grille, dark tan disc wheels, black tires. Horizontal or vertical flange. DG (or Edocar?) base.
1. Brown roof, silver grille, DG18-19 base, vertical flange.
2. Brown roof, gold grille, DG18-19 base, vertical flange.
3. White roof, silver grille, DG18-19 base, vertical flange.
4. Brown roof, silver grille, DG18-19 base, horizontal flange.
5. Brown roof, gold grille, DG18-19 base, horizontal flange.
6. Brown roof, silver grille, DG18-19-22 base, horizontal flange.
7. Brown roof, gold grille, DG18-19-22 base, horizontal flange.
8. Lighter yellow body and chassis, brown roof, silver grille, DG18-19-22-24-25 base, horizontal flange.
9. Edocar base?

020 FORD STAKE TRUCK   90mm 1986
Metal cab, stake body and chassis, plastic load, grille, base and 6-bolt single front and dual rear wheels. Chassis casting can have thick or thin front fenders. Base types:
1. DG20.
2. Lledo Promotional.

20-BBC-LP BBC (no logo)   1986
Dark green cab, body and chassis, silver grille, dark green wheels, black tires. Gold frames but no lettering. Load of six dark brown barrels. LP base. Part of BBC-Radio Times set.
1. As above.

20-BUR-LP BURT'S ALES   1986
Dark green cab and chassis, red chassis, black grille, dark green wheels, black tires. Logo: white "BURT'S" on gold-bordered red horizontal panel, green "BURT'S/ALES and figure on gold vertical panel, gold "VENTNOR/I.O.W.", map and semicircle on door, plus gold "BURT'S—VENTNOR" and frame on front of body. Load of six dark brown barrels. LP base.
1. As above.

20-COC-DG COCA-COLA   020-002 1986
Dark yellow cab and body, black chassis, silver grille, red wheels, black tires. Logo: white "Coca-Cola/BOTTLING/COMPANY" on white-bordered red horizontal panel, yellow-black-white figure, black "Drink" and red "Coca-Cola" on red-bordered white vertical panel, red "DELICIOUS/AND/REFRESHING" on door. Load of six dark brown or red barrels. DG base. Special box.
1. Dark brown barrels.

2. Red barrels.

20-EAG-DG EAGLE ALE   020-001 1986
Dark yellow cab and body, black chassis, black grille, red wheels, black tires. Logo: black-and-white-outlined gold "Eagle Ale" on white-and-gold-bordered yellow horizontal panel, black and gold eagle figure on white disc on vertical panel, black "The/High Flying/Lager" on door. Load of six dark brown barrels. DG base.
1. As above.
2. Lighter yellow cab and body, purplish-brown chassis.

20-GOO-DG GOODRICH   020-004 1986
Ivory cab, navy blue chassis, silver or gold grille, cream wheels, black tires. Logo: white "Goodrich" on white-bordered dark blue horizontal panel, blue-cream-black figure of man and tire on vertical panel, red and green emblem on door. Load of black tires. DG base.
1. Silver Ford grille.
2. Gold Packard grille.

20-LAI-LP LAIRD'S BLENDED APPLEJACK   1986
Tannish yellow cab, dark tan body, dark brown chassis, silver grille, dark tan wheels, gray tires. Logo: brown "BLENDED" and tan-outlined brown "APPLEJACK" on horizontal panel, brown "LAIRD'S", gold and red emblem, and brown "AMERICA'S/OLDEST/BRANDY/DISTILLERS" on vertical panel, red apple and "LAIRD AND COMPANY/SCOBEYVILLE/NEW JERSEY" on door, plus brown "LAIRD'S" on front of body. Load of six dark brown barrels. LP base.
1. As above.

20-LIO-DG LIONEL/NICHOLAS SMITH   1986
Dark orange cab, blue body and chassis, gold grille, red wheels, black tires. Logo: white-outlined red "LIONEL" on horizontal panel, red-white-green emblem and white lettering on vertical panel, black "TRACK/REPAIR" on door, plus white "Nicholas Smith" on front of body. Load of six dark brown barrels. LP base.
1. As above.

20-LOW-LP LOWCOCKS LEMONADE   1987
Magenta cab and body, black chassis, silver grille, black wheels and tires. Logo: black-outlined red "LOWCOCKS" on black-outlined yellow ribbon, yellow "LEMONADE" on horizontal panel, telephone number on vertical panel, yellow and black bottle on vertical panel, yellow "Drink/LOWCOCK'S/Lemonade" and trim on door, plus yellow "W. J. LOWCOCK" on front of body. Load of either six dark brown barrels or black bottle with yellow cap and yellow and black label. LP base. Certificate and postcard.
1. Load of barrels only.
2. Load of barrels plus bottle (barrels must be removed to install bottle).

20-STR-DG STROH'S BEER   020-005 1987
Red cab and body, black chassis, gold or silver grille, white wheels, black tires. Logo: black-outlined gold "Stroh's" and white "America's only/Fire-Brewed Beer" on horizontal panel, gold and black emblem on vertical panel, white "EST./1850" and black "No. 5" on door. Load of six black barrels. DG base. Thick front end with holes and wide slot.
1. Gold grille.
2. Silver grille.

20-UNI-DG UNIROYAL   020-006 1987
Red cab and body, black chassis, gold grille, red wheels, black tires. Logo: black "UNIROYAL" and black and white tire tread design on black-bordered white horizontal panel, black "Manufacturers/of Quality/Tire Products/Since 1895" on white vertical panel, black emblem and "UNIROYAL" on door, plus black "UNIROYAL" on front of body. Load of black tires. DG base.
1. As above.

20-WAT-LP WATNEYS   1987
White cab, body and chassis, silver grille, red wheels, black tires. Logo: white "WATNEYS", "IMPORTED/RED/BARREL/BEER" and other lettering on red panels, red hood lines. Load of six red barrels. LP base.
1. As above, "IMPORTED/RED/BARREL/BEER".
2. "IMPORTED/BARREL/RED/BEER".

20-WHI-DG   WHITBREAD　　　　020-003   1986
Brown cab and body (shades vary), black chassis, gold grille, red wheels, black tires. Logo: gold "WHITBREAD" and red frame on horizontal panel, gold "BREWERS/SINCE 1742" and red frame on vertical panel, gold design and red frame on door, plus gold "WHITBREAD" and frame on front of body and red hood panel outline. Load of six dark brown barrels. DG base.
　1. As above.
　2. Lighter brown (shades vary) cab and body.
　3. Purplish or reddish brown cab and body.
　4. Purplish brown cab, dark brown body.
　5. Dark brown cab, purplish brown body.
　6. Reddish-brown barrels.
　7. Pale brass grille.
　8. LP base.
　9. Disc wheels.
Many combinations of these features may exist.

021   CHEVROLET VAN　　　　80mm   1986
Metal body and chassis, plastic roof, grille and base. Metal 12-spoke, plastic 20-spoke or disc wheels. Chassis castings include die number 1 or 2 under toolbox on left running board; these will not be listed, as any model may exist with either number. In 1987 a roof casting including a header was introduced; no model yet exists both with and without a header; thus if a header is not mentioned for a particular model, it has none. The interior of the body casting was modified to take the new roof. Base types:
　A. DG21.
　B. Lledo Promotional.
　C. Edocar.

21-AAC-LP   AACA NATIONAL FALL MEET　　　　1987
White body, blue chassis, red roof with header, silver grille, 20-spoke red wheels, white tires. Logo: gold scroll with "AACA/National/Fall Meet" and other lettering, gold and black car design, gold emblem. Header: white "Hershey Region". LP base.
　1. As above.

21-ALL-LP   THE ALLENBURYS' DIET　　　　1986
Magenta body, black chassis, pale tan roof, gold grille, dark red 20-spoke wheels, gray tires. Logo: Maroon "The" and "FOR ADULTS", black-outlined maroon "Allenburys' Diet" and black "ALLEN & HANBURYS, Ltd." on pale tan panel, white "Wholesale & Manufacturing Chemists/LONDON & WARE", other lettering and trade mark. LP base.
　1. As above.

21-ANC-LP   ANC PARCEL SERVICE　　　　1987
White body, blue chassis, off-white roof, gold grille, black 20-spoke wheels, black tires. Logo: blue "THE BRITISH PARCEL SERVICE/ANC/NEXT DAY—NATION-WIDE" and other lettering, red and blue design, red frames. No header. LP base.
　1. As above.

21-AUS-LP   AUSTRALIAN MODEL SWAPMEETS　　　　1986
Light orange body, green chassis and roof, silver grille, yellow-orange disc wheels, black tires. Logo: green and orange "AUSTRALIAN MODEL/SWAPMEETS" and design, green "E. G. WHITLAM CENTRE/LIVERPOOL/1986". LP base.
　1. As above.

21-BRE-LP   BRENMARK　　　　1987
Cream body and roof, black chassis, silver grille, 20-spoke black wheels, black tires. Logo: black and red "BRENMARK" and emblem, black lettering. LP base.
　1. As above.

21-CFV-LP   CANADA FRUIT & VINE　　　　1986
Cream body, maroon chassis and roof, silver grille, 12-spoke gold wheels, white tires. Logo: maroon grape design, "CANADA FRUIT AND VINE" and "F.D.M." LP base.
　1. As above.

21-CIM-LP   CITY MUSEUM & ART GALLERY　　　　1986
Cream body, brown chassis and roof, gold grille, 12-spoke gold wheels, black tires. Logo: green "CITY MUSEUM/& ART GALLERY/STOKE-ON-TRENT" and

lines. LP base.

21-CIT-LP   THE CITIZEN/GLOUCESTER JOURNAL　　　　1987
Yellow body, black chassis and roof, 20-spoke black wheels, black tires. No other data.
　1. As above.

21-COC-DG   COCA-COLA　　　　021-003   1986
Cream body, red chassis and roof, gold grille, 12-spoke gold wheels, white tires. Logo: red "KEEP A CASE/Coca-Cola/IN YOUR HOME" on brown-bordered red oval on yellow-brown-cream grid pattern, brown and cream hand holding bottle, brown "The" and "BOTTLING Co." and red "Coca-Cola". DG base. Special box.
　1. As above.

21-COM-LP   CO-OPERATIVE MILK　　　　1987
Light yellow body, brown chassis and roof, silver grille, brown disc wheels and tires. (Lledo's first and so far only model with brown tires!) Logo: blue "CO-OPERATIVE MILK/MILK SERVICE DEPT/PURE BOTTLED MILK", lines, trim and frames. LP base.
　1. As above.

21-DEA-LP   DEANE'S　　　　1987
Green body, dark green chassis and roof, silver grille, green disc wheels, black tires. Logo: silver "DEANE'S/FRESH VEGETABLES/FRESH FRUIT/FLOWERS FOR ALL OCCASIONS", other lettering and frame. LP base. In DG box.
　1. As above.

21-DRB-LP   DR. BARNARDO'S　　　　1986
White body, black chassis, red roof, silver grille, white disc wheels, black tires. Logo: white "Dr Barnardo's/No destitute child/ever refused admission: and design on white-bordered red panel. LP base. Certificate.
　1. As above.

21-DRP-DG   DR. PEPPER　　　　021-006   1987
Red body, black chassis, white roof with header, gold grille, red disc wheels, white tires. Logo: black-outlined white "DRINK/Dr. Pepper", black "GOOD FOR LIFE" on white background, white "Dallas" and "Drink/Bottled/5c", plus red "King of Beverages" and underline on header. Dg base.
　1. As above.

21-EDO-EC   EDOCAR　　　　1986
Blue body, black chassis, white roof, gold grille, white disc wheels, black tires. Logo: black "EDOCAR" on yellow-red-black box design, gold "Finest Diecast/Miniatures". Edocar base.
　1. As above.

21-EXC-LP   EXCHANGE & MART BAZAAR　　　　1986
Brown body, black chassis and roof, black gold grille (first and so far only example thereof), brown disc wheels, white tires. Logo: white "THE/EXCHANGE/& MART/and Collectors'/Weekly" and "THURSDAYS", black-and-white-outlined gold "BAZAAR", brown "2d" on black-outlined gold disc, black and brown stripes, gold designs. LP base. Special box.
　1. As above.

21-FOX-LP   FOX TALBOT　　　　1986
Cream body, brown chassis and roof, gold grille, 20-spoke brown wheels, white tires. Logo: green camera design and "FOX TALBOT/154 Tottenham Court Road/London W1", telephone number and "Quality/Photographic/Equipment". LP base.
　1. As above.

21-HOB-LP   HOBBYCO　　　　1987
White body, red chassis and roof, white disc wheels, black tires. No other data.
　1. As above.

21-HOS-DG   HOSTESS CAKE　　　　021-004   1986
White body, red chassis and roof, silver grille, red disc wheels, white tires. Logo: white "HOSTESS/CAKE" and stripes on blue ribbons, white silhouette on red heart, red "America's/Favorite/Quick/Dessert". DG base.
　1. As above.

21-JEP-LP   JERSEY EVENING POST　　　　1987
White body, black chassis and roof with header, gold grille, 12-spoke gold wheels. Logo: Black "Jersey Evening/Post" and "St. Saviour.Jersey.Channel Islands", pink panel and stripe, plus black "Part of Jersey life" on white header background. LP base.
　1. As above.

21-LCM-DG   LLEDO CLUB MEMBER　　　　021-005   1986
Maroon body, black chassis, pale tan roof, gold grille, maroon disc wheels, white tires. Logo: black "Models of" and "LLEDO.O.R.I.G.I.N.A.L." and black-outlined gold "DAYS GONE" on gold and black emblem, gold "Club Member/Edition/Autumn/1986". DG base. Special box.
　1. As above.

21-LLP-LP   LLEDO PROMOTIONAL　　　　1986
Yellow-orange body, black chassis, roof and grille, yellow disc wheels, black tires. Logo: black "YOUR OWN PROMOTIONAL CAR/PHONE FOR INFORMATION", phone numbers for Belgium and Holland, and "LLEDO/PROMOTIONAL". LP base.
　1. As above.

21-LEI-DG   LEICESTER MERCURY　　　　021-002   1986
Blue body, black chassis and roof, gold grille, 20-spoke black wheels, black tires. Logo: white "LEICESTER/Mercury/LARGEST CIRCULATION/ILLUSTRATED/CHRONICLE and circled "No. 27". DG base.
　1. As above.

21-OKT-LP   OKTOBERFEST TOY SHOW　　　　1986
Cream body, maroon chassis and roof, silver grille, gold 12-spoke wheels, white tires. Logo: green "2nd ANNUAL/TOY SHOW/OCT. 12, 1986" and "OKTOBERFEST" design. LP base.
　1. As above.

21-RDP-LP   RDP LLEDO COLLECTOR GUIDES　　　　1987
Cream body, black chassis and roof, white grille, red 20-spoke wheels, white tires. Logo: red "LLEDO/COLLECTOR GUIDES" and telephone number, "RDP/1987" on doors, on adhesive labels. LP base.
　1. As above.

21-SHA-DG   SHARP'S TOFFEE　　　　021-001   1986
Cream body, brown chassis, tan roof, silver grille, maroon disc wheels, white tires. Logo: Brown "SHARP'S" and emblem with company name and address, orange "SUPER-KREEM/TOFFEE", blue-brown-cream figure. DG base.
　1. Silver plated grille.
　2. Silver painted grille.
　3. Silver plated grille, purplish-brown ridge in place of two pins under grille, .

21-SUN-DG   SUNBAKED RAISINS　　　　1987?
No data. Announced for late 1987.
　1. As above?

21-WPT-LP   WEST POINT TOY SHOW　　　　1986
Light orange body, blue chassis and roof, silver grille, 20-spoke yellow-orange wheels, white tires. Logo: blue and orange coat of arms, red "WEST/POINT", "TOY/SHOW" and "JUNE 22;/1986". LP base. Certificate.
　1. As above.

022   PACKARD TOWN VAN　　　　87mm   1986
Metal body and chassis, plastic roof, seat, windshield, grille, base and disc wheels, including two spares. Chassis has small horizontal rear flange. Base types:
　A. DG18-19-22.
　B. DG18-19-22-24-25.
　C. Lledo Promotional.

22-EXC-LP   EXCHANGE AND MART　　　　1987
White body, black chassis, roof and seat, gold grille and windshield, dark red wheels, black tires. Logo: red-white-black-gold emblem with black-outlined white "EXCHANGE/& MART", red "1987/MOTORING NEWS" and "Est/1868", red and gold frames. LP base. Special box.
　1. As above.

22-FEL-LP   FELTON WORLDWIDE　　　　1987
Light gray body, black chassis, roof and seat, gold grille and windshield, maroon

wheels, white tires. Logo: black "FELTON/worldwide", red lines andframe, plus black "Flavors/Fragrances/Essential Oils" on rear. LP base.
1. As above.

22-FTD-DG FLORISTS TRANSWORLD DELIVERY   022-003 1987
Cream body, black chassis, roof and seat, gold grille and windshield, cream wheels, black tires. Logo: black and gold emblem with gold "FTD" and figure and black "FLORISTS TRANSWORLD DELIVERY/SINCE 1910", red "Say it/with flowers" and "WE/DELIVER/WORLDWIDE". DG18-19-22-24-25 base.
1. Packard grille.
2. Ford grille.
3. Rolls grille.

22-JHC-LP THE JOHN HARVEY COLLECTION   1987
Dark brown body, roof and seat, cream chassis, gold grille and windshield, brown disc wheels, black tires. Logo: gold "The/John Harvey/Collection", emblem, "Harvey House/Tring, Herts." and frame. LP base. Fuji box.
1. As above.

22-JON-LP J. FRED JONES PACKARD   1986
Blue body, navy blue chassis, cream roof and seat, gold grille and windshield, navy blue wheels, black tires. Logo: white "J. Fred Jones/PACKARD SALES & SERVICE/PACKARD MOTOR CAR Co./DETROIT, MICHIGAN", on adhesive label. LP base.
1. As above.

22-LCM-DG CLUB MEMBER EDITION   022-004 1986
Yellow body, brown chassis and roof, gold grille and windshield, red seat, red wheels, red tires. Logo: gold and black Lledo emblem, gold "Club member Edition Winter 1986/87". DG18-19-22-24-25 base. Special box.
1. As above.

22-LTC-DG LORD TED CIGARS   022-002 1986
Black body, chassis, roof and seat, gold grille and windshield, red wheels, cream tires. Logo: gold "Lord Ted/Cigars for Gentlemen/St. James", telephone number and trim. DG18-19-22 or DG18-19-22-24-25 base.
1. Packard grille, DG18-19-22 base.
2. Packard grille, DG18-19-22-24-25 base.
3. Rolls grille, DG18-19-22-24-25 base.

22-STA-DG STAG WHISKY   022-001 1986
Cream body, red chassis, roof and seat, silver grille and windshield, red wheels, white tires. Logo: orange-outlined brown "STAG/WHISKY", black and orange stag design, black "PURE MALT WHISKY/70% PROOF" and "ESTd./1846". DG or LP base.
1. DG18-19-22 base (original issue).
2. DG18-19 base.
3. DG18-19 base, Rolls grille.
4. DG18-19-22-24-25 base, darker red roof, seat and wheels.
5. LP base.

22-TEL-LP TELEMEDIA SPORTS   1987
White body, blue chassis, roof and seat, gold grille and windshield, 12-spoke gold wheels, white tires. Logo: blue and white design, blue "TELEMEDIA SPORTS/RADIO DAY/SEPTEMBER 12, 1987" and Toronto Blue Jays emblem. LP base.
1. As above.

22-WHI-DG WHITMAN'S SAMPLER   022-005 1987
Yellow body, brown chassis, red roof and seat, gold grille and windshield, brown "Started/in/1842" and other lettering and frame. DG18-19-22-24-25 base.
1. As above.

22-WPT-LP WEST POINT MILITARY ACADEMY   1987
Yellow-orange body, black chassis, roof and seat, gold grille and windshield, black wheels, white tires. Logo: black coat of arms, "WEST/POINT", "MILITARY/ ACADEMY", "HOTEL/THAYER" and other lettering, plus, on one version, red red "TOY SHOW" and "JUNE 21, 1987". Black-outlined yellow "HOTEL/THAYER"

and black address on rear. LP base.
1. With red Toy Show lettering.
2. Without red Toy Show lettering.

023 SCENICRUISER   109mm 1987
Metal body and chassis, red-tinted opaque plastic windows, base and single 5-star front and two axles of 6-spoke dual rear wheels including tires. The first Greyhound issues lacked triangular wheel spacers on the base; all subsequent issues have them. Base types (both with ridge around lettering):
A. DG23.
2. Lledo Promotional.

23-ARC-LP ARC OF ALLEN COUNTY   1987
White body, black chassis, black wheels. Logo: blue "arc/LEARNING/LIVING/ GUIDANCE/INDUSTRIES/OF/ALLEN/COUNTY". LP base. Certificate.
1. As above.

23-BAT-LP B & A TOP MARKS   1987
Rose pink body and chassis, black wheels. Logo: Light green "B & A TOP MARKS" on adhesive label. LP base.
1. As above.

23-BMO-LP BANVIL MILTON ONTARIO   1987
Yellow-orange body, black chassis, black wheels. Logo: gold "BANVIL MILTON ONTARIO" on black background. LP base.
1. As above.

23-BUF-DG BUFFALO LUXURY TRAVEL   023-003 1987
Red body, black chassis, black wheels. Logo: white "BUFFALO" and black "Luxury Travel" on red and yellow stripe. DG base.
1. As above.

23-FRA-LP FRANDELLO   1987
Yellow-orange body, black chassis, black wheels. Logo: yellow-orange "FRANDELLO" on green background. LP base.
1. As above.

23-GRE-DG GREYHOUND   023-001 1987
Silver body and chassis, black wheels. Logo: black-outlined silver greyhound figure and black "Greyhound", on white stripe. DG base.
1. No wheel spacers.
2. Wheel spacers.

23-GWT-DG GOLDEN WEST TOURS   023-002 1987
Gold body, black chassis, black wheels. Logo: red and gold "GOLDEN WEST and design, and gold "tours", on light blue stripe. DG base.
1. As above.

23-STA-LP STAGECOACH   1987
Yellow-orange body, black chassis, black wheels. Logo: gold guitar, "STAGE-COACH" and piano keys on black background. LP base.
1. As above.

23-THO-LP THOMAS TOURS   1987
Yellow-orange body, black chassis, black wheels. Logo: yellow-orange "THOMAS TOURS" and design on black background. LP base.
1. As above.

23-TOF-LP TOFF TOFF   1987
Pink body and chassis, black wheels. Logo: black "TOFF TOFF", old car design, "YOUR LLEDO SPECIALIST/IN ESSEN (W. GERMANY)" on yellow adhesive label. LP base.
1. As above.

024 ROLLS ROYCE PLAYBOY   87mm 1987
Metal body and chassis, plastic plain or textured top, interior, trunk, grille, base and wheels, including two side spares. Chassis castings:
1. Small horizontal rear flange.
2. Medium horizontal flange with rounded corners.
Base types (with ridge around lettering):
A. DG18-19-22-24-25.
B. DG18-19-22.

Lledo Promotional.

24-BLK-LP BLACK   1987
Black body, chassis, top, interior and trunk, silver grille, red 20-spoke wheels, black tires. In 3-piece boxed set. LP base.
1. As above.

24-PUR-DG PURPLE   024-002 1987
Metallic purple body (shades vary), dark purple chassis, white top, interior and trunk, silver or gold grille, dark purple disc wheels, light gray tires. DG base. Medium flange.
1. Pale body, silver grille.
2. Pale body, gold grille.
3. Dark body, silver grille.

24-RED-DG RED   024-003 1987
Red body, white chassis, green roof, interior and trunk, gold grille, 20-spoke red wheels, white tires. LP base. Large flange. In special Fuji box.
1. As above.

24-YEL-DG YELLOW   024-001 1987
Dark yellow body, black chassis, light brown top, interior and trunk, gold grille, yellow disc wheels, black or gray tires. DG base. Small or medium flange.
1. Plain roof, black tires, DG18-19-22 base, medium flange.
2. Plain roof, black tires, DG18-19-22-24-25 base, small flange.
3. Plain roof, black tires, DG18-19-22-24-25 base, medium flange.
4. Textured roof, black tires, DG18-19-22-24-25 base, medium flange.
5. Plain roof, gray tires, DG18-19-22-24-25 base, medium flange.

025 ROLLS ROYCE SILVER GHOST   93mm 1987
Metal body and chassis, plastic top, interior, grille and base. Metal 12-spoke or plastic 20-spoke wheels, including two side spares. Chassis types:
A. Small horizontal rear flange.
B. Medium horizontal flange with rounded corners.
Base types (both have ridge around lettering):
A. DG18-19-22-24.
B. Lledo Promotional.

25-BLK-LP BLACK   1987
Black body, chassis, top and interior, silver grille, red 20-spoke wheels, black tires. LP base. Medium flange.
1. As above.

25-BLU-DG BLUE   025-001 1987
Navy blue body, black chassis, top and interior, gold or silver grille, black 20-spoke wheels and tires. DG base. Medium or small flange.
1. Gold grille, medium flange, DG18-19-22.
2. Gold grille, small flange, DG18-19-22-24-25 base.
3. Gold grille, medium flange, DG18-19-22-24-25 base.
4. Silver grille, medium flange, DG18-19-22-24-25 base.
5. Lighter blue body, gold grille, medium flange, DG18-19-22-24-25 base.

25-CON-LP CONGRATULATIONS   1987
Rose pink body, white chassis, top and interior, silver grille, white 20-spoke wheels, black tires. Logo: black "Congratulations". LP base. Medium flange.
1. As above.

25-SIL-DG SILVER   025-002 1987
Silver body, blue chassis and top, cream interior, gold grille, gold 12-spoke wheels, white tires. DG 18-19-22-24-25 base, small or medium flange.
1. Gold Rolls grille, small flange.
2. Gold Rolls grille, medium flange.
3. Gold Packard grille.

25-SLB-DG SILVER/BLACK   025-003 1987
No data.
1. As above.

25-WHI-DG WHITE   025-003 1987
White body and chassis, black top, cream interior, gold grille, gold 12-spoke wheels, black tires. DG 18-19-22-24-25 base, medium flange.
1. As above.

Lledo™ Models

026   CHEVROLET SOFT DRINKS VAN   82mm 1987
Metal cab, body and chassis, plastic load, blade, grille, base and disc wheels. DG21-26 base.

26-LCM-DG   LLEDO CLUB MEMBER   026-002 1987
White body and blade, black chassis and load, silver grille, white 6-bolt wheels, black tires. Logo: black "The/Lledo/COLLECTION and stripes on blade, Lledo emblem on rear, "Club/Member/Summer/Edition/1987" on doors. DG21-26 base.
   1. As above.

26-SCH-DG   SCHWEPPES   026-001 1987
Yellow cab and body, red chassis, brown or black load, yellow blade, gold grille, red

disc wheels, white or black tires. Logo: black "Schweppes" on blade, red and gold emblem on door, red-gold-yellow-black "Schweppes" emblem on rear. DG 21 or DG21-26 base.
   1. Light yellow cab, body and blade, light brown load, white tires, DG21-26 base.
   2. Dark yellow cab, body and blade, black load and tires, DG21 base.
   3. DG21-26 base, otherwise as type 2.

027   MACK BREAKDOWN TRUCK   100mm 1987
Metal body, chassis and boom, plastic rear interior, hook, grille, base, single front and dual rear wheels. Base types:
   A. DG27-28.

27-A1R-DG   A1 24-HOUR RECOVERY   027-001 1987
Orange body, black chassis, rear interior, grille, wheels and tires, white boom. Logo: red "A1" on red-bordered yellow disc and "24-Hour/RECOVERY" on yellow and orange diagonal stripes. DG base.
   1. As above.

028   MACK CANVAS BACKED TRUCK   1988
28-LYO-DG   LYONS TEA   028-001 1988
No data. Announced for late 1987, then postponed.
   1. As above.

Marathon Models

Lledo Marathons are a series of modern commercial vehicles. As I write this, three buses have been produced and two trucks have been announced. The M1 Leyland Olympian is a London doubledecker, the M2 Setra Coach a short singledeck shuttle, and the M3 Neoplan Spaceliner a longer singledeck coach. As of late 1987, each has been issued in three forms.

M1   LEYLAND OLYMPIAN   94mm 1987
Metal body and roof, plastic windows, interior, base, and single front and dual rear wheels. Base: "LLEDO/MARATHONS/M1/MADE IN ENGLAND" within ridge.

M1-LON-MA   LONDON ZOO   1987
Red body and roof, cream windows and interior, black base and wheels. Upper logo: red "LONDON ZOO" and multicolored animal figures on black-cordered yellow panel. Lower logo: white "LONDON TRANSPORT" and underline. M1 base.
   1. As above.

M1-LOP-MA   ENSIGNBUS/LONDON PRIDE   1987
Blue body and roof, cream windows and interior, black base and wheels. Upper logo: white "Ensignbus", red-white-blue design with blue "PINDISPORTS" and red "No. 1 SKI SHOP IN LONDON" and other lettering on white background. Lower logo: white "LONDON PRIDE/SIGHTSEEING". M1 base.
   1. As above.

M1-PAN-MA   PAN AM   1987
White body, windows and interior, blue roof, black base and wheels. Upper logo: blue "Today's Pan Am", white emblem, red "To every corner of America", on gray panel. Lower logo: blue "CORPORATION TRANSPORT". M1 base.
   1. As above.

M2   SETRA COACH   87mm 1987
Metal body and roof, plastic windows, interior, base, and single front and dual rear wheels. Base: "LLEDO/MARATHONS/M2/MADE IN ENGLAND" within ridge.

M2-AIC-MA   AIR CANADA   1987
White body, red roof and interior, clear windows, black base and wheels. Logo: red "AIR CANADA" and emblem, black "09", "COURTESY BUS" and stripe. M2 base.
   1. As above.

M2-GHA-MA   GHANA AIRWAYS   1987
Yellow body and roof, clear windows, red interior, black base and wheels. Logo: red "GHANA AIRWAYS", black "TO WEST AFRICA", green "COURTESY COACH", red-yellow-green-black emblem, orange-green-black city design. M2 base.
   1. As above.

M2-PAN-MA   PAN AM   1987
White body, blue roof, clear windows, red interior, black base and wheels. Logo: white emblem and "PAN AM" on blue background, black "07", "CREW BUS" and stripe. M2 base.
   1. As above.

M3   NEOPLAN SPACELINER   101mm 1987
Metal body and roof, plastic windows, interior, base, and single front and dual rear wheels. Base: "LLEDO/MARATHONS/M3/MADE IN ENGLAND" within ridge.

M3-GAT-MA   GATWICK FLIGHTLINE   1987
Tan body and interior, white roof, clear windows, black base and wheels. Logo: white and yellow "GATWICK FLIGHTLINE", yellow and green stripes and trim. M3 base.
   1. As above.

M3-ISL-MA   ISLAND TOURS   1987
Yellow-orange body and roof, clear windows, red interior, black base and wheels. Logo: blue "ISLAND TOURS", orange-blue-black island design. M3 base.
   1. As above.

M3-SPE-MA   SPEEDLINK   1987
White body and roof, clear windows, red interior, black base and wheels. Logo: yellow "HEATHROW/GATWICK", white "SPEEDLINK" and plane design on blue background, red, blue and yellow stripes. M3 base.

M4   LEYLAND RIGID TRUCK (forthcoming).
M5   LEYLAND TIPPER TRUCK (forthcoming).

Gift Sets & Collector Packs

More has been advertised than, to my knowledge, has been put on the market, and I must confess that I have not kept records of exactly what boxed sets I have bought or seen. But the following boxed sets are known to exist:

GS1: Gift Set: 6 Railway Express, 7 Ford Sales & Service, and 9 New York-Rio; 1984.
GS: unnumbered Gift Set: 6 Barclays, 11 Abels, and 13 Michelin; 1985.
CP1: Collector Pack: 3 Robertsons, 4 Pears, and 6 Daily Express; 1984.
GS: Bus Gift Set: 10 Trailways, 15 Castlemaine, and 17 Eurotours; 1985.
Commonwealth Games 3-piece set, 1986.

Coca-Cola 3-piece set, 1986.
Hershey 3-piece set, 1986.
Hamleys 6-piece set, 1986?
Rolls-Royce 3-piece sets: the first with three black models, the second with other colors; 1987.
Lothian 3-piece bus set, 1987.

Glasgow 3-piece bus set, 1987.
KLM: two 3-piece sets, 1987.
As of October 1987, two forthcoming sets are: Dundee 3-piece bus set.
MM4 Military Gift Set: 4 vehicles in RAF colors.

Matchbox Price Guide

Rather than trying to list every Matchbox model individually, I consider it more practical to make an individual listing only for the Models of Yesteryear, and to put the other series in categories with appropriate price ranges. Please remember that this guide applies only to the 1982-1987 products listed in this book, and absolutely not to any earlier Matchbox products! Prices apply to mint models in original box or bubblepack; for unboxed mint models subtract about 10%; nonmint models are worth considerably less. Since many models exist in more than one variation, and these variations may not be of equal value, and since some people are willing to pay more than others for a model, often depending on how important it is to their collection, a high and a low price will be given.

Matchbox Series

Current 1-75 sold in the USA: $1-2.
Current 1-75 not sold in the USA: $2-4.
Obsolete regular issues: $2-5.
Limited and promotional issues: $2-10.
  (some promos may be worth more)

Superfast Specials/Lasers: $1-2.
Matchmates pairs in bubblepack: $5-10.
Dinky Toys: $2-3.
Twin Packs, current: $2-3.
Twin Packs, obsolete: $3-6.

Matchbox® Series

Convoy, current regular issues: $4-6.
Convoy, obsolete regular issues: $6-10.
Convoy, promotional: $8-12.
Convoy Action Packs: current retail price.
Team Matchbox, current: $5-6.
Team Matchbox, obsolete: $6-10.

King Size, current: current retail price.
King Size, obsolete and foreign: up to twice their retail price when current.
Specials, Turbo Specials, Gift Sets, other series: Current: current retail price.
Obsolete: up to 50% above retail price when current.

Models of Yesteryear

Y1-C8 Jaguar, metallic blue $8-12	Y8-D7 **MG,** blue body 8-10
C9 dark green 7-10	D8 cream body 7-10
C10 yellow-orange 6-8	Y8-E1 **Yorkshire Wagon** 6-8
Y2-D1 Bentley 6-8	Y9-B9 **Simplex,** yellow body 6-8
Y3-D1 Ford Tanker, BP 8-12	Y9-C1 **Leyland,** A. Luff 50-65
D2 **Carnation** 8-12	Y10-C7 **Silver Ghost,** silver body 8-10
D3 **Zerolene** 50-75	Y10-D1 **Maserati** 6-8
D4 **Express Dairy** 8-12	Y11-C7 **Lagonda,** plum body 10-20
D5 **Mobiloil** 7-9	Y11-D1 **Bugatti** 6-8
D6 **Castrol** 6-8	Y12-C13 **Ford Van,** Smiths Crisps 8-12
D7 **Red Crown** 15-25	C14 **Yesteryear Anniversary** 8-12
Y4-D4 Duesenberg, brown & tan 8-12	C15 **Arnotts Biscuits** 25-50
D5 silver & blue 6-8	C16 **Sunlight Seife** 50-75
Y5-D18 Talbot Van, Nestle's 8-12	C17 **Harrods** 15-25
D19 **Wrights Soap** 8-12	C18 **Cerebos** 6-9
D20 **EverReady** 8-12	C19 **Captain Morgan** 6-9
D21 **Dunlop** 7-10	C20 **Royal Mail** 6-10
D22 **Rose's** 6-8	C21 **Pepsi-Cola** 6-9
D23 **Speelgoed Otten** 10-20	C22 **Hoover** 6-10
Y6-D8 Rolls-Royce, red chassis 8-12	C23 **Motor 100** 8-12
D9 black chassis 8-12	C24 **H. J. Heinz** 8-12
Y7=D1 Ford Breakdown Truck 6-8	C25 **Rosella** 6-8

Models of Yesteryear

Y12-D1 **Ford Pickup,** Imbach 15-25
Y12-E1 **Stephenson's Rocket** 20-25
Y13-C9 **Crossley, Carlsberg** 8-12
   C10 **Warings,** white roof 15-25
   C11 **Warings,** cream roof 6-8
Y14-C8 **Stutz,** blue body 8-12
Y14-D1 **E. R. A.** 6-8
Y15-B14 **Packard,** tan & brown 8-12
Y15-C1 **London Tramcar** 6-8
Y16-B8 **Mercedes,** red body 7-10
Y16-C1 **Ferrari** 6-8
Y17-A7 **Hispano-Suiza,** blue body 7-10
   A8 green body 6-8
Y18-B1 **Atkinson,** Sand & Gravel 8-12
   B2 **Portland Cement** 7-10
   B3 **Bass & Co.** 15-25
Y19-A5 **Auburn,** cream body 8-12
   A6 white body 7-10
Y19-B1 **Fowler Showman's Engine** 20-25
Y19-C1 **Morris Van,** Brasso 6-8
Y20-A1 **Mercedes,** silver gray body 8-12
   A2 white body 7-10
   A3 red body 6-8
Y21-A1 **Woody,** no logo 8-12
   A2 **A. & J. Box** 7-10
   A3 **Carter's** 6-8
Y21-B1 **Steam Roller** 20-25
Y22-A1 **Ford Van,** Oxo 8-12
   A2 **Palm Toffee** 7-10
   A3 **Toblerone** 7-10
   A4 **Maggi Soup** .... 10-15?
   A5 **Canada Post** 8-12
   A6 **Spratts** 7-10

A7 **Lyons Tea** 6-8
Y23-A½ **Bus,** Schweppes 8-12
A3 **R. A. C.** 7-10
A4 **Maples** 10-20
A5 **Haig** 6-8
Y24-A1 **Bugatti,** black/yellow 7-10
   A2 gray & red body 6-8
Y25-A1 **Renault,** Perrier 8-12
   A2 **James Neale** 20-30
   A3 **Duckhams Oils** 10-20
   A4 **Eagle Pencil** 6-8
   A5 **St. John Ambulance** 15-25
   A6 **T. Tunnock** 10-20
   A7 **Delhaize & Co.** 6-8
Y26-A1 **Crossley, Löwenbräu** 8-12
   A2 **Romford** 6-8
   A3 **Gonzalez Byass** 6-8
Y27-A1 **Foden,** Pickfords 7-10
   A2 **Hovis** 7-10
   A3 **Tate & Lyle** 6-8
   A4 **Spiller's** 15-25
Y27-B1 **Foden & Trailer,** Frasers 20-30
Y28-A1 **Unic Taxi,** red body 7-10
   A2 blue body 6-8
Y29-A1 **Walker Van,** Harrods 8-12
   A2 **Joseph Lucas** 6-8
Y30-A1 **Mack Truck,** Acorn 8-12
   A2 **Consolidated** 10-20
   A3 **Arctic Ice Cream** 6-8

Naturally, to a collector who wants particular variations, those that are harder to obtain will be worth more. This guide is intended to give a general idea of the value of a basic model, and cannot be applied to every minor variation.

Lledo™ *Price Guide*

Instead of giving one price which practically no one will agree with, I am giving two prices—a low and a high—in U. S. dollars, and hoping some of you will agree with some of them. The situation is, of course, complicated by the fact that some variations will be worth more than others, and we cannot list every variation separately—so please don't assume that any variation of a given model must be worth the higher price. The best way to find out what models are worth is to go to toy shows and see what they are actually selling for.

Code 3 models will not be listed, and I have no way of saying what some very rare models are worth.

001 HORSE DRAWN TRAM
DOW-DG **Downtown** $3-8
MAI-DG **Main Street** 3-8
MAN-LP **Manly Jazz** 10-20
NAT-DG **National Tramway** 5-8
WES-DG **Westminster** 3-8

002 HORSE DRAWN MILK FLOAT
CEL-DG **Celtic Dairies** 3-6
CHA-DG **Chambourcy** 3-6
CLI-DG **Clifford** 3-6
EXP-DG **Express Dairy** 3-6
GRY-SP **Gray** 15-20

003 HORSE DRAWN DELIVERY VAN
COC-DG **Coca-Cola** 3-6
FIN-DG **Fine Lady** 3-6
GRY-SP **Gray** 15-20
HAM-DG **Hamleys** 3-6
LCM-DG **Club Member** 6-10
LSW-DG **LSWR Parcels** 3-6
NOR-DG **Matthew Norman** 3-6
PEP-DG **Pepperidge Farm** 3-6
PHO-LP **Phoenix Dye** 20-30
ROB-DG **Robertson's** 3-6
ROY-DG **Royal Mail** 3-8

007 **FORD WOODY WAGON**

In other words, DG issues start at $3 and don't usually go much higher (except for rare varieties); LP issues start at about $10 and can go a lot higher, and View Vans and Edocars start around $5 and rarely go beyond $8. The Fantastic Set o' Wheels issues are in the same price range as DG isues, and so are the Marathons. The big problem comes in evaluating obsolete or extremely hard-to-get promotionals. In some cases I have no idea what they might sell for, as there seem to be absolutely none on the market.

If you disagree with some of the evaluations in this guide, you will not be alone. I fully expect every collector or dealer who reads it to disagree with something! But I hope it will be of some use to someone.

Notes

Notes

Notes